JUST ENOUGH
SOFTWARE TEST AUTC

ISBN 0-13-008468-9

90000

9 790130 084681

ABOUT THE SERIES

In today's world of ever-improving technology—with computers that get faster, cheaper, smaller, and more powerful with each passing month—there is one commodity that we seem to have less and less of: time. IT professionals and managers are under constant pressure to deliver new systems more quickly than before; and one of the consequences of this pressure is that they're often thrown into situations for which they're not fully prepared. On Monday, they're given a new assignment in the area of testing, or risk management, or building a new application with the latest tools from IBM or Microsoft or Sun; and on Tuesday, they're expected to be productive and proficient. In many cases, they don't have time to attend a detailed training course; and they don't have time to read a thousand-page *War and Peace* tome that explains all the details of the technology.

Enter the Just Enough Series of books from Yourdon Press. Our mission is, quite literally, to provide just enough information for an experienced IT professional or manager to be able to assimilate the key aspects of a technology and begin putting it to productive use right away. Our objective is to provide pragmatic "how-to" information—supported, when possible, by checklists and guidelines and templates and wizards—that can be put to practical use right away. Of course, it's important to know that the refinements, exceptions, and extensions do exist; and the Just Enough books provide references, links to Web sites, and other resources for those who need it.

Over time, we intend to produce "just enough" books for every important aspect of IT systems development: from analysis and design, to coding and testing. Project management, risk management, process improvement, peopleware, and other issues are also covered while addressing several areas of new technology, from CRM to wireless technology, from enterprise application integration to Microsoft's .NET technology.

Perhaps one day life will slow down, and we'll be able to spend as much time as we want, learning everything there is to be learned about IT technologies. But until that day arrives, we only have time for "just enough" information. And the place to find that information is the Just Enough Series of computer books from Prentice Hall PTR/Yourdon Press.

ABOUT THE SERIES EDITOR

Edward Yourdon is an internationally recognized consultant, lecturer, and author/coauthor of more than 25 books, including *Managing High-Intensity Internet Projects, Death March, Time Bomb, The Rise and Resurrection of the American Programmer, Modern Structured Analysis*, and others. Widely known as the lead developer of the structured analysis/design methods in the 1970's and the popular Coad/Yourdon object-oriented methodology in the early 1990's, Edward Yourdon brings both his writing and technical skills as Series Editor while developing key authors and publications for the Just Enough Series/Yourdon Press.

Selected Titles from the
YOURDON PRESS SERIES
Ed Yourdon, *Advisor*

JUST ENOUGH SERIES
DUÉ Mentoring Object Technology Projects
MOSLEY/POSEY Software Test Automation
THOMSETT Radical Project Management
ULRICH Legacy Systems: Transformation Strategies
YOURDON Managing High-Intensity Internet Projects

YOURDON PRESS COMPUTING SERIES
ANDREWS AND STALICK Business Reengineering: The Survival Guide
BOULDIN Agents of Change: Managing the Introduction of Automated Tools
COAD AND MAYFIELD with Kern Java Design: Building Better Apps and Applets, Second Edition
COAD AND NICOLA Object-Oriented Programming
COAD AND YOURDON Object-Oriented Analysis, Second Edition
COAD AND YOURDON Object-Oriented Design
COAD WITH NORTH AND MAYFIELD Object Models, Strategies, Patterns, and Applications,
    Second Edition
CONNELL AND SHAFER Object-Oriented Rapid Prototyping
CONSTANTINE The Peopleware Papers: Notes on the Human Side of Software
CONSTANTINE AND YOURDON Structure Design
DEGRACE AND STAHL Wicked Problems, Righteous Solutions
DEMARCO Controlling Software Projects
DEMARCO Structured Analysis and System Specification
FOURNIER A Methodology for Client/Server and Web Application Development
GARMUS AND HERRON Measuring the Software Process: A Practical Guide to Functional
    Measurements
HAYES AND ULRICH The Year 2000 Software Crisis: The Continuing Challenge
JONES Assessment and Control of Software Risks
KING Project Management Made Simple
PAGE-JONES Practical Guide to Structured Systems Design, Second Edition
PUTNAM AND MEYERS Measures for Excellence: Reliable Software on Time within Budget
RUBLE Practical Analysis and Design for Client/Server and GUI Systems
SHLAER AND MELLOR Object Lifecycles: Modeling the World in States
SHLAER AND MELLOR Object-Oriented Systems Analysis: Modeling the World in Data
STARR How to Build Shlaer-Mellor Object Models
THOMSETT Third Wave Project Management
ULRICH AND HAYES The Year 2000 Software Crisis: Challenge of the Century
YOURDON Byte Wars: The Impact of September 11 on Information Technology
YOURDON Death March: The Complete Software Developer's Guide to Surviving "Mission
    Impossible" Projects
YOURDON Decline and Fall of the American Programmer
YOURDON Modern Structured Analysis
YOURDON Object-Oriented Systems Design
YOURDON Rise and Resurrection of the American Programmer
YOURDON AND ARGILA Case Studies in Object-Oriented Analysis and Design

JUST ENOUGH
SOFTWARE TEST AUTOMATION

Daniel J. Mosley

Principal Consultant and Owner, CSST Technologies, Inc.

&

Bruce A. Posey

Principal Consultant and Owner, Archer Group

With Carl Nagle's Data Driven Engine Framework for Rational Software's Suite TestStudio

&

Keith Zambelich's "Test Plan Driven" Testing Framework For Mercury Interactive's WinRunner

PRENTICE HALL PTR
UPPER SADDLE RIVER, NJ 07458
www.phptr.com
www.phptr.com/mosley

Library of Congress Cataloging-in-Publication Data

Mosley, Daniel J.
    Just enough software test automation / Daniel J. Mosley, Bruce A. Posey.
        p. cm. — (Just enough series)
    Includes bibliographical references and index.
    ISBN 0-13-008468-9 (paper)
    1. Computer software—Testing—Automation. I. Posey, Bruce A. II. Title. III.
Series.

QA76.76.T48 M673 2002
005.1′4—dc21

                            2002072366

Editorial/production supervision: *BooksCraft, Inc., Indianapolis, IN*
Acqusition Editor: *Paul Petralia*
Editorial Assistant: *Richard Winkler*
Marketing Manager: *Debby VanDijk*
Manufacturing Manager: *Alexis R. Heydt*
Cover Design Director: *Jerry Votta*
Cover Designer: *Anthony Gemmellaro*
Series Interior Design: *Gail Cocker-Bogusz*
Full Service Production Manager: *Anne Garcia*

© 2002 Pearson Education, Inc.
Publishing as Prentice Hall PTR
Upper Saddle River, New Jersey 07458

Prentice Hall books are widely used by corporations and government agencies for training, marketing, and resale.

For information regarding corporate and government bulk discounts please contact:
Corporate and Government Sales (800) 382-3419 or corpsales@pearsontechgroup.com

Company and product names mentioned herein are the trademarks or registered trademarks of their respective owners.

Printed in the United States of America
10 9 8 7 6 5 4 3 2 1

ISBN 0-13-008468-9

Pearson Education LTD.
Pearson Education Australia PTY, Limited
Pearson Education Singapore, Pte. Ltd.
Pearson Education North Asia Ltd.
Pearson Education Canada, Ltd.
Pearson Educación de Mexico, S.A. de C.V.
Pearson Education—Japan
Pearson Education Malaysia, Pte. Ltd.

Contents

CHAPTER 8
The Control Synchronized Data-Driven Testing Framework in Depth

151

CHAPTER 9
Facilitating the Manual Testing Process
with Automated Tools   201

Preface

There has been a glut of test automation books on the market as of late. They all espouse different approaches to, and different levels of, software test automation implementation. There is even an attempt to describe an automated software testing life cycle in the most popular offering (see the Dustin reference in Chapter 2). Traditionally, authors of information systems (IS) industry publications typically try to force a hypothetical model to describe the processes we use. Sometimes it works and sometimes it doesn't. The problem is that there is no empirical evidence to support that the approaches put into practice in these models work in the real world. The majority of the recommended approaches in software testing and software development practices are based on anecdotal evidence and project management fads that are started by so-called experts in the IS field and perpetuated by chief information officers (CIOs) in health club steam rooms.

We do not believe in an *automated* testing life cycle. This is an artificial construct that we find of little use. Nor do we believe in a software testing life cycle. What we do believe is that software testing occurs as a set of integrated activities in the software development process. We also believe that good software testing requires a special form of project management and its own set of operational techniques. Testing also requires a set of tools that a test engineer can rely on during test activities. These tools can be testing artifacts such as printed test scenarios that a test engineer follows or printed test logs that the engineer fills out while executing the tests.

We are not saying that we have to wait until a body of empirical evidence has been compiled before we accept and use the tools and techniques advocated by the IS authorities. We are saying that we have to evaluate the tools and methods ourselves and weed out the fluff. The real experiment is this: which techniques work and which do not when practitioners (you and we) attempt to use the technology.

Dan Mosley, the first author, explored his first automated testing tool back in 1985 and the technology was pretty crude. He was able to obtain an evaluation copy of that product while he was teaching one of the earliest undergraduate software testing courses (Washington University in St. Louis, 1985–1992). In the mid-1990s, he had long telephone conversations with Eric Schurr, then of Software Quality Automation (SQA), now of Rational Software Corporation, which subsequently absorbed SQA and its products, concerning automated software testing tools and what, functionally, they should provide for software test engineers' use.

They discussed what a good automation tool should do and what features it should include. Because of Dan's contacts with Eric, he acquired and used copies of SQA's (now Rational's) automated testing tool, which came out after that early Version 1.0. The most current version (at the time of this writing) is Rational Suite TestStudio 2002. Dan's experiences with this product have shown that test automation is not an easy overnight fix for a faltering testing effort. Furthermore, his experiences have proven that automated testing is not a substitute for manual testing. Glen Myers published the fundamental concepts of software testing in the late 1970s. Even today his *Art of Software Testing* (1979) is considered the premier dialogue on software testing. We still need to apply his recommendations when we test manually and when we build an automated testing infrastructure.

Our pet peeve with test automation as it is currently practiced is the lack of emphasis on front-end test planning and test design activities. We keep repeating the classic mistake that software developers have perpetuated since the first program was written—we start testing (in the case of automated testing, writing the test scripts) without doing the proper analysis of the problem and design of the testing infrastructure. It brings to mind a cartoon from years ago—a manager is talking to the programmer: "You start writing code and I'll go find out what it is supposed to build." Automated tests that "test" the wrong things can have only one result: unsuitable tests are executed much faster.

The ultimate goal of any automation effort should be a set of planned tests that corresponds to a set of test requirements that in turn are reflected in the automated tests. Furthermore, the heart of the testing effort is not the test scripts, but the test data. This is why there is so much hype about data-driven automated testing as an automation implementation framework. The underlying premise is that data should drive the tests and should exercise the application under test's (AUT) features. The test scripts are just delivery vehicles. Automated tests are effective only when the test data are designed well.

An operational goal of an automated testing framework is to minimize test script maintenance. The traditional capture/playback model that testing tool vendors have championed for years leads to inordinately high script maintenance because the test data are hard coded in the body of the test script. Mosley's first experiences developing automated test scripts intuitively demonstrated that strictly using capture/playback is not the way to go. Furthermore, the built-in test cases the tools provided were essentially useless for anything but testing the application's graphical user interface (GUI). True functional testing requires the test engineer to write test data that probe the AUT in depth. GUI testing should be done, and it can be automated with minimal effort. In actual practice, we usually have a single test script that exercises the GUI objects. It baselines and validates the properties of all GUI objects. The test script is executed for each GUI screen.

Automating functional testing requires sophisticated test data that explore the AUT. The test data must reproduce test scenarios that exercise important system features. Consequently, automated functional testing is more complicated and difficult. It requires the test engineer to write a significant portion of the test script as opposed to recording it. It also means designing effective test data. Understanding what to test (having a documented set of test requirements) and designing test data that verify the requirements are the keys to writing valuable automated functional tests.

Understanding how to verify the test results is as important as knowing what to test. Automated test verification is also data dependent. As their primary verification method, automated tests frequently capture and store baseline data that are later compared against the same data captured during regression tests. More sophisticated tests access and manipulate database records before, during, and after the tests are executed.

A powerful automated testing framework must provide tools that address test planning, test design, test construction, test execution, and test results verification. An effective infrastructure is one that is predicated on an integrated central repository where testing artifacts can be stored and reused. The infrastructure should also provide customizable reporting capabilities.

We have a history prior to coauthoring this book. We met in 1996 when we worked together on the first really successful automated testing project we had encountered up to that point. Since then, we have worked together on a plethora of test automation projects. We have developed a sense of what is required to implement a successful automation project and what is required to propagate automated testing in an IS development and testing organization. We know as much about what *won't* work as we do about what *will* work.

Working together, we implemented a data-driven automated testing paradigm before we had even heard of this now prolific industry phrase (we were unaware of the paper that Richard Strang had given at the STAR conference in 1996; see the Chapter 1 references). We pioneered and perfected our implementations of the data-driven approach while others were just beginning to discuss and write about it. Of course, as with any new hot-button technology, it is not really new, just rediscovered. Data-driven testing is no exception. Beizer, in *Software Testing Techniques* (1983), described "Data-Base-Driven Test Design." This was late in the mainframe era and early in the PC revolution, so it was an idea related to testing mainframe applications. He presented it as a procedure not for testing the database, but for using the database structure to derive test data. He argued that it "is best suited to the verification of functional requirements as set down in the system specification." It is a simple step to expand this approach to include tests that are based on business rules supported by the database table structures. Add data that test the GUI objects and their behaviors and you have data-driven testing.

We also discovered structured test script writing (also known as framework-based testing) during this period. Again this is not new technology. Test scripts are programs written in modified versions of common programming languages such as Visual Basic and C. They are different in that they have special features to accommodate software testing tasks. There is a vast literature base that addresses *structured programming* concepts such as functional decomposition, module cohesion, module coupling, and modular (functional) reusability. As a test script constitutes a software program that tests another software program, it is subject to the same design and construction rules as the programs it is testing. Thus, structured programming concepts also apply to automated test scripts.

Because automated test scripts are also subject to the same baggage that other software programs carry, they can contain logic flaws; they can contain spaghetti (convoluted) code; they can contain hard-coded variables; and they can be implemented with both procedure and data in the test script itself. All of this adds up to increased costs related to test suite maintenance, just as there are costs associated with maintaining the software systems these test scripts test. Creating structured component-based test scripts that are separate from the data they execute is the only way to create an effective software test automation infrastructure, one that maximizes testing accuracy and that minimizes testing maintenance.

There have also been recent efforts to develop high-level test automation languages that can be used to design and implement automated tests by nontechnical personnel such as business and product analysts and system customers. These efforts are advocated as the next step in the evolution of automated testing. As yet, we have not seen an approach that simplifies test script development enough to be really useful. We can see the value of this as long as we are striving toward a set of universal script libraries that will support a common Java-like test scripting language; however, most frameworks to date have been written to support contrived high-level command languages, not object-oriented ones. In addition, the supporting libraries are as yet immature in the functionality they offer to the scriptwriter. To accomplish their testing needs, organizations have to add additional code to the existing library subroutines and functions.

Because we are practitioners, the aim of this book is to offer useful advice on test automation from the test automation developer's/user's perspective. It includes pragmatic advice on what to do and caveats concerning what not to do when designing and implementing a test automation infrastructure. It also contains advice on what current popular testing approaches can and cannot do for your testing endeavors.

Our examples were developed on the Rational Suite TestStudio platform, but we feel they can easily be adapted for use with other automated testing platforms. In addition, an FTP site (*www.phptr.com/mosley*) supports this book. That site contains template files from the Archer Group's Control Synchronized Data Driven Testing (CSDDT) approach (for the Rational environment), Carl Nagle's Data Driven Engine (DDE) approach (for the Rational environment), and Keith Zambelich's Totally Data-Driven approach using Mercury Interactive's WinRunner automated test tool, which is based on Zambelich's Test Plan Driven framework that uses his Toolkit For WinRunner. These resources can be used to easily jump-start your data-driven automated testing effort.

What Is Just Enough Test Automation?

This is not going to be a discourse on how to select and implement an automated testing tools suite. There are a number of articles and books available today that offer practical advice on tool selection. It is also not an introductory book on software testing automation. If you are reading this book, we'll assume you have some level of previous experience with test automation. We will also assume that you have some serious questions about the practical aspects of test automation. You may, or may not, have a successful implementation under your belt. In any case, you most probably have experienced the operational, political, and cultural pitfalls of test automation. What you need is a how-to book that has some practical tips, tricks, and suggestions, along with a proven approach. If this is what you want, read on. Our perspective on test automation is what you will be getting in the remaining chapters of this book.

No New Models, Please!

"Read My Lips: No New Models!" echoes a sentiment with which we wholeheartedly agree (14). As mentioned in the Preface, there has been a plethora of models of the software testing process (6,10,11) and models of the automated software testing process (4,7,8,9,12,15), including a software test automation life cycle model (2). While these ideas are all right and in some aspects useful when discussing software testing and test automation, they are of little use to real-world practitioners.

The Software Engineering Institute at Carnegie Mellon University has established a Software Testing Management Key Process Area (KPA) that is necessary to achieve Level 2: Repeatable in the Software Process Capability Maturity Model (CMM) (11). Such a model is useful for general guidance, but it does not define a process that is useful to the test engineer proper. It does give test managers a warm and fuzzy feeling when they pay lip service to it but in reality the testing process activities do not reflect the model at all. The same things hold true for the software test automation life cycle model. We do not believe in life cycles. Instead, we believe in processes that direct workflows. Every testing group has a process. In some instances it is a chaotic process, and in other instances it is more organized.

Krause developed a four-level maturity model for automated software testing (3) that he ties to the software testing maturity model (1) and the SEI Software Process Maturity Model (4) that evolved into the CMM. The levels he specified are Accidental Automation, Beginning Automation, Intentional Automation, and Advanced Automation. While this model may describe what happens from a conceptual standpoint, it offers no practical advice that will facilitate test automation implementation. It merely describes what the author has noted happening in typical organizations.

Dustin, Rashka, and Paul published an Automated Test Lifecycle Methodology (ATLM)—a "structured methodology which is geared toward ensuring successful implementation of automated testing."(2) It identifies a four-phased methodology: Decision to Automate Test; Introduction of Automated Testing; Test Planning, Design, and Development; Execution and Management of Automated Test.

While this model is useful from a management and control perspective, it is not practical from the test automation engineer's point of view. Powers offers practical advice that can be very helpful for software testing engineers who are responsible for building and implementing a test automation framework. It includes common-sense discussions of programming style, naming standards, and other conventions that should be applied when writing automated test scripts (9).

There is a comprehensive discussion of the principle of data abstraction, which is the basis of the data-driven approach to automated software testing. He discusses alternatives for coding how data are defined and used by the test script. According to Powers, "The principle is one of depending less on the literal value of a variable or constant, and more on its meaning, or role, or usage in the test." He speaks of "constraint for product data." He defines this concept as "…the simplest form of this data abstraction is to use named program constants instead of literal values." He also speaks of "variables for product data" and says, "…instead of the literal name 'John Q. Private,' the principle of data abstraction calls for the programmer to use a program variable such as **sFullName** here, with the value set once in the program. This one occurrence of the literal means there's only one place to edit in order to change it."(9)

The immediate impact of the statement Powers makes is that you begin to see the possible benefits derived from data abstraction when it comes to the maintenance of automated test scripts. He further suggests that these values be stored in a repository that will be accessible from the test script code: "All that's required is a repository from which to fetch the values, and a program mechanism to do the retrieval."(9)

This is the underlying principle of Strang's Data Driven Automated Testing approach. His approach uses a scripting framework to read the values from the test data repository. It uses a data file that contains both the input and its expected behavior. His method has taken data abstraction from storing just the literal values to also storing the expected result values. This approach can accommodate both manual and automated data generation. The test script must be coded in such a way that it can determine *right* results from the *wrong* results (12).

Powers's and Strang's work is reflected in the data-driven approaches discussed in Chapters 7 and 8 of this book. Archer Group's Control Synchronized Data Driven Testing (CSDDT) is an example of one such approach that employs the concepts discussed here.

Rational Software Corporation has authored the Rational Unified Process (RUP), which contains specific test phases that are designed to support its automated testing tool suite (10). Even if you are not a Rational user, the testing process information provides a solid base for doing even manual testing. RUP itself comprises process documentation that addresses all of software development, not just testing. It is relatively inexpensive—the RUP CD-ROM sells for under $1,000. The most important aspect of RUP's testing approach is that it can be used to support a data-driven automated testing framework. That is why we have used it in the past and why it is mentioned in this book.

A Life Cycle Is Not a Process

The problem with the approaches taken by the authors cited thus far and other industry gurus is the same problem we have with all life-cycle models—they are management oriented, not practitioner oriented. Again, this approach offers very little in the way of an operational process that we can term an automated testing process. Other approaches, e.g., data-driven automated testing, which these authors have criticized, offer much more in the way of methods and techniques that can actually be applied in day-to-day test automation activities. What this line of thinking really offers is a model to give testing managers the same warm and fuzzy feeling mentioned above with respect to the testing maturity model.

Although purported to be an experiential model, this representation of automated testing has not been developed on a deductive basis. It is a theory based on inductive reasoning, much of which is founded on anecdotal evidence, as are many of the models advocated in information systems (IS) literature. On the other hand, nonmanagement techniques, which are operational, not managerial, and which are applied to specific tasks in the automation process, are based on deductive reasoning. Data-driven testing is an example of a nonmanagement technique. These techniques have evolved through practitioner trial and error—how many of the traditional engineering methods have come to be that are used today.

A Tool Is Not a Process

The most recent results for the minisurvey on the CSST Technologies, Inc., Web site indicate that 40% (102 out of 258 respondents) see software testing methods/process implementation as doing the most to facilitate their testing work. Twenty-four percent (63 respondents) see improved software requirements documentation as the most important facilitation factor. Nineteen percent (50 respondents) believe that software test standards implementation is the most important aspect. Ten percent (25 respondents) cite improved test planning as the most important consideration. Only 7% (18 respondents) think that more time to test would facilitate their work.

Purchasing a software testing tool suite does not constitute implementing a software testing process. Processes are steps that are followed that result in a goal being achieved or a product being produced. The process steps implement testing activities that result in test execution and the creation of test artifacts. Automated software tools support existing processes and, when the process is chaotic, impose some much-needed structure on the activities. One of the primary reasons software testing tool implementations fail is because there is little or no testing process in place before the tools are purchased.

When we are designing and building automated tests, we do not even see a process. What we see are tasks, a schedule, and personal assignments to complete. For us, just enough software test automation is the amount we need to do our jobs effectively. If we do not have commercial software testing tools we can use, we build our own or use desktop tools that our clients routinely load on workstations.

Figure 1.1 illustrates a testing process that was defined for one of our clients that is loosely based on the RUP testing approach (10). Our process approach differs from Rational's in that we view test script design as part of test implementation whereas in RUP it is still considered to be a test design activity. The reason we differ is we believe that the skill set required for test design does not include previous programming experience, but the one for test implementation does.

How Much Automation Is Enough?

This is the question that has been asked since the inception of automated test tools. The tools vendors have presented us with one point of view, and industry experts have given us varied viewpoints. Vendors began with basic capture/playback tools that have evolved into some very sophisticated and highly integrated tool suites. They seem to have left it to the practitioner to determine what lies beyond the basic capture/playback model. The experts in test automation have written many articles and books. They have cited case studies of both successful and failed automation attempts. In the end there has been a modicum of agreement about what we must do, but not how we have to do it. In this text we will give you our point of view on how to do test automation. We believe the industry has debated what to do long enough. Until the tool suites reach a new plateau and until they possess even more sophistication, we have a working archetype for an automation framework that we can use.

To find out how much test automation is enough, we have to look at the areas of the software testing process that *can* be automated followed by the areas that *should* be automated. There is a difference between a tool and a process. Tools are used to facilitate processes. A tool can be used to implement a process and to enforce process standards. In many instances, the built-in procedures that tools bring with them can be construed as processes.

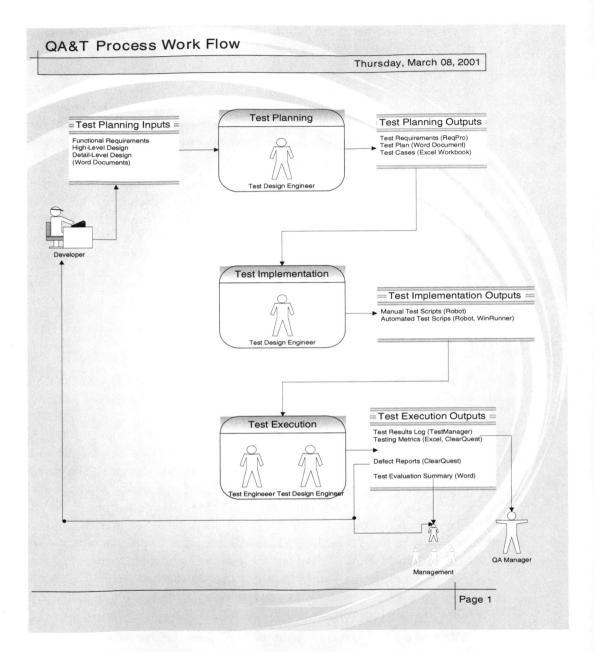

FIGURE 1.1
Quality Assurance and Testing (QA&T) Process

They are, however, frequently incomplete and ill-thought-out processes. The best software testing tools are the ones you can mold to your testing needs. They are the ones that offer a high degree of customizability with respect to workflow and to their tracking and reporting capabilities.

What are the types of tests that can be automated? They include unit, integration, and system testing. Subcategories of automated system tests include security, configuration, and load testing. Automated regression testing should be implemented at the unit, integration, and system levels during development and for use against major and minor system production releases.

What are the regions of the testing process that we should consider? They include the general spheres of test planning, test design, test construction, test execution, test results capture and analysis, test results verification, and test reporting. There are other activities that are closely associated with the testing activities proper. They include problem (defect) tracking and resolution, software configuration management, and software test metrics. Overall, the activities of the testing process are glued together, as is the software development process, by good project management techniques.

All of these areas should be automated to the degree that it makes sense for your organization in terms of time and costs. The more automation you can implement, the better and more effective your process will be. Realize that this statement holds true only if the tools are the appropriate ones and if they have been properly implemented. By *implemented* we mean that an integrated test automation framework has been constructed and is being used.

Testing Process Spheres

Let's look at each component of the testing process individually.

Test Planning

We'll begin our discussion of the testing process with test planning, the most important activity in the testing process. It involves assessing risk, identifying and prioritizing test requirements, estimating testing resource requirements, developing a testing project plan, and assigning testing responsibilities to test team members. These ingredients can be structured as a formal test plan or they can be developed individually and used at the appropriate times.

The traditional idea of a test plan is the *who, what, when, where, how,* and *how long* of the testing process. Since using Rational RequisitePro's capabilities, we have adjusted our thoughts on what a test plan is and how it is used. We can import the software requirements document into tools such as Rational RequisitePro and then develop test scenarios directly from such tools into a test plan that is constructed using the RUP test plan template, which we have modified extensively (see Figure 1.2). From the test plan scenarios, we can create test requirements. They can be constructed directly in the scenario tables in the test plan document, or they can be created in a separate test requirements document using the RUP template. From either of these documents, we can create a test requirements view that we can export to a Comma Separated Values (CSV) file. Then we can open the test requirements during testing in Microsoft (MS) Excel and update it online with the test results and import it back into RequisitePro. This is how we defined our manual testing process. We do not yet have this fully implemented, but have piloted it and it works very well.

The point is that we now see the test plan as a working document derived from software requirements and linked to test requirements and test results. It is a dynamic document used during testing. The old idea of test plan is that it is a planning document. It is a document that forces the tester to think about what he is going to do during testing. From this perspective, it becomes a document that, once the planning stage is finished, sits on the shelf. In our experience, very few people refer back to the test plan during test execution. In fact, we have worked in several companies where test plans were actually created after the fact. With our approach, the test plan is created up front, and it is updated when the software requirements are updated; subsequently, the updates are reflected in the test requirements, which can actually be used for testing. The test plan standard is based on a modified version of the template contained in RUP, which accompanies the Rational Suite TestStudio.

The following is how we defined the manual system testing process at one client organization. We have also piloted this and it works very well. From the test plan scenarios, we create test case requirements. They are constructed directly in scenario tables created in the test plan document, as well as in separate test requirements documents (requirements grids). From either of these sources, we can create test requirements views that can be exported to CSV files. For manual testing, we open the CSV files in MS Excel. We use the information to guide manual test execution activities, and we update it online with the test results. We import the updated files back into our automated tool for results analysis and reporting.

Figure 1.2 contains a modified version of the RUP test plan template document table of contents (TOC). The TOC has been simplified in that the number

1. INTRODUCTION
   1.1 PURPOSE
   1.2 BACKGROUND
   1.3 SCOPE
   1.4 PROJECT IDENTIFICATION
2. SCENARIOS FOR TEST
3. TEST STRATEGY
   3.1 TESTING TYPES
      3.1.1 Function Testing
      3.1.2 Business Cycle Testing
      3.1.3 User Interface Testing
      3.1.4 Performance Profiling
      3.1.5 Load Testing
      3.1.6 Stress Testing
      3.1.7 Volume Testing
      3.1.8 Security and Access Control Testing
      3.1.9 Failover and Recovery Testing
      3.1.10 Configuration Testing
      3.1.11 Installation Testing
   3.2 TOOLS
4. RESOURCES
   4.1 WORKERS
   4.2 SYSTEM
5. PROJECT MILESTONES
6. DELIVERABLES
   6.1 TEST MODEL
   6.2 TEST LOGS
   6.3 DEFECT REPORTS
7. APPENDIX A: PROJECT TASKS

FIGURE 1.2
RUP Test Plan TOC with Modifications

of testing types has been reduced to include only Function Testing, Business Cycle Testing, Setup and Configuration Testing, and User Interface Testing.

The purpose of the test plan is to assemble the information extracted from the requirements/design documents into test requirements that can be implemented as test scenarios. The test scenarios are the portion of the test plan that will directly feed the development of test conditions, test cases, and test data.

Desktop tools such as MS Office and MS Project can be used to automate test planning and project management. For example, checklists created in MS Excel spreadsheets can be used to assess and analyze risk and to document test requirements; MS Project can be used to produce the project plan; MS Word can be used to create a formal test plan that ties it altogether. These documents are test-planning *artifacts*. Just as software development artifacts need configuration management, so do test objects.

Test Design

Test design includes identifying test conditions that are based on the previously specified test requirements, developing all possible functional variants of those conditions, divining the expected behavior(s) of each variant when executed against the application under test (AUT), and executing manual tests during the design process prior to test automation. The manual testing allows the test design engineer to verify that the test data are appropriate and correct for the automated test in which they will be used. It also allows the test designer to become a "human" tester who can identify errors automation might miss. Test design also embraces the layout of the test data that will be input to the AUT. When designing from a data-driven perspective, these same data also control the navigation of the automated test scripts. Last, the test scripts themselves have to be designed.

Designing the tests and the test data is the most time-consuming portion of the testing process. It is also the most important set of activities. If the tests do not test what the requirements have indicated, then the tests are invalid. If the test data do not reflect the intent of the tests, once again the tests are invalid. Test case design is so important that we have included a section in the appendices devoted to test design techniques and their use.

Test designers can use MS Excel to design and build the tests. If you use this approach, it is best to keep everything in a single workbook and to include one test conditions spreadsheet, one test data spreadsheet, and as many detailed test spreadsheets as are needed to adequately describe the environmental, pretest, and posttest activities that are related to each test. For manual testing, a test log should be constructed that will be used during test execution (used online, not as a printed test log). There are integrated tool suites available that support test data design and creation with mechanisms known as *data pools*. In all cases the data are stored as CSV files that can be read and interpreted by automated test scripts. Those data can be used for either manual or automated testing.

Test Implementation

Test implementation can be subdivided into Test Construction, Test Execution, Test Results Capture and Analysis, and Test Result Verification. We'll discuss each activity separately.

Test Construction   Test construction is facilitated using the same set of tools that test design employs. The test data are constructed in a spreadsheet in the same workbook as the test conditions. Those data can then be exported to CSV files that can be used at test execution. When the tests are executed via an automated framework, test construction also includes writing the test scripts. Automated test scripts are software programs. As such, they have their own programming languages and/or language extensions that are required to accommodate software testing events. The scripting language is usually embedded in a capture/playback tool that has an accompanying source code editor. The flavors of the languages vary by vendor and, as the associated syntax/semantics vary, so does the difficulty of using a specific product. In addition, some vendors' scripting languages and their recording tools are more robust than others.

The more specialized the commands available as part of the language, the more control the test engineer has over the test environment and the AUT. Specialized tests are built into the languages as commands that, when executed, test specific items—for example, graphical user interface (GUI) object properties and data and window existence—and do file comparisons. Some of the built-in test cases are useful and most are very powerful for GUI testing, but they are not all useful for functional testing. We implement many of the tests through executing external test data (data that reflect the test requirements) and verification of the results. Those data control how the test script behaves against the application; the data contain values the test script uses to populate the target application input data fields.

The design and implementation of the test scripts is left to the scriptwriter. If there are no guidelines for developing test scripts, the scripts that are created will most likely be badly structured and each will be the product of the personality of the individual who coded it. We have seen this happen when several people on the test team were given specific sections of an application and asked to write automated test scripts for their portion. We even gave them basic templates as starting points and, still, no two were alike. We have written and implemented a set of automated test script writing guidelines that is described in Chapter 8.

If possible, test script coding should be completed in parallel with test data development. Using an approach such as Archer Group's CSDDT allows the test scriptwriters to work independently of the test data designers. This is doable because the data drive the test scripts. The scripts are designed and built to specifics that create a general test-processing engine that does not care about test data content.

It is very important to have test script coding conventions in use if the workload is spread across a number of scriptwriters. It is also important that the right personnel are assigned to this set of activities. We have found that test designers do not like coding test scripts and that test implementers do not enjoy designing and building test conditions and test data. In fact, they both do crappy work when their roles are reversed.

Script writing, as it is used here, is the *coding* of test scripts in a test tool's proprietary test scripting language, in one of the extant application programming languages such as Java or Visual Basic; in one of the standard scripting languages such as Perl, CGI, or VB Script; or in the operating system's command procedure language (for example, coding Unix shell scripts that execute test procedures). As far as test script writing is concerned, you really need people who enjoy programming. Bruce was an engineer who moved into the software industry as a programmer before becoming a test scriptwriter. That type of experience makes a person a natural test scriptwriter. Test script coding requires either prior programming experience or current training in programming concepts such as logic, syntax, and semantics. It also requires an eye for developing complex logic structures. Because of these requirements, don't expect nontechnical testers to write test scripts and, furthermore, don't expect them to be able to create effective test scripts using the capture/playback facilities most tool suites provide. Test scripts developed by that method are a maintenance nightmare.

Test Execution   Test execution can be manual, automated, or automated-manual. It is common wisdom in the testing industry that manual tests and automated tests each find different classes of errors. Thus, the experts say that we should do both. We agree to a great extent—that to do full-blown manual system tests and then follow up with automated regression tests is a neat idea, but most testing efforts have the resources to do only one or the other. What we suggest is a combination of both where manual testing occurs in parallel with test case design and construction.

The test designers should have the application open as they design and construct the test data, and they should execute it against the application feature(s) it is designed to test. This accomplishes two things. First, it performs a validation of the data that will eventually be used in the automated regression tests and, second, it implements manual functional (system-level) tests of each application feature prior to the automated regression tests. Many errors can and will be found during test case design and construction when this process is followed. We have successfully applied this approach.

Test Results Capture and Analysis For manual testing, a test log should be developed and implemented online. At the very least it should be a spreadsheet in the same workbook where the test conditions and test data are stored. Ideally, a test results database is used as a central repository for permanent storage. This is the case when the tests are executed using capture/playback tools such as Rational Robot or Mercury Interactive's Win-Runner. The test results are trapped as they occur and are written to the repository where later they can be viewed and reports can be printed.

Bruce has developed an automated manual test script (using Rational Robot and the SQABasic language) that does this very thing for manual tests (this tool is fully described in Chapter 9). It displays the manual test scripts much as a teleprompter does, and each step in the script can be selected during test execution. When execution is completed, the test can be logged as pass, fail, or skipped. The manual test script is based on one that was published several years ago by the Phoenix Arizona SQA Users Group (13). It has been completely rewritten and enhanced to add custom comment entries in the test log. This test script is included with the utilities that are on the FTP site that supports this book. It can easily be adapted to scripting languages other than SQABasic.

Test Results Verification Test results verification can be accomplished either manually or through test automation. Manually eyeballing the results and making subjective assessments of correctness is one way of verifying the test results. Test results can further be compared to sets of expected output data values, compared to values that should have been created in database rows based on the transactions tested, and compared against stored files and reports.

Test results verification is a task ripe for automation. Test results should be captured in a test log that is stored in a test repository. The test log should store results from previous test runs that can serve as baseline behaviors with which to compare the current test results. For manual tests, the test log can be an MS Excel workbook where new spreadsheets are created for each new test iteration. It does not matter how the test results are stored. What is important is that comparisons can be made. If a baseline is not established, then the assessment of a pass or fail status is based on a guess at what the results should be. Being able to define and store baseline behaviors is an important advantage and a strong argument for automated testing.

Commercially available automated testing tool suites offer a variety of automated verification methods. For example, Rational Robot uses SQA-Basic, which has special test cases called *verification points* that can be used to trap AUT characteristics; these can then be used as baselines for future regression tests.

Test Reporting   Test reporting is an essential part of the testing process because it documents the test results and their analysis. Two levels of reporting are required—a summary report should be generated for middle- and upper-level technical managers and for customers, and a detailed report should be compiled and presented to the development team members as feedback.

These reports should be presented in standard formats that can be edited and tweaked for each individual test project report. We have employed the reporting template that is in RUP's documentation, but you can create your own. Two versions of this report can be created—a summary report and a detailed report. You can also find templates and examples of test reporting on the World Wide Web.

An important reporting item is also defect tracking information. Defect tracking reports can be generated separately using tools such as Rational ClearQuest and/or MS Excel. Defect information should also be summarized and included in both the detailed and summary test evaluation reports. It is imperative to include a list of known defects that have not been addressed and that will be in the software upon its release. The information in the list should be grouped according to severity. Information such as this can be used to make intelligent release decisions, and help desk personnel can use it after the software goes into production.

Support Activities

Testing Is a Team Effort

Because software testing is done at the team level, it requires tools that support and enhance team member communication and that present an integrated interface allowing team members to share common views of testing process activities and artifacts. One of the predominant problems at all stages of the testing process is artifact control and storage. One of the areas that provide the most payback to the testing process is automated configuration management of testing deliverables. There are many documents and executables that are created that must be available to all of the test team members. Team members frequently work these entities in parallel. They must be protected from concurrent updates that may overwrite each other when more than one team member is working on the same deliverable. Furthermore, there must be a central repository where the artifacts are stored for public use.

We have worked on many testing projects where there was no central storage and where everyone on the team created and updated the documents on their local desktops. We created rules defining directories for specific deliverables and stating that everyone was supposed to place their work in these shared public directories. This solution was better than no solution, but it still did not provide versioning with check-out and check-in control of the documents.

First and foremost are testing management and requirements management. Testing management can be implemented using a tool such as MS Project. It allows tasking identification, resource management, and progress assessment through the setting of testing milestones. A requirements management tool is also essential because software requirements must be documented and updated during the development process and test requirements must be documented and updated in parallel with development activities and during testing activities.

Our tool of choice for requirements management has been RequisitePro because it integrates software requirements gathering with test requirements specification. Furthermore, its test requirements grids can be exported to MS Project and then used to guide and monitor the test process. There are other requirements management tools available, some of which are integrated with testing tool suites. While this book is not about tool evaluation, there are two essential considerations when assessing these products. First, is the product already integrated with a testing tool suite? Second, if it is not, does it have an open application programming interface (API) that can be used to create your own integration code?

Software configuration management is next. There are products available that can be used to implement configuration management of testing artifacts. They include MS Visual SourceSafe, Rational ClearCase, and Merant's PVCS, just to name a few. It is imperative that all testing artifacts be stored in an automated configuration management database. It is just as important that the particular configuration management tool you have chosen communicate with the other tools you are using to support test process activities at all levels of testing. If the tool does not, then it must offer and open an API to build the software bridges you need.

Software testing metrics are a necessary component in test evaluation reporting. The metrics should include defect metrics, coverage metrics, and quality metrics. There are many useful defect tracking measures. Defect metrics can be generally categorized as defect density metrics, defect aging metrics, and defect density metrics: the number of daily/weekly opens/closes, the number of defects associated with specific software/test requirements, the number of defects listed over application objects/classes, the number of defects associated with specific types of tests, and so on. Defect reporting should be automated using at a minimum an Excel workbook because Excel has the capability to summarize spreadsheet data in charts and graphs. Defect reporting can also be automated through tools such as Rational ClearQuest, among others.

Testing quality metrics are special types of defect metrics. They include (8):

- Current state of the defect (open, being fixed, closed, etc.)
- Priority of the defect (importance to its being resolved)
- Severity of the defect (impact to the end-user, an organization, third parties, etc.)
- Defect source (the originating fault that results in this defect—the *what* component that needs to be fixed)

Coverage metrics represent an indication of the *completeness* of the testing that has been implemented. They should include both requirements-based coverage measures and code-based coverage measures. For examples of these metrics, see Chapter 9 in reference (6) and the Concepts section under "Key Measures of Testing" in reference (10).

A Test Automation Group's Scope and Objectives_____

The Scope

A test automation group's purpose should be to develop automated support for testing efforts. This group should be responsible for the design and implementation of a data-driven automated testing framework. They should design and construct suites of automated tests for regression testing purposes. Figure 1.3 illustrates an automated testing infrastructure that was designed for a well-known company by CSST Technologies, Inc.

The test automation framework should be deployed specifically to support automated test script development and the maintenance related to all levels of testing. The framework should support unit and integration testing and system/regression testing endeavors. This does not imply that other

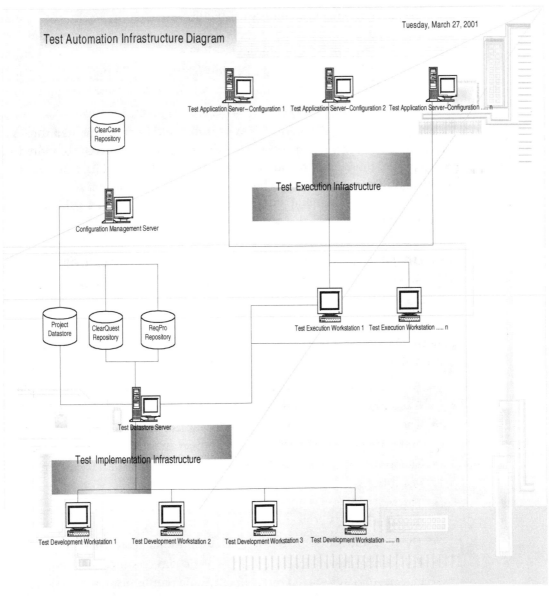

FIGURE 1.3
A Sample Automated Test Infrastructure

areas not included in this scope cannot take advantage of the test automation framework and tool suites. Other departments that may be interested in using the test automation scaffolding and the automation tool suite should fund and coordinate deployments with the automation team. An automation effort should focus on the identified areas of deployment.

The chosen approach should cover the test automation activities that will be performed by an automated tools group. Manual testing activities can serve as precursors to test automation. The goal for manual test efforts should be to manually test all application features and, while in the process, to develop test conditions and data that can be implemented using the automation framework for regression testing.

As an example, the data-driven approach could be implemented through structured test scripts that make use of functions and procedures stored in library files, the primary goal being to separate the test data from the test scripts and the secondary goal being to develop reusable test script component architecture. Meeting these goals substantially reduces the maintenance burden for automated test scripts.

Assumptions, Constraints, and Critical Success Factors for an Automated Testing Framework

The following assumptions should be applied.

Assumptions   The following assumptions form the basis of the test automation strategy.

- An integrated tool suite must be the primary test management, planning, development, and implementation vehicle.
- The tool suite must be used to direct and control test execution, to store and retrieve test artifacts, and to capture/analyze/report test results.
- The tool suite must include a tool of choice for defect tracking and resolution.
- The tool suite must include a component for test requirements management.
- The tool suite must include a configuration management tool of choice.
- The configuration management tool of choice must be used to put manual and automated test artifacts under configuration management.
- All of the tools described above must be integrated with desktop tools such as MS Office.

- The proper automated testing workspaces must be created on test servers that are separate from development servers.
- The required test engineer desktop-script-development configuration must be defined and implemented.
- Testing standards must be documented and followed.

Constraints   These constraints limit the success of the automation effort if they are not heeded.

- The automated tools group resources must remain independent of any manual testing group.
- There may not be a large enough number of available staff on the automation team.
- The level of cooperation of the software development group and their management with respect to automated tool use may be too low.
- There may be a lack of cooperation and information exchange with developers in creating testable applications.
- The release schedules for major versions of the AUT and for customer-specific releases of the AUT can be too tight.
- There is uncertainty associated with the GUI updates in AUT.
- There may be corporate mandates on what tools must be used.

Critical Success Factors   We based the following critical success factors on a set of test automation guidelines developed by Nagle (7).

- Test automation must be implemented as a full-time effort, not a sideline.
- The test design process and the test automation framework must be developed as separate entities.
- The test framework must be application independent.
- The test framework must be easy to expand, maintain, and enhance.
- The test strategy/design vocabulary must be framework independent.
- The test strategy/design must hide the complexities of the test framework from testers.

Strategic Objectives   These objectives are based on the critical success factors listed above.

- Implement a strategy that will allow tests to be developed and executed both manually (initial test cycle) and via an automation framework (regression test cycles).

- Separate test design and test implementation to allow test designers to concentrate on developing test requirements, test planning, and test case design while test implementers build and execute test scripts.
- Implement a testing framework that both technical and nontechnical testers can use.
- Employ a test strategy that assures that test cases include the navigation and execution steps to perform, the input data to use, and the expected results all in one row or record of the input data source.
- Realize an integrated approach that applies the best features of keyword-driven testing, data-driven testing, and functional decomposition testing.
- Implement an application-independent test automation framework.
- Document and publish the framework.
- Develop automated build validation (smoke) tests for each release of the application.
- Develop automated environmental setup utility scripts for each release of the application.
- Develop automated regression tests for
  - ✘ GUI objects and events
  - ✘ Application functions
  - ✘ Application special features
  - ✘ Application performance and scalability
  - ✘ Application reliability
  - ✘ Application compatibility
  - ✘ Application performance
  - ✘ Database verification

Test Automation Framework Deliverables

The following represents a minimal set of test automation framework artifacts that must be created in order to assure success.

- An integrated suite of automated tools that can be used by both technical and nontechnical individuals to test application software
- A strategy for training and periodic retraining of framework users
- A set of reusable test scripts and test script utilities
  - ✘ Automated environmental setup utility scripts

- ✗ Automated smoke test scripts
- ✗ Automated GUI test scripts
  - ✔ Events and objects
  - ✔ Object properties
- ✗ Data-driven automated functional test scripts
  - ✔ GUI-level data validation
  - ✔ Server-level data validation
- ✗ Automated reliability test scripts
- ✗ Automated compatibility test scripts
- ✗ Application performance test scripts
- ✗ Automated test utility libraries (files that contain reusable called procedures and functions) to implement activities such as pretest database loading and posttest database verification

An Automation Plan

Some do not believe that a plan for automating software testing activities is necessary. In fact, it has been said that such a plan is a waste of time and money and that it can impede an automation effort. Our experience has been that it is important to go through the exercise of writing a plan because it directs your thinking, and, if you follow a plan template, it reduces the chances of omitting important details. Appendix C illustrates an automation plan that was developed for one major company. You could say that it was a waste of time from a management perspective because the plan was submitted to executive-level management in the IS group and was never heard from again. It was not a waste of time for those of us who had to get the effort moving; it gave us guidance and perspective concerning what we thought we could accomplish given the time we had.

Appendix D is a template for a test automation project work breakdown plan. Even if you do not write a formal work breakdown plan, you should at least ponder what you are going to do for each of the areas that are listed in the template.

Categories of Testing Tools _____

A number of different types of automated and manual testing tools are required to support an automated testing framework. Marick has categorized them in a manner that makes sense because it is based on when and how they are used during testing (5).

Test Design Tools. Tools that are used to plan software testing activities. These tools are used to create test artifacts that drive later testing activities.

Static Analysis Tools. Tools that analyze programs without machines executing them. Inspections and walkthroughs are examples of static testing tools.

Dynamic Analysis Tools. Tools that involve executing the software in order to test it.

GUI Test Drivers and Capture/Replay Tools. Tools that use macrorecording capabilities to automate testing of applications employing GUIs.

Load and Performance Tools. Tools that simulate different user load conditions for automated stress and volume testing.

Non-GUI Test Drivers and Test Managers. Tools that automate test execution of applications that do not allow tester interaction via a GUI.

Other Test Implementation Tools. Miscellaneous tools that assist test implementation. We include the MS Office Suite of tools here.

Test Evaluation Tools. Tools that are used to evaluate the quality of a testing effort.

Appendix B is a list of automated testing terms and definitions included for your convenience.

Conclusion

Your job is to look at each testing sphere and, given the scope, goals, and objectives of your organization's automation effort, to decide what category(ies) of test tools (manual or automated) should be implemented to support that sphere. You will find that you have to make compromises and concessions and that an ideal test automation framework is just that: an idea. What you will finally implement is a mélange of tools and techniques that are appropriate for your needs.

References

1. Bender, Richard. *SEI/CMM Proposed Software Evaluation and Test KPA*. Rev. 4, Bender and Associates, P.O. Box 849, Larkspur, CA 94977, April 1996.

2. Dustin, Elfriede, Jeff Rashka, and John Paul. *Automated Software Testing*. Addison-Wesley, Reading, MA, 1999.

3. Humphrey, W. S. *Managing the Software Process*. Addison-Wesley, Reading, MA, 1989.

4. Krause, Michael H. "A Maturity Model for Automated Software Testing." *Medical Device and Diagnostic Industry Magazine*, December 1994.

5. Marick, Brian. "Testing Tools Supplier List." *www.testingfaqs.org/tools.htm*

6. Mosley, Daniel J. *Client-Server Software Testing on the Desktop and the Web*. Prentice Hall PTR, Upper Saddle River, NJ, 1999.

7. Nagle, Carl. "Test Automation Frameworks." Published at *members.aol.com/sascanagl/FRAMESDataDrivenTestAutomationFrameworks.htm*

8. Pettichord, Bret. "Seven Steps to Test Automation Success." Rev. July 16, 2000, from a paper presented at STAR West, San Jose, November 1999. Available at *www.pettichord.com*

9. Powers, Mike. "Styles for Making Test Automation Work." January 1997, Testers' Network, *www.veritest.com/testers'network*

10. Rational Software Corporation. *Rational Unified Process 5.1, Build 43*. Cupertino, CA, 2001.

11. The Software Engineering Institute, Carnegie Mellon University. "Software Test Management: A Key Process Area for Level 2: Repeatable." Available in the "Management Practices" section of *www.sei.cmu.edu/cmm/cmm-v2/test-mgt-kpa.html*

12. Strang, Richard. "Data Driven Testing for Client/Server Applications." Fifth International Conference on Software Testing, Analysis and Reliability (STAR '96), pp. 395–400.

13. Weimer, Jack. *Manual Test User Interface Program*. Touch Technology International, Inc., *www.touchtechnology.com*. Available from Phoenix, Arizona, SQA Users Group. This code is free and can be passed on to anyone who wishes to use it, provided the copyright, credits, and instructions stay with the code. *www.quanonline.com/phoenix_sqa/tips.html*

14. Wiegers, Karl E. "Read My Lips: No New Models!" Whitepaper, Process Impact, (716)377-5110, *www.processimpact.com*

15. Zambelich, Keith. "Totally Data-Driven Automated Testing." Whitepaper, Automated Testing Specialists (ATS), *www.auto-sqa.com/articles.html*

Knowing When and What to Automate 2

In General

Zambelich has this to say with respect to test automation:

> The case for automating the Software Testing Process has been made repeatedly and convincingly by numerous testing professionals. Most people involved in the testing of software will agree that the automation of the testing process is not only desirable, but in fact is a necessity given the demands of the current market. (3)

Developing an automated testing framework can be an expensive and time-consuming project. The creation and implementation of this framework must be done far in advance of the AUT's delivery to quality control (QC) and thus may be built and tested early in the project's life cycle. Unfortunately, once that framework is in place, you may find that it is not appropriate for all of your organization's software testing needs. Knowing when to use such a framework is an important part of test automation. We have hotly argued this subject in online discussions with other members of the automated testing community. The portion of our argument that follows alludes to the value of data-driven testing, given the effort expended to develop the framework. It was taken from the discussion held on the SQA users group Web site the week of May 17–21, 1999. Although there were many participants, in the excerpt here Elfriede Dustin, Carl Nagle, and Dan Mosley are the debating parties. You can find the full online discussion in Appendix A.

Elfriede:

I have to agree with Mark, in that there is a time for data driven testing and then there isn't. I will always use data driven testing using "test data" (see *www.autotestco.com* for one example of how we've used Robot for Y2K data testing), but very rarely will use data driven testing using "control data." The reason being is that it's tedious to implement and the effort only pays off if the test can be reused many times over in subsequent releases.

I inquired with Ed Kit after his presentation at the STAR and he agreed with me that the efforts of implementing this approach often don't pay off until after the 17th run. (Yes, that's the number he gave.)

A while back, one of my coworkers in a previous job had just received training on this data driven testing approach. It took that person 3 weeks to implement the data driven approach. There were lots of nice tables with commands/controls and data to read. But in the end it boiled down to that the test would have been much more efficient using simple record and playback and modification of the recorded script, since the test wasn't used repeatedly. The effort in this case was a waste of time. You will have to use your judgment and remember that it does not always pay off to implement a complex data driven framework for automated testing.

Carl:

I would have to agree on almost every aspect of this, but must also argue that no amount of automation is cost effective if it is not *INTENDED* to be repeated. In fact, to break even on a 17th iteration sounds great. On a build verification performed nightly that's 17 business days (or less) and all in the same release!

Dan:

I beg disagree with you (Elfriede). Data-driven testing does require the up front investment that you indicated, but it does pay off big dividends during build-level regression testing. I have been there and I have seen it. We had to test 100+ transaction screens (each one was a window in itself) for a financial application. We developed over 7000+ data-driven tests which each took approximately 3 to 5 days to create and debug, but which ran in 1–2 hours when played back between builds. We usually received one build a week and we were able to replay 100+ test scripts and 7000+ test records each week and finish on time.

As you can see from this discussion, there are differing opinions as to the value of automated testing in general and of the data-driven approach specifically. The main question is this: When does it make sense to implement an automated testing framework? For some smaller testing projects, the effort may be too much given the size of the venture. Even for larger testing efforts, test automation does not seem sensible if the tests are not going to be reused in a regression test suite.

Another way to break down this issue is to view it by type of testing to be automated. For unit and integration testing, automation is indispensable. Why? Without automation, the quality of the builds given to testing is horrible. What happens is that defects, which should have been found during the development, are left for system testers to find. In today's world of Web development, Java is the language of choice and object orientation is the approach. Developers should be using test tools such as JUnit to embed test cases as classes that can be saved with the rest of the code and used/reused to test the Java objects prior to integration through the build process. Doing this eliminates many of the error types that are currently getting through to system testing. Furthermore, an automated integration-level smoke test should be prepared and executed for each build before it is accepted into system test. Chapter 5 discusses these issues in more detail.

Hancock argues:

> Test Automation is an investment. The initial investment may be substantial, but the return on the investment is also substantial. After the number of automation test runs exceed 15, the testing from that point forward is essentially free.(1)

He sees automation versus manual testing as basic cost-benefit analysis. He quotes Kaner's premise that it takes 3 to 10 times as long to build, verify, and document an automated test (2). Hancock uses 15 as a worst-case scenario in his example of the potential return from test automation in order to produce a conservative estimate of the potential benefits.

To calculate the return on investment (ROI), Hancock says the "multiple" must be determined; that is, how many times the set of tests needs to be executed—the number of platforms, operating systems, and foreign languages to be accommodated by the software multiplied together as well as by the number of builds/versions against which the tests will run (1).

If you use Hancock's ROI approach, automation during unit and integration tests is more of a bargain than automation of system testing because system tests have less of a chance of reuse than the other two types. If the system-level test cases are not implemented in an automated regression suite that will experience a high level of reuse, there is not much ROI from system test automation. The ROI for unit and integration tests can be much higher.

Very few companies fully realize the true value of automated testing. They seem to want it, and know they need it, but in the end they cannot convince upper management of its cost benefits.

When to Automate System Tests

There are several additional elements to consider in determining when to automate. The following is based on practical experience developed through having worked on multiple projects at several companies since 1996.

Time to Automate Is Always the Number One Factor

It will cost you more time up front in the project to set up an automated testing project than it will to set up a manual test project. Automation offers no shortcuts in the beginning. You must still perform all of the same steps that you would perform for a manual testing project. Automation begins after all the test cases are defined against the finished (this is being optimistic) requirements and after a build of the AUT is delivered.

In addition, the application features to be tested via automation must work. You cannot create a valid, completed automated test against a requirement or application feature if it does not work at 100%. The primary purpose of an automated test is to verify that a requirement, once validated, functions properly in successive builds or modifications of the AUT. Furthermore, because automated testing reduces the time necessary to perform regression testing, this is where its benefits are realized the most.

If you are on a fast-track project where the project management has a very tight delivery schedule, you can pretty much forget about automation unless adequate time has been allocated specifically for it.

An Extreme Example

Let's focus on the number of AUT builds that will be delivered and on their complexity. If you are going to receive only one build of a project of mediocre size and complexity, there is probably little benefit to automating your testing effort. In fact it would be absurd due to the fact that it would be reused only during the repair cycle(s), which may be very few. Even if the project is relatively complex in nature, if the number of rebuilds and deliveries to testing are limited to fixes only, it is probably not worth the time to automate.

If the project is going to be delivered to testing in an iterative process, where sets of new features are to be delivered at multiple intervals and the feature set is fairly complex, it is likely that automated testing will offer a significant benefit. The generally accepted rule of thumb is that it takes three to four times the amount of time to automate testing as it does to perform manual testing. If you can predetermine early in the project that there will be more than three to four significant testable builds delivered to you, then your project is a likely candidate for automated testing.

There is no magic combination or precise formula to determine when automation should and should not be performed. Here are a few points to consider.

- Is the feature set in the AUT simple or complex in nature?
- Is the feature set in the AUT subject to significant change during the development process and its phases?
- Is the feature set in the AUT currently working as stated in the requirements?
- Does the feature set in the AUT require a significant number of data combinations to validate all of the business rules?
- Is the test tool being utilized for automated testing capable of interacting with all of the necessary attributes of the feature for test purposes? (For example, can it interact with it as well as the users will be able to? Can we capture all of the necessary data from the GUI and child objects?)

As you can see, these issues can be very complex and difficult to determine. In general, here are a few practical criteria to use to determine whether or not to automate testing.

1. If the AUT is not complex and not very large, don't automate.
2. If you will receive only a few (three or less) builds, don't automate.
3. If a feature doesn't work at 100%, don't perform automated testing on it, regardless of the size or complexity of the AUT (you can plan for it,

but don't create the actual automated test scripts until it is finished and working at 100%).

4. If the development cycle is on a high-speed schedule with short times between deliveries, you simply won't have time to automate it.

5. If a feature cannot be tested with 100% accuracy via automated testing, don't bother unless it saves a considerable amount of manual test time. This does not mean that the feature has to be 100% tested. Remember that software testing almost never provides 100% coverage of each and every feature of an AUT. Don't try to go there. What testing you *do* perform should never be subjective. The results should always be predictable and should be able to produce a pass or fail condition.

A Quantitative Example

A feature set in the AUT takes 6 hours to test manually. If it takes 6 hours to perform these test(s), then it will take a minimum of 6 hours (most likely more because you will be interchanging between manual testing and test data/test script creation) to record the tests using an automated test tool. The accepted rule of thumb states that it will take an additional 12 hours of work to organize and set up the automated test script(s). This being the case, automating testing of this feature set will cost 18 hours up front. The tester would be required to perform the manual test 3 times to total up to 18 hours. In general, playing back a test script takes only about 1/10 the amount of time it took to execute it manually. The test is running nearer to machine speed, usually limited only by the application's reaction time and any delays that have to be inserted into the test script such as those used to simulate user "think" time.

This being said, the automated test should execute in approximately 36 minutes. Therefore, on the fourth test execution of the feature set, test automation starts saving a little under 5.5 hours of test time and will then continue to save that amount each time regression testing is performed for this AUT's feature set. Automation costs more up front, but pays off rapidly each time regression testing is performed. Not only is there a savings of time, but also the tests are performed with more accuracy when the human interaction factor is removed.

What to Automate

If time permits, automate testing of the entire project. Practical experience has shown that on average you can automate 60% of the overall project. Your objective should be to automate testing of the critical path(s) of the AUT. First, automate the primary functions that will be performed by the targeted end-users. Slowly, but surely, add the not-so-critical portions of the application as time permits. Be sure to develop a test coverage matrix showing requirements on one axis and developed tests on the other so that you constantly have a good picture of what has and what has not been automated.

Early in the project do not bother to automate testing of such things as login, user preferences, or other options. Do not automate testing of status bars, help screens, or any other areas of the application that development will pay little attention to until later in the project. Plan for the automation strategy for these items early in the test development phase, but do not implement them until the development effort focuses on them. A bit of common sense tells us that we automate testing of those items that development considers finished or complete.

Hancock says to automate "what makes sense."(1) The answer to this question will vary from project to project and from environment to environment. You will have to develop an assessment strategy for your testing organization that can be used to determine what to automate. We believe our tips will assist you during your decision process.

A Word About Creating Test Scripts

You will discover more defects when you are developing the automated tests (because you must perform manual testing first to verify that your automated test will work properly) than you will running the finished test scripts. This is normal. Automation is used to help uncover those defects that are created accidentally or inadvertently after the feature being tested has already been tested and delivered. The speed at which you can uncover these newly introduced defects is the issue at hand. Automated testing is your insurance in that it is used to verify that what functioned properly once still functions properly.

Conclusion

This chapter includes practical advice on whether or not to automate, as well as when and what to automate. The advice is based on our practical experience as employees and consultants.

The general advice and that related to unit and integration testing are based on the experiences of coauthor Daniel Mosley and his testing in Web-based Java environments. The advice can also be applied in non-Web development environments such as Visual Basic.

The system test automation tips are based specifically on the work of coauthor Bruce Posey, whose specialty is test script design and construction.

References

1. Hancock, James. "When to Automate Testing A Cost-Benefit Analysis," June 1998, Testers' Network, *www.veritest.com/testers'network*

2. Kaner, Cem. "Improving the Maintainability of Automated Test Suites." *Software QA* 4, no. 4, 1997. (Also published in *Proceedings of the 10th International Software Quality Week*, San Francisco, May 1997.)

3. Zambelich, Keith. "Totally Data-Driven Automated Testing." Whitepaper, Automated Testing Specialists (ATS), *www.auto-sqa.com/articles.html*

Start at the Beginning, Define the Test Requirements, Design the Test Data

3

Software/Test Requirements

In an informal survey taken at *www.csst-technologies.com*, we asked the question, "As a software tester, what would facilitate your work the most?" The answers were grouped as follows:

Improved system requirements documentation	33% (28 responses)
Software testing methods/process	31% (27 responses)
Software testing standards	16% (14 responses)
Improved test planning	13% (11 responses)
More time to complete testing	7% (6 responses)

It is obvious that the two most important improvements software test engineers want are improved software requirements and improved testing methods. This is not so obvious with software development managers.

In good economic times, major corporations employ a fair number of Quality Assurance & Testing (QA&T) personnel, as well as hiring consultants from outside. The year 2001, however, was a very depressed year for quality assurance and software testing employment. Economic circumstances in 2001 affected employment patterns, revealing a problem that in better times had remained hidden. Furthermore, by trying to get the most bang for their buck, employers have exacerbated that problem. Employers are using the same personnel to do test planning and test design as they are using for test implementation. This has led to a blurring of the roles of test engineers, the test design engineer, and the test implementation engineer.

Misunderstanding of how these engineers work is caused by two factors. The first is a lack of understanding of the software testing process and how automation fits. The second is a lack of understanding of the roles of test engineers as they change throughout the testing process. We have reached the age of specialization, and software testing is no exception. Test engineers can specialize in test planning, test design, and/or test implementation. Each role requires a different set of manual and automated testing skills. Test planners and test designers may work in parallel or may be the same person; they should possess similar abilities to define and document testing artifacts. Test implementers, on the other hand, are either nonprogramming manual testers or are programmers who are doing automated testing. The latter write and execute automated test scripts. Both categories capture and analyze the test results. As previously stated, it is desirable to have the test designer act as a manual tester during design activities. Therefore, the test design engineer must be a "generalist" who can do test planning and design as well as test implementation while the test implementation engineer must be a "specialist" in writing and executing automated test scripts. The test implementation engineer must be an expert in test script design and not in test/test data design.

As for the automation aspects of testing, we have worked for the past 10 years implementing test automation at many local companies, and we have emphasized that an automated test script is not intelligent in and of itself. The intelligence is in the test data. The test data must contain smart tests that are based on the software's requirements definitions and design specifications. The term *intelligent* refers to the data's ability to stress known/ expected application weaknesses. Prior to test implementation, the test designers must build the intelligence into the test data where they will be used manually or with automated test scripts.

The test data must include values that the script needs to navigate the AUT. The only other way to insert smarts into a test script is to hard code the data values in the test script proper or in a function/subroutine that the script calls. This is what happens when the traditional capture/playback automation approach is used. During the recording process, two types of test data are collected—first, the data points that are used to set the context of the test and to navigate the AUT; second, the data values that will be submitted to the application to test its functionality, performance, security, etc. The result of having all of this data embedded in the test script is a test script maintenance nightmare.

Automated test scripts are not necessarily any better unless they execute intelligent test data. Again, it is important to couple the development of test data design for automated tests with manual testing so that the manual tests are also smart. A good way to design test data is to use the requirements and design documents while you have the application running on a test machine and MS Excel open on your desktop machine. When you identify a test requirement, you then document the test conditions and the environmental prerequisites for that requirement in an Excel spreadsheet. Then manually execute the test data on the test computer. If it gives the expected results, document it in the spreadsheet and move on to the next test condition/ requirement. If you use this approach, you will identify the test data and document the pretest environmental variables and whatever posttest cleanup is needed to assure that each test is independent. The test data are exported to a format that an automated test script can use.

Test designers must also specify the test preconditions, navigation of the AUT, the aspects to be tested, and the necessary posttest cleanup. This is all necessary information that the test implementer (scriptwriter) must have to construct an effective automated test script. Designers must use the requirements definition documents and the design documents to identify potential test conditions (areas of the application that may have a predisposition toward having defects) and their expected results. The test designers also use any other information that describes the application that might be available.

Those of you who frequent such user groups as the Software Quality Automation (SQA) users group and the Data Driven Engine (DDE) users group know that we are advocates of the data-driven framework. Coauthor Bruce Posey has developed his own flavor of this paradigm that he has dubbed Control Synchronized Data Driven Testing. Carl Nagle of the SAS Institute has a different perspective in that he has developed his DDE model using Rational Software's SQABasic language platform and MS Excel. Even though both approaches were developed using Rational Software's Test-Studio tool suite, they are adaptable to other commercially available tool suites such as those offered by Mercury Interactive and Seque.

The primary difference in the two approaches is that CSDDT stores test context, navigation rules, and special test procedures as subroutines used directly by the main procedure in the test script, whereas in the DDE model these tasks are executed by a special set of test script libraries that constitute the engine. In a sense the DDE is test automation middleware. The second difference is that the DDE is driven by a set of test tables that are developed as Excel spreadsheets, but that contain special commands that tell the engine where to go and what to test. In the CSDDT approach, this information precedes the actual test data in each test record. The test records are stored as CSV files or in data pools.

The problem with both approaches is that they depend on the test data and extraneous information about those data to execute the actual test(s). If the data are not focused, the tests that are conducted are ineffective. The only way to focus automated testing is to develop test data from the software development process artifacts available to the Test Planner/Designer or to pick the brains of the system analysts and designers.

Other than one or two openings for manual testers, the only current opportunities in IT organizations are those that involve coding automated test scripts. Employing only test implementers means companies are forcing test engineers to play both roles in the testing process, that of test design engineer and that of test implementation engineer. This was happening to some extent even before the current economic downturn; however, employment opportunities for test designers have all but evaporated. Even companies that advertise asking for a broad background in test automation really want people only to code test scripts. Now, coding test scripts is an honorable profession, but most individuals we have encountered who enjoy implementing the tests by writing and executing the test scripts do not enjoy planning and designing the tests. Consequently, they do not put forth a good effort when asked to do so.

This is how we as authors have come to a division of labor. Dan's personal work preference is test planning and design; Bruce's is test implementation. When we consult within local IT organizations, the service we provide is that of test requirements identification and documentation (Dan), test data design and construction (Dan), and test implementation (Bruce). Since the beginning of the summer of 2001, test designer consulting positions have virtually dried up. All of the preemployment screening interviews have focused only on test script writing with an emphasis on how quickly the potential consultant/employee can develop a suite of automated test scripts that will provide automated regression testing. According to Kit's definitions of the generations of automated test tool (capture/playback tools) use (9), we are functioning at the level of the third generation.

For example, the job description in Figure 3.1 is for the position of software test engineer with a Fortune 500 company for which Dan was interviewed. During that interview, it came to light that there were actually two positions and that both were for test implementers, not test designers. From the description in Figure 3.1 it is clear that the individuals who wrote it have no idea about who does what testing activities, or when those activities occur, because the description calls for a single person who has both the skill sets of a test design engineer and a test implementation engineer. They wanted someone to come in and start coding test scripts right away. Of course, you can see the problem with the situation. They were violating the testing process by skipping or haphazardly planning the tests and the test data. The only relevant parts of the job description were that it called for experience in creating manual and automated test scripts and knowledge of SQL as required skill sets because they would be required to code the scripts. The rest of the verbiage refers to test planning and test design rather than test implementation.

Why does a test scriptwriter (an implementation engineer) need to have a working knowledge of the software development Capability Maturity Model (CMM)? There is no reason. This knowledge will help the test manager in the quest to formalize and structure the testing process and its management, but it is of little use to the test implementer. Needless to say Dan was not contracted for either of those openings. One reason was because he proceeded to explain to the interview committee that its automated testing effort was doomed to failure because it was ignoring a most important aspect of automated test development—the design of intelligent tests. I explained why and offered my services in that area, but to no avail. They were determined to start writing test scripts without doing the planning and design that leads to a successful automated testing implementation. They did, however, hire Bruce.

The point is that a suite of automated tests created without first designing the test data shoots in the dark at the AUT and is no better than random testing or no testing at all. With respect to our geographic area and the companies that service it, this situation is QA&T management's fault. When will these individuals take up the torch and do what it takes to implement software quality control procedures that are effective? As we said earlier, we have worked in a number of IT organizations and QA&T departments as contactors and, with one exception, we have yet to see test automation done properly.

With their tight/reduced budgets, and by not employing test designers to create intelligent tests, these same managers are not specifying which targets the test scripts must assault. Think about the war in Afghanistan. If the spot-

Information Technology Team:	TCC QA
Date Posted:	10/2/01
Start Date:	11/1/01
Assignment Length:	12 Months
Status:	Open
Location:	St. Louis

Description/Special Requirements:

Work as a key team member in the development of software systems for Xxxxxxx Company.

Responsibilities:

As a Software Tester, the qualified candidate would take a large role in ensuring that our systems meet quality standards before they are released to the field. This position would be involved throughout the project lifecycle to ensure that requirements are verifiable and the system is integration-and-system tested.

Required Skills:

Minimum of 3–4 years experience in software testing. In-depth knowledge and experience in integration and system testing, development of test plans, test processes and techniques, and the creation of manual and automated test scripts. Experience with Rational Suite TestStudio for automated testing and Rational RequisitePro for test requirement traceability necessary. Demonstrated proficiency in MS Office for the completion of test plans and manual test scripts. Individual must have a strong technical aptitude, strong problems solving and decision-making skills, good communications skills, result oriented, and works well in a team environment.

Optional Skills:

Knowledge of Capability Maturity Model, SQL, Oracle, and Team-Share's track desirable.

Hires / No. of Positions: 0 / 1

FIGURE 3.1

Software Test Engineer Job Description from a Local Fortune 500 Company ters were not on the ground to guide the high-tech laser bombs, they would not hit the terrorist targets. All of the bombing would be ineffective unless the military resorted to carpet bombing, a technique which was used in World War II. This required dropping tons of bombs at generalized targets in order to achieve results similar to those derived today through using a much smaller number of so-called smart bombs. Carpet bombing requires a much higher level of effort and resources; in the same manner, so does random testing. For the position in the job description (Figure 3.1), management wanted someone to come on board and automate their random testing.

Laser bombs are focused on specific targets much as data-driven tests are focused on specific test conditions when they attack the application you are testing. Laser-bomb accuracy is unprecedented, and its target demolition rate is very high. The same can be said for the defect-finding rate of data-driven tests. Automated test suites that run unintelligent tests (those that are not based on knowledge of how the application works and where the application might display weaknesses) are more akin to carpet bombing the application. A much larger number of tests are required and the defect-finding rate of the tests is much lower—statistically less than one-third of random tests will find a discrepancy in the AUT.

One reason for opting to use the data-driven approach (smart tests) is software testing economics. The more effective the tests are at finding defects, the bigger the ROI in their design and construction. This is much the same as the ROI of smart bombs compared to those used in carpet bombing runs. The smart bombs cost more up front, but hit more targets; ordinary dumb bombs are cheaper, but many more are required to achieve the same result. Designing intelligent tests costs more up front than simply jumping in and creating automated test scripts, but the true cost of quality is seen *after* the system is released. The lower the number of defects that survive in production software, the higher the quality and the lower the maintenance costs.

The moral of this dissertation—if there is one—is that, even in bad economic times, QA&T managers must understand that there are no shortcuts to test automation and that to forgo hiring the talent needed to do test planning and test design is to risk much higher costs after the software is released to the customers.

Requirements Gathering and Test Planning Automation

Identifying and defining software requirements in general is a difficult job. Requirements management is seen as the key to success in software development (9,18). Over the years the American National Standards Institute (ANSI) and the Institute of Electrical and Electronics Engineers (IEEE) have defined standards such as

- ANSI/IEEE 830-1984: Software Requirements Specifications
- ANSI/IEEE 830-1998: Recommended Practice for Software Requirements Specifications
- IEEE Std 1362-1998: (incorporates IEEE Std 1362a-1998) IEEE Guide for Information Technology—System Definition—Concept of Operations (ConOps) Document

While the first two documents are technical standards for requirements specifications by software engineers, the third is aimed at defining software requirements from the user's point of view.

A formal approach to specifying test requirements goes a long way toward satisfying the two major complaints cited in the survey at the outset of this chapter. It formalizes the translation of software requirements to test requirements and makes the process repeatable (CMM Level 2). Even with the availability of the ANSI/IEEE standards, Gerrard holds that the majority of requirements documents are "often badly organized, incomplete, inaccurate and inconsistent." (9) He also believes that the majority of documented requirements are "untestable" as written because they are presented in a form that is difficult for "testers" to understand and test against their expectations. It is up to the test engineers themselves to translate those requirements into testable ones.

There are no standards documents to guide the specification of requirements for software testing (and/or to guide the translation of existing software requirements specifications). Refining existing software requirements into software testing requirements is a very difficult task. The information a test engineer must have in order to properly test a software component is highly detailed and very specific. Granted, there are different levels and approaches to testing and test data specification (Black Box, Gray Box, and White Box views of the software); for detailed information on these concepts and their application, see (14,15,16). The nature of the test requirements depends on the point of view of the test engineer. The stance of the test engineer is also dependent on the level of depth and details contained in the software requirements specification. Thus, it is possible to specify test requirements from both Black Box and White Box perspectives.

In many instances, there isn't a software requirements specification document to be translated into test requirements. When this is true, test engineers have two options. One is to try to capture the test requirements on their own, and another is to tell the project manager that the software cannot be tested because there are no documented requirements. Unfortunately, in the real world, many software requirements specification documents are written only after the software has been constructed. When this is the case, test engineers must ferret out the test requirements themselves, prior to and during testing activities.

Why are test requirements so important to the testing process? First, they are necessary because test engineers must predict the expected outcome of their tests. As Myers so aptly stated in his landmark book, *The Art of Software Testing*, "If there are no expectations, then there can be no surprises."(16)What Myers meant is that there must be some set of prior beliefs about the behavior of the software if anything it does is to be conceived as incorrect. He also wrote, "If the expected result of a test case has not been predefined, chances are that a plausible, but erroneous, result will be interpreted as a correct result because of 'the eye seeing what it wants to see.'" Without test requirements, there is no way to predefine the software's behavior devoid of prestidigitation.

As for the second issue, test results verification cannot be done unless there is a set of predefined application behaviors. This is because test engineers must verify the results of each test. It is not enough to know what to expect, so one must capture the AUT's actual behaviors and compare them to the expected behaviors that are based on the definitions of what the software should do (the requirements). Prediction and verification cannot be done with prespecified test requirements. This is a major point of consideration for software development managers, who want to know how the test results will be verified. They want to see written proof of the test result. There are many ways to verify test results. For example, simply observing the AUT's behavior may be enough, but development managers want more substantial proof. That is where test requirements play a crucial role.

A *test requirement* is a testing *goal*. It is a statement of what the test engineer wants to accomplish when implementing a specific testing activity. More than this, it is a goal that is defined to reflect against an AUT feature as documented in the software requirements specification. A test requirement is a step down from the software requirement. It must be *measurable* in that it must be able to be proven. *Measurable* means that the test engineers can qualitatively or quantitatively verify the test results against the test requirement's expected result. In order to achieve this, test requirements must be further decomposed into test case requirements. These low-level requirements contain more elemental detail than software requirements and high-level test requirements do. Test Case Requirements describe specific test conditions in such detail that there is a direct relation from each test case requirement to each test data record that is actually executed. The relationship from software requirement to test requirement can be one-to-one (one test requirement per software requirement), one-to-many (one software requirement resulting in many test requirements), and many-to-one (more than one software requirement relating to one test requirement). Using the same line of thinking, the relationship of test requirement to test case requirement can be one-to-one (one test condition per test requirement), one-to-many (one test requirement resulting in many test conditions and therefore many test case requirements), and many-to-one (more than one test case requirement relating to one test condition). In all instances, many-to-many relationships are also possible, but they make testing so complex that the results are difficult to interpret, so this type of relationship should be avoided. When it occurs, consider using a decomposition approach to split the test requirement into one or more less complex requirements.

Test requirements must also be associated with manual or automated scripts. For example, a test requirement may produce 50 test conditions that represent functional variations of the baseline test data. Those data are stored as test data records in a text file. An automated (data-driven) test script that navigates the AUT and reads in the data inserts each record into the appropriate GUI screen and the AUT saves the record to its database. For test coverage metric purposes, it is important to *attach* the test script to the test requirement.

From Software Requirement to Test Requirement to Test Condition: An Automated Approach

In automated development tool suites such as Rational Enterprise Suite, requirements management tools are used to specify a number of different types of software requirements. Automated test tool suites such as Rational Suite TestStudio 1.0/1.5 offer the test engineer the ability to work with software requirements entered via Rational RequisitePro and to translate them into test requirements for the design and construction of automated test scripts.

Rational's development/test tool suites are designed around an internal process—Rational Unified Process. RUP describes several general software requirement types (20):

Functional Requirement—defines the input and output behavior of a system

Usability Requirement—defines aesthetics, and consistency in the user interface, documentation, and training materials

Reliability Requirement—defines failure and recoverability

Performance Requirement—defines response time

Supportability Requirement—defines testability and maintainability

In addition to these, RUP also describes several software construction-oriented requirement types that take into account physical constraints (20):

Design Requirement—places limitations on the software design

Implementation Requirement—places limitations on software construction

Interface Requirement—places limitations on software interaction with other systems, users, etc.

Physical Requirement—places limitations, such as hardware type, on implementation

In addition, Rational RequisitePro offers the ability to specify custom requirement types designed around specific project needs. As far as test requirements go, RUP 1.0 asserts the following:

> Test cases are ways of stating how we will verify what the system actually does, and therefore they should be tracked and maintained as requirements. We introduce the notion of requirements type to separate these different expressions of requirements.(20)

RequisitePro has two default requirement types that relate to testing. They are a Test Requirement type (prefixed with TR) and a Test Case Requirement type (prefixed with TCS). Both kinds of test requirements can be entered either through the RequisitePro interface or through the Test-Manager GUI. Requirements can also be gleaned from MS Word or from standard text documents using a keyword search and include algorithm.

Once entered, requirements are stored in linked project and test repositories and are visually and structurally presented as a hierarchy of parent and child requirements. As you can infer, there should be a relationship between a test requirement and a test case requirement. This relationship should be implemented by including test case requirements as children of related test requirements. Test requirements can in turn be linked to other types of requirements by making them children of those requirements.

Products such as Rational RequisitePro and Rational TestManager organize and link test requirements; they also can track test requirement revisions and do general housekeeping around the requirements. However, they do not specify the content of those requirements; that is, the details required for test script design, for test data design, and for test results verification purposes are not prespecified. Test engineers must use their skills and experience to develop the subject matter of the Test Requirements. To do so, they must address specific issues for Test Requirements and even more detailed issues for Test Case Requirements. For our purposes, we will classify Test Requirements as Black Box and Test Case Requirements as White Box.

Test Requirement specifications should include at a minimum the following sections and subsections:

1. The Test Objective(s)
2. Associated Risk Factors
   a. From Project Risk Assessment
   b. From Expected Usage Profiles
3. Associated Priority Level

For Test Requirements, the sources of information include the software requirements specification documentation; the results of high-level project risk assessment analysis; the prioritization of the test requirements based on assessed risk; and, when obtainable, software usage profiles for establishing the probability of potential use of specific application functions (this information can be obtained only from observing user behavior with existing manual and/or automated business systems and may not be readily available).

The test objectives should include both Black Box and White Box statements describing the testing goals for each documented requirement.

Test Case Requirement specifications should include these sections and subsections:

1. Pretest Setup
2. Test Conditions
   a. Valid Conditions
   b. Invalid Conditions
3. Test Data
   a. For Valid Conditions
   b. For Invalid Conditions
4. Expected Behaviors for Test Conditions
   a. For Valid Conditions
   b. For Invalid Conditions
5. Test Execution
   a. Manual
      i. Associated Test Scripts

  b. Automated

   i. Attached Test Scripts

 6. Test Results Verification Procedures

 7. Posttest Cleanup

  Specification of pretest setup restrictions should include a description of any and all environmental conditions that must exist in order for the test to execute properly. This includes specification of data values that the test data (test input records) require for validation purposes or that the test script uses for navigation and/or control purposes. For example, a test to reactivate a deleted customer account cannot be executed unless the customer table contains at least one customer record that has been flagged as deleted. If one does not exist, part of the test setup is to select an existing customer record and set its status to deleted. On the average there may be several such interactions that must be established prior to test execution. The information in Tables 3.1 and 3.2 can frequently be used to determine what the pretest setup data relationships are.

TABLE 3.1

GUI Edit Examples

GUI Field	Database Column	Edits	Error Message	Error Ovrrd (Y/N)
Activity Date	ACTIVITY_DATE	Cannot equal spaces	G001A	Y
		Must be numeric	G001B	Y
		Must be greater than zeros	G001C	Y
		Must be a valid date	G001C	Y
Date of Note	INV_NOTE_DT	Cannot equal spaces	G005A	Y
		Must be numeric	G005B	Y
		Must be greater than zeros	G005C	Y
		Must be a valid date	G005C	Y
Invoice Number	INV_NBR	Cannot equal spaces	G006A	Y
Mfg. Code (Master)	MFG_NBR	Cannot equal spaces	G007A	Y
Plan No.	PLN_NBR	Cannot equal spaces	G008A	Y
		Must be numeric	G008B	Y
		Must be greater than zeros	G008C	Y

TABLE 3.2
Example of Server Edits

GUI Field/ Data Value	Database Column	Edits	Error Message	Error Ovrrd (Y/N)
Activity Date Date of Note	ACTIVITY_DATE INV_NOTE_DT	Both dates are reformatted if they are European. If the Date of Note's month = Activity Date's month then skip the following month edit If Activity Date's month = 01 Date of Note's month must equal 11 or 12		
			R004C	Y
		If Activity Date's month = 02 Date of Note's month must equal 01 or 12	R004C	Y
		ELSE Activity Date's month must be greater than Date of Note's month AND (Activity Date's month -1) or (Activity Date's month -2) is equal to Date of Note's month.	R004C	Y
		NOTE: *Date of Note cannot cross into a future month.. For example: If Activity Date is 5/15, Date of Note can be 5/20, but if Activity Date is 5/30, Date of Note cannot be 6/1. Error message is not consistent with the edit.*		
		Date of Note must be a valid date	G005C	Y
		Date of Note cannot be greater than Activity Date + 5 days	R004A	Y
		Date of Note cannot be more than 60 days older than the Activity Date.	R004B	Y

TABLE 3.2
Example of Server Edits (Continued)

GUI Field/ Data Value	Database Column	Edits	Error Message	Error Ovrrd (Y/N)
Plan No. Date of Note	PLN_NBR INV_NOTE_DT	If Plan found on TPLAN: If PLN_DISC_DAYS = 0 (a date was entered) Compare the Date of Note to PLN_DISC_DATE If the Date of Note is > PLN_DISC_DATE, plus an extra error message:. "Date is" followed by PLN_DISC_DATE Else bypass this edit	R198 plus	Y
Invoice Number	INV_NBR	Invoice must not exist on TINVOICE table except for the following condition: If the invoice does exist, and the status code = '8' and current balance = 0, it is not an error.	R005	Y
Mfg. Code (Master)	MFG_NBR	Must exist on the TMANUFAC table . Cannot be flagged for delete—MFG_DEL_CODE = 'D' . NOTE: Removed 2d edit which checked repurchase code for 'C'. TC93 moves a "D" to the MFG_DEL_CODE when flagging a mfg for delete.	R006 G007I	Y N
Plan No.	PLN_NBR	Plan must exist on the TPLAN table. Cannot be flagged for delete— PLN_DEL_CD = "D".	R007 R335	Y Y

As for sections 2 (Test Conditions), 3 (Test Data), and 4 (Expected Behaviors for Test Conditions) of the Test Case Requirement specification, the necessary information comes from many and varied sources. Consequently, it is more difficult to find, identify, and organize. We have, in our wanderings as consultants, come across one document that is as close to containing the information needed to write a good test case specification document as we have seen. It was actually intended as a design specification document for mainframe application features that were to be ported to a client-server environment. It included both written and tabular descriptions of application features that could be translated into test conditions and test data, as well as assisting in the verification of test results (as it turned out, we were able to use the information to develop and implement a data-driven automated test system). The format of the document is not what is important, but the content (the tables) can be included in any Word document that is used as a Test Case Requirement source text. This is the Test Requirements Note (TRN) document.

In practical use, one TRN document is constructed for each application feature/GUI screen under test. It includes a number of sections that are relevant to that test case specification document. The "edits" section lists global, relational, and file edits; edits for required fields (single only, not cross-field edits); edits for correct data type (alpha, numeric, date) that will be performed on the client side (GUI); as well as other edits (including cross-field validations and reads to the database) that are performed on the server.

Table 3.1 is an example of how the client-side edits are specified. The included information can be used to build test data to execute against GUI-level data validations and to guide an automated test script while executing the test data. Table 3.2 illustrates how business (rules) edits performed on the server side are specified. Tables 3.1 and 3.2 contain the information needed to detail the test conditions and, from there, to develop test data. They also indicate under what conditions error messages are generated and what messages should be displayed. These tables provide all of the information necessary to identify and document Test Requirements and to develop (decompose the Test Requirements into) test conditions that are the Test Case Requirements. Then the Test Case requirements can be used to create the test data.

With respect to test results verification, it is necessary to determine what level of verification is acceptable and what methods will be used to perform the verifications. Table 3.3 defines a CRUD (Create, Read, Update, Delete) Matrix that identifies each database table and defines the types of

TABLE 3.3
Example of a CRUD Matrix

Database Table Name	Create	Read	Update	Delete
TPRODUCT	X			
TPLAN	X			
TCOMPANY	X		X	
TINVOICE	X	X		
Config File	X			
CMFLOG File				X
Help File	X			
TCSERROR	X			

accesses that are made by the application feature being tested. This information is important because it is frequently necessary to go directly to a specific column/row in a particular table to verify test results. This information may also be necessary to identify table values that must be modified during pretest setup as well.

For manual tests, the results are verified by the test engineer's efforts. For automated tests, results verification is frequently accomplished via the automated test script that is executed. This is a much more efficient and effective method. It also requires information about the application that cannot be obtained from the traditional software requirements specification. The test engineer must look toward the design specification documents to obtain the necessary information. The most accurate way to verify is to have a set of expected interactions with database tables and then go to those tables and verify that those actions occurred.

The database accesses in Table 3.4 include calls to each table in the database; listing each call (retrieve, save, etc.); including arguments, expected return values (e.g., status—found or not found, row count); the reason for the call; and the database table column names. The information in Table 3.4 also facilitates automated results verification.

Another area that must be described for verification purposes is output processing. This includes log files, files for export, reports, html pages, and values displayed to GUI fields. Table 3.5 illustrates output values as they might be specified for a specific GUI screen.

TABLE 3.4
Detailed Database Access Examples

Ref #	Table	Reason	Arguments	Return	Order by #
4	TPLAN	File edit	OFC_NBR, PLN_NBR, PLN_DISC_DAYS = '0'	Status (Found/Not found) and column: PLN_DISC_DATE	N/A
5	TINVOICE	Existence check and file edit	OFC_NBR, OFC_DL_NBR, INV_NBR	Status (Found/Not found) and columns: INV_CUR_BAL INV_STAT_CD	N/A
7	TPLAN	Existence check	OFC_NBR, PLN_NBR	Status (Found/Not found)	N/A
11	TPRODUCT	Existence check	PRD_CD	Status (Found/Not found)	N/A
12	TCOMPANY	File edit	First two characters of OFC_NBR	Status (Found/Not found) and column: DATE_FORMAT_CD American Date Format = MDY, European Date Format = DMY	N/A

TABLE 3.5
Example of GUI Output

Column Name	GUI Default	User-Entered	Program Modifies	Output Value	Order on GUI
ACTIVITY_DATE	Current system date, format for U.S. or UK	X	N/A	From screen, formatted for U.S.	1
TRAN_CODE	01	N/A	N/A	GUI default	5
OFC_DI_NBR	N/A	X	N/A	User-entered value	4

TABLE 3.5
Example of GUI Output (Continued)

Column Name	GUI Default	User-Entered	Program Modifies	Output Value	Order on GUI
INV_NBR	N/A	X	N/A	User-entered value	2
CREATE_SW	N/A	N/A	N/A	Always spaces	3
INV_NOTE_DT	N/A	X	N/A	From screen, formatted for U.S.	6
PLN_NBR	N/A	X	N/A	User-entered value	8
INV_ORG_AMT	N/A	X	N/A	User-entered value	7
INV_CURT_OVRRID_CD	'N'	X	N/A	User-entered value	9
APPROVAL_ID	N/A	X	N/A	User-entered value	10

Other general areas that should be addressed in a Test Case Requirement specification include

1. Security
2. Audit Logging
3. Error Handling—for GUI, business rules and database errors
4. Help Processing
5. CONFIG File logic

One final area that should be addressed is unit test data. Describe in detail any special data requirements identified during unit testing that could be used for integration, system, and user acceptance testing. Include the list or point to a document that describes the special data needs.

As far as posttest cleanup goes, everything that was manipulated during the pretest setup and during test execution must be reset to its initial state. The step to do this should be described as the last part of the Test Case Requirement specification.

Requirements Management and Traceability _____

Requirement traceability is a part of requirements management. Requirements management also includes the handling of test requirements. Councill and Councill are right on the money with their assessment of what a requirements management application should do. According to them, a requirements management application should offer or support these features:

1. The tool's capability to accept input of, or conduct queries on, relationships among the following lifecycle work products—
   a. Business rules
   b. Business models
   c. Requirements
   d. Use cases
   e. Other object-oriented or component-based design diagrams
   f. Test cases
2. Seamless integration with the following tools—
   a. OOAD [object-oriented analysis and design] or component-based analysis and design application
   b. Defect and test case management application
3. The ability to establish and compare baseline requirements for selected builds or versions
4. The ability to add, modify, and delete attributes by requirement type (3)

The Councills also stress the importance of traceability.

The ability to create test cases through transfer of data from the RM [requirements management] application to the test management tool was well received by the software development organization. The decreased time in writing test cases and the ability to ensure that all requirements were associated with "traced to" test cases was viewed as decreasing time to deployment.(3)

The ability to link software requirements to test requirements is crucial to the development and use of software testing metrics. It allows the test group to report on the number (percentage) of requirements that were tested. It allows test engineers to indicate the quantity and quality of the test automation effort. For instance, the percentage of tests that were automated can be compared to the percentage of tests that were not automated. The quantity of test data that were represented by test conditions in those tests can also be reported.

Another important feature is the ability to embed test requirements into other test artifacts such as the test plan. Rational RequisitePro is an example of one such requirements management tool that creates requirement traceability matrices in which individual requirements can be linked to and embedded in test plan documents written in MS Word and linked to/exported to MS Excel workbook spreadsheets.

We have used this tool's capabilities to enforce structured manual testing. A custom requirements matrix was developed which included only the fields necessary to conduct the test and a pass/fail field with options for recording the test results. The matrix was exported to MS Excel, which was opened and used by the testers who were conducting the manual tests. They executed manual tests according to the direction in the test plan and recorded the results in the test requirements matrix spreadsheet. When the tests were completed, the spreadsheet was exported back to RequisitePro, and the matrix now included the test results for each test requirement. This made test results analysis and reporting a lot simpler.

Functional Test Data Design

We believe that it is important that test design engineers have a basic knowledge of test case design techniques. If you are already familiar with these techniques and do not need to review them, skip to the beginning of the next chapter. If this is your first exposure to them, you will want to read this overview and review Myers (16) and Mosley (15), which contain detailed examples of how the techniques are used.

Black Box (Requirements-Based) Approaches

Cause-Effect Graphing   This approach involves identifying specific causes and effects that are outlined in the requirements document. *Causes* are conditions that exist in the system and account for specific system behaviors known as effects. *Effects* can be states that exist temporarily during the processing or system outputs that are the result of the processing. The causes and effects are transformed into a cause-effect diagram that can be used to create test cases.

Equivalence Partitioning   This approach uses the system requirements to identify different types of system inputs (input domains). Each input type is defined as an *Equivalence Class*. Rules are derived to govern each Equivalence Class. The rules are used as a basis for creating test cases.

Boundary Analysis   This approach strives to identify Boundary Conditions for each equivalence class. The conditions are used to create test cases containing input values that are on, above, and below the edges of each equivalence class.

Error Guessing   This approach uses the tester's experience and intuition to plug any gaps in the test data developed with the other approaches.

Gray Box (Both Requirements- and Code-Based) Approaches

Decision Logic Tables   This approach looks at combinations of equivalence classes. It can be used to develop test cases from any portion of the requirements containing complex decision logic structures that would result in If/Then/Else logic in the system processing.

White Box (Code-Based) Approaches

Basis Testing   This approach designs test cases that exercise all control flow paths through each program module. It addresses control flow as it occurs due to branching within the module. In Visual Basic, branching is the result of If/Then/Else/Endif statements, GoTo statements, For/Next loops, While/When loops, and Select Case statements. Source code listings or program flowcharts are used to identify the branch points in each module, and this information is used to construct Control Flow Diagrams that are used to design the test cases.

The objective is to test the *basis set* of logic paths. The basis set consists of a set of control paths that have path elements common to all of the paths through the module. The total set of module paths can be constructed by disassembling the basis paths and reassembling them in different combinations. Each different combination accounts for one of the module's logic paths.

Each module has a finite number of unique logic paths; however, the number may be quite high. The philosophy in testing only the basis paths is that, if the building blocks that are common to all paths are tested, it is not necessary to test all of the module's logic paths. This results in a significant savings in the number of test cases needed to test each module.

Requirements-Based Approaches

Requirements-Driven Cause-Effect Testing

Elmendorf describes the Cause-Effect graphing method as "disciplined specification-based testing." (4,5) Based on Elmendorf's work, Myers defines a Cause-Effect Graph as "a formal language into which a natural-language specification is translated." (16) The graph is a "combinatorial logic network" using notation similar to, but simpler than, standard electronics notation. More precisely, it is a Boolean graph describing the semantic content of a written functional specification as logical relationships between causes (inputs) and effects (outputs).

Because Cause-Effect graphing is a Black Box technique, it can be used early in the development process in conjunction with review procedures such as Desk Checking and Walkthroughs. It is a versatile approach because the test cases generated can be used during all subsequent levels of testing from unit testing to system testing.

The Cause-Effect Graph   Cause-Effect graphs are models of complex narrative software descriptions such as digital logic circuits. They can easily be used to develop *functional* test cases (4). Each circuit is a pictorial representation of the *semantics* portrayed in the written specifications. The semantic information in the Cause-Effect graphs is translated into Limited Entry Decision Tables (LEDT), which are used to construct the actual test cases. A LEDT is a binary truth table in which each rule represents a logical path through a program segment.

The only requirement for using and understanding Cause-Effect graphs is knowledge of Boolean logical operators. The most commonly encountered operators are AND, OR, and NOT; however, NAND and NOR may be required in some instances. There are four fundamental configurations and two infrequently used negative forms. Comprehensive examples of cause-effect graphing can be found in Myers (16) and Mosley (14,15). See Tables 3.6–3.10.

TABLE 3.6
Truth Table for Logical AND

A	B	
	1	**0**
1	1	0
0	0	0

Note: The ANDed variables are "A" and "B."

TABLE 3.7
Truth Table for Logical OR

A	B	
	1	**0**
1	1	1
0	1	0

Note: The ORed variables are "A" and "B."

TABLE 3.8
Truth Table for Logical NOT

	B	
	1	**0**
A	0	1

Note: The NOTed variables are "A" and "B."

TABLE 3.9
Truth Table for Logical NAND

A	B	
	1	**0**
1	0	1
0	1	1

Note: The NANDed variables are "A" and "B."

TABLE 3.10
Truth Table for Logical NOR

A	B	
	1	**0**
1	0	0
0	0	1

Note: The NORed variables are "A" and "B."

Identity defines a situation in which node Y is true if node X is true. In Boolean terms, if $X = 1$, $Y = 1$, else $Y = 0$.

AND defines a circumstance where X and Y must be true for Z to be true. Again, in Boolean logic, $Z = 1$ only if $X = 1$ and $Y = 1$, else $Z = 0$.

OR defines a condition in which either X or Y must be true if Z is to be true. In Boolean format, $Z = 1$ if $X = 1$ or $Y = 1$, else $Z = 0$.

NOT defines the instance where Y is true only if X is false. In Boolean logic, $Y = 1$, if $X = 0$, else $Y = 1$.

NAND defines the situation where if both X and Y are false Z is true. In Boolean, $Z = 1$, if $X = 0$ and $Y = 0$, else $Z = 0$.

NOR defines the condition where, if neither X nor Y is true, Z is true. In Boolean notation, if $X = 1$ nor $Y = 1$, $Z = 1$, else $Z = 0$.

A word of caution: The use of negative logic can lead to unnecessarily complex logical combinations and should be avoided when possible. If the situation is a NAND or NOR, try to restate the logic in the positive before developing the Cause-Effect Graph.

From a cause-effect perspective, some combinations of causes may be impossible because of semantic or syntactic **constraints**. In addition, certain effects may mask other effects and, when this occurs, it must be indicated on the graph. Consequently, the notation for constraints must be used in conjunction with the basic Cause-Effect notation (see Figure 3.2).

Constraints on Causes

Exclusive Constraint defines the situation where cause X and cause Y cannot simultaneously be true. If $X = 1$, $Y = 0$; if $Y = 1$, $X = 0$; however, both causes X and Y can simultaneously be equal to 0.

Inclusive Constraint defines the situation in which either X or Y must always be true. If $X = 0$, $Y = 1$; if $Y = 0$, $X = 1$. Causes X and Y may simultaneously be equal to 1, but the state where $X = 0$ and $Y = 0$ is not a possibility.

Requires Constraint defines the circumstance where Y must be true if X is to be true. If $X = 1$, $Y = 1$. The states where $X = 0$ and $Y = 0$ simultaneously, and where $Y = 1$ but $X = 0$ are also possible.

Only Constraint defines the instance where one and only one of X and Y must be true. If $X = 1$, $Y = 0$; if $Y = 1$, $X = 0$. Causes X and Y cannot both be simultaneously equal to 1 or simultaneously equal to 0.

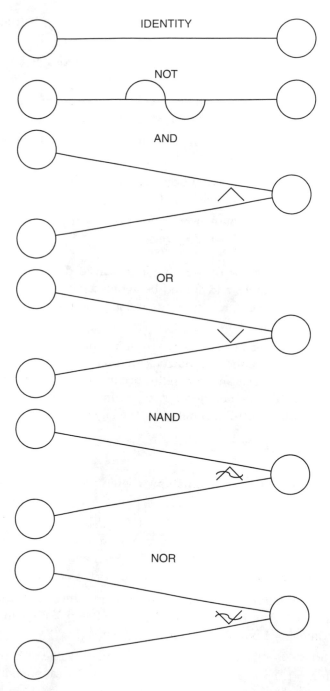

FIGURE 3.2
Cause-Effect Graphing—Basic Notation

Constraints on Effects

Masks defines the circumstance where, if effect V is true, effect Z is forced to be false. If $V = 1$, $Z = 0$.

The Inclusive, Only, and Requires constraints are used with the logical AND operator. The Exclusive constraint is used with the logical OR operator (see Figure 3.3).

Developing Test Cases   The following procedure for deriving test cases using the Cause-Effect method is adapted from Myers's work (16).

1. Divide the specification into workable pieces. Do not attempt to create a single graph for the entire specification. Large specifications are too complex and must be taken in smaller (less complex) segments that are more understandable.

2. Identify the causes and effects in each specification segment.

   A cause is a unique input condition or class of input conditions (an equivalence class).

   An effect is an output condition or a system transformation (an alteration of the system database).

3. Translate the semantic relationships in each segment into Boolean relationships linking the causes and effects in a Cause-Effect Graph.

4. Annotate each graph with the constraints affecting the causes and effects.

5. Trace the binary condition states (which can be perceived as true-false or 1-0 at each node in the graph) and identify each unique combination of binary states that link a cause to an effect.

   Draw a limited-entry decision table summarizing all of the possible condition-state combinations.

   List the Causes in the Condition Stub of the table and the effects in the Action Stub (see the discussion of Decision Logic Tables for definitions of these terms).

   Describe each combination of condition states (causes) in the condition entry quadrant of the table.

   Divide the entry side of the table into *Rules*, one for each unique combination of condition states in the Cause-Effect Graph.

   Indicate which state combinations are associated with specific effects by placing an X in the column that represents the condition-state combination (rule) next to the invoked effect.

6. Convert each column (rule) in the decision table into a test case.

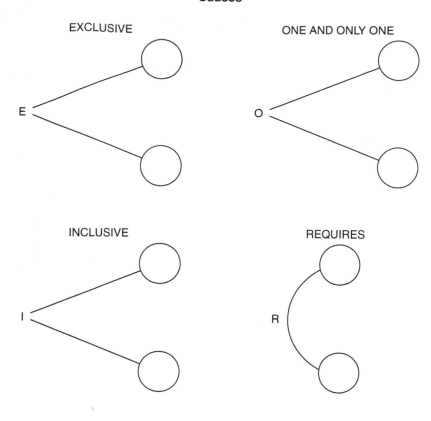

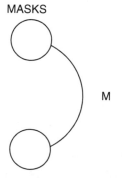

FIGURE 3.3
Cause-Effect Graphing—Constraint Notation

Identifying the unique combinations of condition states in the Cause-Effect Graph (see step 5, above) is a reasonably difficult task. Furthermore, there is no check for completeness as there is for the Decision Logic Table (DLT) procedure described later in the chapter. However, tracing backward from an effect through each of the possible combinations of intermediate input values using the primary input values will yield a set of distinct condition states. This procedure is also adapted from Myers (16).

1. Work with a single effect (output) at a time.

2. Set that effect to the true (1) state.

3. Work backward through the graph and identify all the combinations of causes (inputs) that will force this effect to the true state. The number of possible combinations may be reduced because of the constraints on the causes.

4. As stated in the previous guidelines, create a column in the decision table for each combination.

5. Determine the states (true or false, 1 or 0) for all other effects for each combination.

Equivalence Partitioning, Boundary Analysis, and Error Guessing

Equivalence Partitioning and Boundary Analysis are complementary Black Box test case design strategies that are very useful early in the development life cycle. They are techniques that translate written specifications into function-based test data. Restrictions upon input that are described in the functional specification document are used to define *classes* of input and output. Equivalence Partitioning describes categories of input only, while Boundary Analysis can define both classes of input and classes of output.

Both techniques result in two basic kinds of input classes: *valid* input classes and *invalid* input classes. In the majority of instances, there will be a single class describing the valid input; there will be one to several classes describing invalid types of input. Test cases representative of each class are created and added to the test data set.

Myers has established a set of guidelines for identifying equivalence classes and a set of rules for constructing test cases that cover each class. An additional set of rules governs the creation of test cases for the boundaries of the equivalence classes (16).

Defining Equivalence Classes   Defining equivalence classes is to some extent a trial-and-error process. It is based largely upon intuition and past experience and is something you may have done or are currently doing as part of your testing activities. There are, however, general guidelines that can expedite the process (again adapted from Myers [16]).

1. For input descriptions that specify a range of possible values (continuous input), identify *one* valid equivalence class that is representative of the values included in the range; also identify *two* invalid equivalence classes—one for values that lie above and one for values that lie below the range.

2. For input descriptions that define a set of values, each of which is processed differently (discrete input), identify *one* valid equivalence class for each value and *one* additional equivalence class that represents a value not included in the set.

3. For input of data types (e.g., the data types Numeric and Alphebetic) create *one* valid equivalence class representing the correct data type and at least *one* equivalence class representing a data type that would be considered incorrect.

4. For mixed data types (e.g., Alphanumeric) with specific mandatory conditions (e.g., as in PART-NUMBER where the first position in PART-NUMBER must always be an alphabetic character), identify *one* equivalence class in which the conditions are met and *one* equivalence class in which the conditions are not met.

5. Review the equivalence classes looking for instances where the classes may be further subdivided. The classes are subdivided only if values discovered in a class are not all processed in the same manner.

Myers says it is helpful to create a table with three columns—a left-hand column where each external input restriction is separately listed, a center column where the valid equivalence classes are described, and a right-hand column where the invalid equivalence classes are placed. Arbitrarily number all equivalence classes in the table. Organizing and numbering the equivalence classes in this manner simplifies the test case construction (16).

Constructing Test Cases from the Tabled Equivalence

Classes   The rules that follow for building test data are predicated on testing economy. They allow for the smallest number of test cases that can be created and executed safely with a reasonable level of confidence that we are testing effectively. It is possible to create fewer test cases, but these collapsed test cases will be less effective because of the *error-masking* phenomenon.

Error masking can occur when a test case contains more than one invalid value. During testing, the software evaluates each value separately, so, when the first invalid value is discovered, the evaluation process may be terminated. If this happens, the remaining invalid values do not get processed, which means we don't know what would have happened had they been processed. An example of this might be (in some computing languages) the ANDing operation (a Boolean operation) found in conditional actions. If the first condition is in the false or **off** state, the state of the second condition is not checked. The problem is that we do not know what the system's behavior would be regarding the second condition unless its condition state is evaluated.

An abbreviated version of the test case construction guidelines Myers proposed has been heuristically defined:

1. All of the valid equivalence classes can be incorporated into a single test case.

2. Each invalid equivalence class must be represented by a separate test case.

Defining Boundary Conditions for Equivalence Classes

Myers has defined Boundary Conditions as values that fall *on*, *above*, or *below* the edges of Equivalence Classes (16). An immediately obvious conclusion is that those values above and below the edges will have already been identified if the rules, as set forth above, are used to develop the Equivalence Classes. So, the only new test cases we will create are the ones representing the values on each of the bounds. Consequently, Boundary Analysis is secondary to Equivalence Partitioning in implementation order. In addition, there is one major difference between the two techniques: Boundary Analysis can also be applied to the output domain.

The following guidelines are once again adapted from Myers's work (16).

Input Domain

1. For continuous input, write test cases that represent the lowest and highest valid values within the range.

2. For discrete ordered sets of input, construct test cases that represent the first and last elements in the set (e.g., a sequential input file).

Output Domain

1. For continuous output, construct input test cases that will cause output values to be generated for the highest and the lowest values in the output range.
2. For discrete ordered sets of output, write input test cases in such a way that you can be sure that the first and last output elements will be processed (e.g., ensure that the first and last detail lines in an output report are printed).

Error Guessing

Error Guessing is the process of using intuition and past experience to fill in gaps in the test data set. There are no rules to follow. The tester must review the test records with an eye toward recognizing missing conditions. Two familiar examples of error-prone situations are dividing by zero and calculating the square root of a negative number. Either of these will result in system errors and garbled output.

Other cases where experience can lead us to be error prone are the processing of variable-length tables, the calculation of median values for odd- and even-numbered populations, cyclic master file/data base updates (improper handling of duplicate keys, unmatched keys, etc.), overlapping storage areas, overwriting of buffers, forgetting to initialize buffer areas, and so forth. I am sure you can think of plenty of circumstances unique to your hardware/software environments and use of specific programming languages.

Error Guessing is as important as Equivalence Partitioning and Boundary Analysis because it is intended to compensate for the inherent incompleteness of those functions. As Equivalence Partitioning and Boundary Analysis complement one another, Error Guessing complements both of these techniques. Figure 3.4 illustrated the controlled results from these approaches.

Hybrid (Gray Box) Approaches _____

Decision Logic Tables

DLTs are unique in the fact that they can be constructed from segments of the system's functional specification, or they may be based on program flowcharts or source code listings. From a testing perspective, this approach could be classified as either White Box or Black Box; hence, the Gray Box classification.

Equivalence Partitioning/Boundary Analysis Table 1 GLOBAL_TBL Test Conditions		
Input Conditions	**Valid Equivalence Classes**	**InValid Equivalence Classes**
Connect_Type	Character "P," "I," "F," "D"	Not "P," "I," "F," or "D"
		Empty
Start_Time	HHMM Value 24 Hour Clock	Empty
		Not HHMM value
End_Time	HHMM Value 24 Hour Clock	Empty
		Not HHMM value
Pause_All	"N," "Y," or Space	Not "N," or "Y," or Space
Stop_All	"N," "Y," or Space	Not "N," "Y," or Space
Poll_Increment	Integer Value in Seconds	Non-Integer Value
Redial_Increment	Integer Value Set to 900 Seconds	Value Less than 900 Seconds
		Value Greater than 900 Seconds
		Negative Value
		Non-Integer Value
Site_Loop_Time	Integer Value Set to 60 Seconds	Value Greater than 60 Seconds
		Value Less than 60 Seconds
		Negative Value
		Non-Integer Value
Connection_Loop_Time	Integer Value Set to 60 Seconds	Value Greater than 60 Seconds
		Value Less than 60 Seconds
		Negative Value
		Non-Integer Value
Connection_Wait_Time	Integer Value Set to 600 Seconds	Value Greater than 600 Seconds
		Value Less than 600 Seconds
		Negative Value
		Non-Integer Value

FIGURE 3.4
An Example Black Box Test Case Design Diagram

But the DLT is a design tool, so why should it be included in a discussion of test case design strategies? Because the DLT can be viewed as a *path coverage* approach that has an advantage not offered by Basis Testing. The DLT format allows a test for completeness—this ensures that no path in a particular module is omitted.

The structural complexity of the module is computed as the product of the number of possible states for each condition for each decision. This produces a much larger complexity value than the value of C (the Cyclomatic number) that would be obtained if McCabe's metric were used ([11,12,17]; see the subsequent sections on Basic Testing. The value that is produced represents the total number of possible logical combinations of condition states, not the number of independent combinations. Thus the value of the total table complexity will differ from the Cyclomatic complexity (8). The advantage in knowing the total table complexity is that logical *completeness* can be verified. Thus, the DLT approach addresses a major criticism of White Box strategies—that they cannot account for missing paths.

Developing one test case for each rule in the embedded DLT can create a complete set of test cases for a specific program module. One DLT diagram is constructed for each program module. Test cases from each DLT are subsequently merged to form a test data set that may in turn be merged with other test data sets created using other White Box and/or Black Box methods.

Many of you are probably already familiar with DLTs and may wish to skip this section; however, if you do read it, it will refresh your knowledge of DLT concepts.

From a testing perspective, the DLT is an important tool for software reliability (1,14). The DLT is a tabular diagram that is used to clarify complex logic that has previously been specified in a design narrative. DLTs deal only with conditional logic, allowing the designer to easily understand a situation containing many decision steps. Such decisions will ultimately end up in If/Then/Else form in the final program. A distinct advantage is that the decision-making logic of DLTs is void of the If/Else nesting that often occurs in the narrative description and is perpetuated in the program code. Even Structured English descriptions may contain If/Else nesting.

The problem with If/Else nesting is that of increasing structural complexity. Our ability to deal with complexity falls off rapidly after a certain level has been reached (13,19). When this happens, we begin to introduce errors into our work. The goal of a decision table can be stated formally as follows:

The purpose of a decision table is to reduce a narrative to a set of *conditions* and *actions* that can easily be implemented in If/Then/Else form.

Conditions and the actions dependent on those conditions represent everything except simple Sequence (straight-line execution of the program logic). Any software program can be designed by applying Sequence, Selection, and Iteration and constructed by implementing the corresponding programming language constructs. In the Selection construct, the actions are dependent upon the state of the condition being evaluated (If/Then/Else logic). Most selections are limited to two mutually exclusive alternatives. However, some decisions involve evaluating conditions with more than two mutually exclusive alternatives. The DLT format does not distinguish between *limited entry* and *extended entry* conditions. It merely organizes the conditions and actions so that the proper actions are associated with the appropriate condition-state combinations.

The Iteration construct (looping logic) can also be modeled using conditions and actions. What is a *loop*? It is a repeated set of actions. In some instances the set is repeated if the condition that represents the exit criterion is true (the While or pretest loop), and in others the set is repeated until the condition that represents the exit criterion is false (the Until or posttest loop). Any loop can be specified if two things are known: the actions that are going to be repeated (those that are conditional on the exit criterion) and the condition state required to exit the loop (exit criterion). Consequently, Iteration can be portrayed with a DLT.

DLT Format   A DLT is a tabular diagram that has four quadrants: Condition Stub, Condition Entry, Action Stub, and Action Entry (see Figure 3.5). Conditions are listed in top-down fashion in the Condition Stub in order of their impact on the processing logic. More comprehensive conditions are listed first. For instance, End-Of-File is the most comprehensive condition of all because processing stops when this condition is reached. Consequently, it should be listed first. Another example: in *control break* processing, the inner-

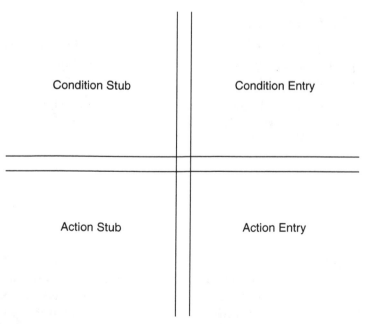

FIGURE 3.5
Decision Table Format

most processing level would be represented in a DLT by being the last condition listed in the Condition Stub; the condition representing the outermost level would be listed first.

Condition-state names are placed in the Condition Entry quadrant at a level corresponding to the condition they define. The number of condition states for a specific condition defines the *Condition Complexity* of that condition.

Actions are entered in the Action Stub. They are listed in the order in which they will execute from top to bottom. Which actions are dependent on which condition-state combinations is specified in the Action Entry quadrant, which is divided into *Rules*.

A rule is a vertical column through the entry side (both condition and action) of the table. It represents one unique combination of condition states and the actions that are executed when that combination occurs. The number of rules in a DLT is a function of the product of the condition complexities for all of the conditions in the Condition Stub. A DLT containing 3 conditions with each condition having 2 possible states would contain 8 rules ($2 \times 2 \times 2 = 8$). The value 8 also represents the *Table Complexity*. Table complexity is a measure of the total number of logic paths through the table.

Enumerating the Rules

Step 1 To determine the rules in a DLT, divide the entry side of the table into the same number of rules as there are condition states for the first (most comprehensive) condition in the Condition Stub.

Step 2 Divide each of the previously created subdivisions into the same number of rules as there are condition states in the second (next most comprehensive) condition.

Step 3 Repeat Step 2 for each of the remaining conditions in the Condition Stub.

Developing the table in this manner ensures that all possible condition-state combinations are present.

Specifying Actions   When all of the rules have been enumerated, the actions dependent on each rule may be specified. More than one action can occur as a consequence of a particular rule. If several actions are dependent on a single rule, list them in top-down sequence in the Action Stub. Placing an X in the column that represents the rule across from the action indicates which actions are executed.

Condition-State Indifference   Certain condition states, when they occur, overrule other condition states. When this happens, the dominant condition state is *indifferent* to the values of subsequent condition states that may finish out the logical combination of states defining the rule.

Indifference is important because, when it occurs, the table can be *collapsed*. In a collapsed table, rules that have different logical significance, but which result in the same set of actions, are combined into a single rule. The table is thus stated more precisely. From the standpoint of software testing, one test case must be generated for each rule in the table; when rules can be collapsed because of condition-state indifference, fewer test cases have to be constructed.

Collapsing the table in no way changes the total table complexity. Collapsed rules account for more than one logic path. *Rule Complexity* is defined as the number of logical combinations of condition states (paths) for which the rule accounts.

Gane and Sarson have defined a set of guidelines for collapsing DLTs (8).

1. Find a pair of rules for which the action(s) is (are) the same and the condition-state values are the same except for one condition in which they differ.

2. Replace that pair of rules with a single rule using the indifference symbol (~) for the condition that was different.

3. Repeat guidelines 1 and 2 for any other pair of rules meeting the indifference criteria.

Proof of Completeness   Proof of completeness for given DLT lies in the fact that the total table complexity can be computed as the product of the condition complexities, or it can be computed as the sum of the rule complexities. If the product of the condition complexities equals the sum of the rule complexities, the table is proved complete. No logical combinations of condition states are missing.

The reason completeness can be proven is because of the fundamental premise of DLTs:

> Given a finite number of conditions with a finite number of condition states, a known number of combinations exist.(8)

DLT as a Software Testing Tool

The DLT is an excellent tool for developing test cases based on path coverage criteria because the number of paths is dependent on the number of decisions in a module (see the discussion of Basis Testing below). It is also excellent because the DLT incorporates all the decisions in a module in a DLT format—every possible combination of condition states (each combination is a logic path) is covered (6,7). Moreover, the completeness check discussed previously ensures that no paths are forgotten.

Thus, each table results in a finite number of test cases being added to the test data set. Because a test case is generated for each of the rules in the table, the tester can be confident of testing the module's logic completely from a path coverage perspective. Furthermore, if the embedded DLT can be collapsed, complete coverage can be attained with even fewer test cases. From the standpoint of testing economics, the smaller the number of test cases required for adequate coverage, the better.

Using the conventions set forth by Myers concerning the development of test data records using Equivalence Classes (16), we can generate heuristics that we can use to fill in the test data set.

1. For all DLTs, assign an arbitrary number to each rule in the embedded DLT, continuing until all of the rules across tableaux are uniquely identified.

2. Until each rule representing a valid input value is covered, write a single test record covering as many of the valid rules as possible.

3. Until each rule representing an invalid input value is covered, write a single test record covering one and only one of the rules.

Because the rules set forth by Myers for creating test cases for equivalence classes (16) are also applicable to the tabular format of the DLT diagram, a set of test data that are similar to and in some instances redundant with the test data from equivalence classes is produced. The advantage of the DLT method over the equivalence class method is primarily the ability to prove completeness. Equivalence Partitioning has no inherent way to determine that all possible classes have been identified. From a Black Box perspective, each equivalence class identifies a unique type of input to the module, and each unique kind of input will invoke a distinct pathway through the module. A rule in a DLT identifies a unique set of circumstances (which, in turn, defines a unique kind of input). In this sense, the two test case design methods are the same, with the difference being in the guidelines for establishing equivalence classes versus the guidelines for enumerating the rules in the DLT.

For a complete discussion and comprehensive examples of DLTs as a tool for generating test data, refer to Mosley (15). You may also want to investigate an extension of the DLT term *Structured Tableau Methodology* (1,2,6,7,15).

An Automated DLT Design Tool

Logic Technologies offers LogiCASE 1.1, an automated reengineering and design tool based on DLTs. The Designer module allows users to construct DLTs from requirements and design specifications. The Designer is fully functional, including a completeness check that will add missing rules to the table and a Reduce command that will collapse the table to its most concise form. The Designer can translate the finished decision tables into the target programming language statements and/or English language statements.

The Reengineering module allows DLTs to be developed from selected C source code segments. It does not support reengineering for any other languages. The reengineering component automatically removes contradictions and redundancies from the source code and the table using a process called *disambiguation*.

While each table is limited to 20 conditions, 20 actions, and 10,240 rules, LogiCASE supports a nested table structure that allows users to decompose larger tables into a set of smaller, less complex tables. It accomplishes this by allowing *include* files, which contain other tables, to replace actions and conditions.

You can obtain the LogiCASE product from Logic Technologies, 56925 Yucca Trail, Suite 254-A, Yucca Valley, CA 92284, Phone 1-800-776-3818, Fax 1-619-228-9653.

Code-Based Approaches

Basis Testing Overview

Basis Testing is a White Box test case technique employing control flow graph representations of program module logic. Control flow graphs are network diagrams graphically depicting the logical pathways through a module. Test cases are created based on a set of independent paths enumerated from the graph. Thomas J. McCabe developed this method, formally known as *Structured Testing* and informally called *basis* testing. McCabe's approach will be discussed as a White Box test case development strategy and not as a testing methodology. For a comprehensive discussion of McCabe's methodology, see his original work (11,12).

The major advantage of McCabe's approach is that it incorporates the Cyclomatic Number as a measure of program/module complexity. The disadvantage is that the control flow charts are generated either from a flow chart before a module is coded or from the source listing after construction is completed. There are two problems with this approach. First, control flow graphs are logical in nature, while flowcharts and source listings are inherently physical or implementation dependent. Second, there are no explicit guidelines for systematically converting the physical information contained in flow charts and source listings into the logical detail depicted in control flow graphs.

Control flow graph construction occurs earlier in the design process, and test case design happens before physical design (via flowcharts) and coding. This facilitates design reviews, Walkthroughs, and Inspections; more important, however, is the fact that program and module testing are placed within the framework of a formal structured systems design methodology.

The Basis Testing Technique

Basis Testing, as described by McCabe, uses source code or flowcharts to generate *Control Flow Graphs* of program modules. The flow graphs are used to enumerate the independent control paths and to calculate the Cyclomatic number $V(G)$, a measure of procedural complexity (see Myers's extension to the Cyclomatic complexity measure [17]). A *basis* set of test cases covering the independent paths is then created (11).

A Control Flow Graph is a network diagram in which nodes represent program segments and edges are connectors from given segments to other program segments. *Edges* depict a transfer of control from one node to another and can represent any form of conditional or unconditional transfer. A *node* represents a decision with multiple emanating edges. A *loop* is a node with an emanating edge that returns to the node. A *region* is an area within a graph that is completely bounded by nodes and edges. Each graph has entry and exit nodes. A *path* is a route through a graph that traverses edges from node to node beginning with the entry node and ending with the exit node (11).

A node is a block of sequentially executed (imperative) actions, and an edge is a transfer of control from one block to another. The If/Then/Else/Endif and nested If/Then/Else/Endif are also examples of statements that conditionally transfer control to specific groups of actions.

Internal structural complexity in program modules is a consequence of the number of functions the module implements, the number of inputs to the module and outputs from the module, and the number of decisions in the module. Structured programming doctrine dictates that a module should implement *one and only one function* (21,22). If this basic rule of thumb is followed, complexity due to the number of functions is minimized. Structured programming dogma also stands on the premise that each module has but a single entry point and a single exit point. If such is the case, complexity due to the number of inputs and outputs can be controlled because the module interface is simplified. This leaves the number of decisions as the major structural dimension contributing to module complexity.

McCabe's complexity measure is an indication of a module's decision structure—it measures procedural complexity as a function of the number of decisions in the Control Flow Graph (11,12). Cyclomatic complexity is a useful metric because it is also representative of perceived complexity. Miller found that the maximum amount of information the human mind can simultaneously process is 3 bits (defining a *bit* as the amount of information required in order to discriminate between two equally likely alternatives). The total number of alternatives is 2 raised to a power equal to the number of discriminations that are involved in a complex decision (13).

Based on his findings, Miller formulated the *seven ± two* rule. Seven alternatives is optimal for memorization, because each choice is a discrimination alternative. Miller determined that the maximum number of alternatives humans can handle simultaneously is 9 (13). If this principle is applied to the decision structure of program modules, the number of bits a programmer must process to understand a complex decision is a function of 2 raised to a power that represents of the number of conditions contained in the decision. An If/Else nest three levels deep has 2^3, or 8, alternatives to comprehend, which is below the limit established by Miller. Adding one more nested decision raises the number of alternatives to 16—well beyond the inherent limit. Consequently, a module with a Cyclomatic complexity greater that 10 is too complex for human short-term memory to comprehend all at one time. If C is greater than 10, a module should be reconstructed or it may be untestable.

The Cyclomatic Number can be calculated using any of three simple equations. The first equation representing the Cyclomatic number is

$$C = E - N + 2$$

where C is the Cyclomatic Number (C has been substituted for $V(G)$, 2 is used instead of $2P$ (P is usually 0) to simplify and make the notation more meaningful), E is the number of edges, and N is the number of nodes. The Cyclomatic Complexity is computed as a function of the relationship of edges to nodes.

Complexity can also be computed as a function of the regions in the control flow graph. Edges cannot cross one another, and regions formed by violations of this rule are not legitimate regions. Only legitimate regions can be included in the calculation of complexity.

The equation based on the number of regions is

$$C = R + 1$$

where C is again the Cyclomatic Number, and R is the number of legitimate regions.

The Cyclomatic Number can also be computed based upon the number of primitive decisions in the graph. A primitive decision is one evaluating the condition states associated with a single condition. Nested conditions and conditions connected by logical operators (AND, OR, etc.) should be treated as though they were completely separate decisions.

The equation is

$$C = D + 1$$

where D is the number of primitive decisions.

The advantage of the latter two equations is that they are easier to understand and use. In fact, the control flow graph does not have to be constructed to use the third equation. The number of decisions in the program flowchart or source listing can be counted and substituted for D in the equation.

These three equations are applied to individual program modules. A measure of the total program complexity can be derived based on the sum of the individual module complexities with a factor subtracted for redundant nodes. A *redundant node* is a node in a high-level module, such as the mainline module, that would be replaced by a subdiagram if the called module were called in line as part of the superordinate module.

The equation is

$$C_t = C_i + 2 - (N - 1)$$

where C_t represents the total program complexity, C_i represents the individual module complexities, and N is the number of modules in the program.

The value of C in each module represents the upper boundary for the maximum number of independent paths through a given program unit. If a set of control paths is constructed equal to C, test cases that exercise those paths will adequately test the module and constitute the basis set of test cases. The basis set does not necessarily execute all possible paths through a segment, but rather a subset from which all other paths can be fabricated.

Once the Cyclomatic Number is known, the independent paths can be enumerated. To enumerate the basis set of paths:

1. Identify all nodes with either a unique letter or number.
2. Begin at the entry node and travel the network using the leftmost path to exit node. List the nodes contained in the path and indicate on the diagram the edges traversed.
3. Follow the previous path backward until a node is encountered that has one or more unmarked emanating edges. Begin at the entry node and follow the preceding path to the node with an unmarked edge. Continue from that point to the exit node using the leftmost unmarked edge.
4. If the new path at any time intersects a previous path, follow the latter path to the exit node.

When no unmarked edges remain, the basis set of paths is complete. The total number of paths must equal C. If a set of paths cannot be created which equals C, then the module is poorly designed and overly complex. It is best to redesign such modules.

It is extremely helpful when constructing the test cases to annotate the decision nodes with the condition being tested and to label the true and false branching edges. One test case is created that will execute each independent path at least once. The basis set of test cases must also exercise each conditional branch at least once. A test case is an input data record containing either a valid or an invalid value for each data field. Figure 3.6 illustrates this technique.

Conclusion

Creating Test Requirements and Test Case Requirements specification documents requires a standard format. The structure should include the types and levels of information described in this chapter, and the documents should be imported into Rational RequisitePro or another similar product that defines test requirements and links them to other products of the testing process. At a minimum, test requirements must be linked to test data specifications. For test execution coverage purposes, they should also be linked to the automated test scripts that execute those data.

The Test Case Requirements should be translated into test conditions in a spreadsheet. The test conditions should be constructed following the guide-

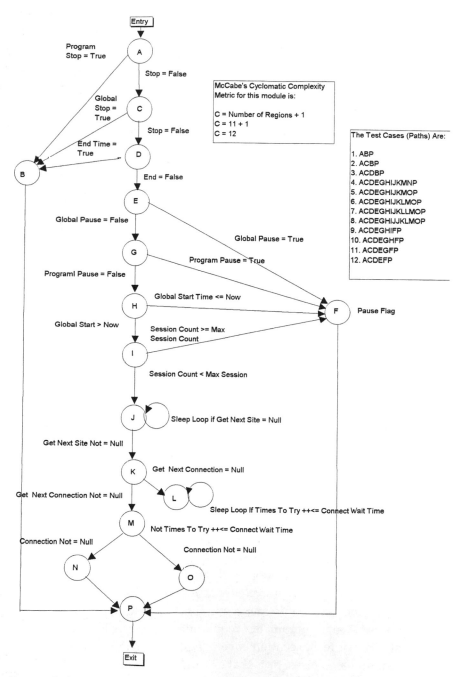

FIGURE 3.6
Arc Polling Software Main Module Control Flow Graph

lines that are described in the functional test data design section of this chapter. Test design engineers should use the Black Box (requirements-based) procedures to develop test data for automated system/regression tests. Software developers should use the White Box (code-based) approaches to construct unit and integration test data using tools such as JUnit.

The key to success is that requirements and test data must all be linked together in a test dynamic test plan document that is developed using an automated requirements gathering tool such as RequisitePro (included as a component in Rational Suite TestStudio). The test plan is created and maintained as a document in a RequisitePro project; by being associated with the project, the test plan can see the requirement matrices that are also in RequisitePro.

References

1. Bartusiak, Marcia. "Designing Drugs with Computers." *Discover,* August 1981.
2. Couger, Daniel. "The Structured Tableau Design Methodology (STDM)." *Computer Newsletter,* University of Colorado, Colorado Springs, 1983.
3. Councill, Bill, and Carol Councill. *Automating Requirements Traceability* Conducting verification and validation to help you build the right software product in the right way, *www.stickyminds.com,* > Software Testing > Test Automation Zone > Articles & Papers.
4. Elmendorf, William. *Cause-Effect Graphs in Functional Testing.* TR-DD.2487, IBM System Development Division, Poughkeepsie, NY, 1973.
5. ———. "Functional Analysis Using Cause-Effect Graphs." *Proceedings of Share XLIII,* New York, 1974, pp. 577–87.
6. Franz, Don. *Information Systems File Structure and Program Design Workbook and Problems.* Unpublished.
7. Franz, Don, and D. Gamble. *Structured Tableau Design Methodology.* Specialized On-Line Systems, Inc., 1981.
8. Gane, Chris, and Trish Sarson. *Structured Systems Analysis: Tools and Techniques.* Prentice Hall, Englewood Cliffs, NJ, 1979.
9. Gerrard, Paul. "Testing Requirements." A paper presented at EuroSTAR '94, Brussels, Belgium, October 1994, pp. 10–13.
10. Kit, Edward. "Integrated Effective Test Design and Automation." *Software Development* 7, no. 2, February 1999.

11. McCabe, Thomas J. "A Complexity Measure." *IEEE Transactions on Software Engineering* SE-2, no. 4, 1976.

12. ———. *Structured Testing: A Testing Methodology Using the McCabe Complexity Metric*, NBS Special Publication, Contract NB82NAAR5518, 1982.

13. Miller, George. "The Magical Number Seven, Plus or Minus Two: Some Limits on Our Capacity for Processing Information." *The Psychological Review* 63, no. 2, March 1956, pp. 81–97.

14. Mosley, Daniel J. *Client-Server Software Testing on the Destop and the Web*. Prentice Hall PTR, Englewood Cliffs, NJ, 1999.

15. ———. *The Handbook of MIS Application Software Testing: Methods, Techniques, and Tools for Assuring Quality Through Testing*. Prentice Hall Yourdon Press, Englewood Cliffs, NJ, 1993.

16. Myers, Glenford. *The Art of Software Testing*. Wiley-Interscience, New York, 1979.

17. ———. "An Extension to the Cyclomatic Measure of Program Complexity." *ACM SIGPLAN Notices*, October 1977, pp. 61–64.

18. Oberg, Roger, Leslee Probasco, and Maria Ericsson. "Applying Requirements Management with Use Cases." Technical Paper TP505, Rational Software Corporation, 1998.

19. Poole, Bernard, and Noreen Prokop. "Miller's Magical Number: A Heuristic Applied to Software Engineering." *Information Executive*, 1989.

20. Rational Software Corporation, *Rational Unified Process 5.1.1*. Cupertino, CA, 1999.

21. Stevens, Wayne, Glenford Myers, and Larry Constantine. "Structured Design." *IBM Systems Journal* 13, no. 2, 1974.

22. Yourdon, Edward, and Larry Constantine. *STRUCTURED DESIGN: Fundamentals of a Discipline of Computer Program and Systems Design*. Prentice Hall, Englewood Cliffs, NJ, 1979.

A Look at the Development of Automated Test Scripts and at the Levels of Test Automation

4

Developing Automated Test Scripts

You can either record or program automated test scripts using a test tool's test scripting language. If you don't have an automated test tool, you can record test scripts using the Windows macro recorder function. Regardless of what method you choose, if you follow a few simple test case design rules, your result will be more robust, easier-to-maintain test cases. Adhikari cites four test case design principles that are in use at Charles Schwab. The design engineers are told to do the following (1). We have applied these rules and found them to be effective when developing automated tests/test data.

1. Design independent test cases.
2. Design self-contained tests.
3. Design home-based test cases.
4. Design nonoverlapping test cases.

Test case independence ensures that one test case does not depend on the successful completion of another test case in order to run (it does not depend on the results of the previous test case). It also ensures that automated test suites will run to conclusion when left unattended.

The scientific method was founded on testing. When scientists conduct experiments, they test only one condition for each experimental repetition. This ensures that the results of each trial are a direct function of the condition that was varied. If two or more variables are changed simultaneously, it is very difficult to pinpoint the one responsible for the observed outcome of the experiment. Of course, in science as in applied endeavors, it is sometimes not possible to create ideal experimental conditions.

In testing software, if two test cases are not independent, two things may happen. First, the subsequent test case may fail to execute, and, second, isolating the cause of any failure is extremely difficult. It is possible, though sometimes very difficult to almost impossible, to design independent test cases.

The purpose of software testing is to identify new errors, while the purpose of debugging is to locate and remove known errors (5,6,7). *Fat* test cases (test cases that cover many test conditions) are used to identify new errors. *Lean* test cases (test cases covering only a single test condition) are used to locate and remove known errors. So, test cases that are not independent are better and more economical for finding errors because fewer are required, but additional test cases that are independent are frequently required to find and remove the errors.

It becomes a trade-off. If your purpose is to have automated test cases that are executed in batch mode via shell procedures, then you want independent test cases. The major drawback is that more test cases may be required to find the same number of errors than would be needed if we were using fatter manual test cases. Another drawback: the higher the number of test cases, the more maintenance the test suite requires. In short, the more test cases, the more testing will cost.

Self-contained tests use test cases that have testing requirements implemented in baseline databases. Maggio described the need for base states in test scripts. Base states eliminate linear dependence among test cases. He argued that, because an initial precondition surrounds the verification process within each test script and ends with a postcondition, it is isolated from other test scripts. Furthermore, it will pass or fail regardless of previous or future application conditions. Setting up base states requires using home-based test cases (4).

Home-based test cases all start from the same point in the application. According to Maggio, the application must be in a specific state, such as its initial state, when it is first executed (the precondition) (4). This means that the application should be open with all menus enabled but no child windows or dialog boxes open. The corollary to this is that when the test cases finish they must return the application to home base (the postcondition).

Constructing home-based test cases is very important because there is less chance of test case execution failure when each test case begins from a known point and cleans up after itself. In an automated suite of test scripts, this ensures that each script begins under the same set of conditions as its predecessors, and it helps ensure that the test scripts are independent. This does not mean that there will not be instances where the results from one test are used as preconditions for another test.

No gap and no overlap means that test cases should cover all aspects of all system functions, and that test case redundancy should be eliminated. Testers sometimes have a tendency to test everything. They will even test for conditions that can never occur. Mosley and Myers have explicitly argued that comprehensive testing is not possible (5,6,7). Thus the tester is charged with testing as much as possible given the available time and resources.

Testing economics dictate the use of fat test cases to identify new software errors. These test cases are not just randomly selected. They are designed and constructed according to guidelines that ensure adequate testing coverage with a limited number of test cases. Techniques such as those discussed in the previous chapter (Cause-Effect Graphing, Equivalence Partitioning, Boundary Analysis, Error Guessing, Decision Logic Tables, and Basis Testing), when used in combination, result in a test database that covers all system functions and that minimizes test case redundancy.

Automated tests should

- Test that the application does what it is intended to do (known as either *constructive* or *positive* testing)
- Test that the application does not do anything that it is not supposed to do (known as either *destructive* or *negative* testing)
- Test that the application is robust (i.e., that it can handle spurious data without crashing); when possible, specific positive and negative results should be identified as expected outputs of specific test scripts.

Fuchs, who prefers writing automated test cases to recording them, offers a three-step approach for creating automated test cases, a discussion of which follows (2).

Step 1. Design the test case. Fuchs says each test case should contain from 1 to 10 closely related scenarios. Test cases with more than 10 scenarios should be separated into multiple test cases. Each scenario should be associated with a unique expected result.

Step 2. Run the test manually. Fuchs argues that automated tests are best for finding errors during regression tests and that manual testing is better for finding them in the first go-round. The first set of test should be the most productive at finding new errors, whereas the regression tests should find more errors that are related to the evolution of the software. Regression tests do, however, find errors that were missed originally. We have personally seen regression testing identify errors that were in software systems since their inception (in one case, this amounted to more than 20 years of use with the error present in the system until regression testing led to its discovery).

Step 3. Automate the test cases. For each test scenario, the test script should contain sections that

- Perform setup
- Perform the test
- Verify the result
- Log the results
- Handle unpredictable situations
- Decide to stop or continue the test case
- Perform cleanup

The setup activities the test script must perform include defining common variables, constants, and procedures the test will use; starting the AUT; and creating any required directories and data files.

The testing activities should simulate how a user would use the AUT. An important point to make here is that scenarios must execute in the order in which they are written because this represents how the user will perform the work. The functional requirements documentation can be a place to start when identifying typical business scenarios for business use. A better way is to observe someone actually using the system; however, in many cases, this will not be possible until the system is under test.

Verifying results involves checking the initial and final states for the controls involved in each user action. It also means checking the database for changes that are both expected and unexpected. The only way to verify application functionality with respect to business rules and business rule interactions is to confirm that changes have actually occurred to associated data values.

Logging results means keeping a record of the pass/fail status of each test case. Then you can review the results after the tests are finished and compare test logs from different test executions.

Handling unpredictable situations involves trapping unexpected events and recovering from them. The kinds of unexpected events that can occur include unexpected keystrokes, unexpected windows, windows that are expected but not present, and system-level interrupts.

The decision to stop or continue is made at the end of each scenario. This decision depends on the pass/fail status of the scenario just executed. In some instances the subsequent scenario can still run even if the preceding one fails, but in other situations the later scenario(s) would provide invalid test results if the earlier one(s) has(have) failed.

Performing the cleanup involves closing the AUT, deleting any directories and data files that are no longer needed, and performing any other miscellaneous cleanup activities. This usually means returning the test case to home base.

Test scripts should be organized into test suites that are executed from shell scripts (2). The MS Visual Test online documentation suggests designing a functional area test suite, a regression test suite, a benchmark test suite, a stress test suite, and an acceptance test suite. We have added three more classes of tests—the unit test suite, the integration/smoke test suite, and the system test suite.

Unit-Level Tests

- **Unit Test Suite**, implemented and used by software developers during the development process, is a suite of reusable tests run by each developer prior to integration of the software components at build time. These tests should be automated and constructed using environments such as JUnit for Java.

- **Integration/Smoke Test Suite** is an automated test suite that is run after the software build is completed. Its purpose is twofold: First, it should initialize the environment in which the AUT will execute, setting up environmental variables, initializing database tables, and so on. Second, it should test the basic functionality of the build. Other types of testing should not process until the AUT passes the integration/smoke tests.

- **Unit-Level Regression Test Suite** tests previously tested features to determine if they continue to function correctly as corrections, tuning, and enhancements are added to the builds during the unit testing phase—these additions can introduce new defects.

- **Functional Area Test Suite** should be developed for each functional area you can identify in the AUT. Execute this test suite manually the first time. Later, automate it and reuse it as the regression test suite.

System-Level Tests

- **System Test Suite** should perform cross-function tests that are designed to simulate user interactions with the system during normal business processing activities. In addition, the system test suite should include security tests, configuration tests, usability tests, and so forth. As with the functional test, execute the system tests manually the first time. Automate both the functional and system test suites and use them as part of the regression test suite.

- **Acceptance Test Suite** tests the software to determine if it meets the minimum standards for user acceptance of the system. The purpose is to determine if the system is ready to withstand the rigors of beta testing and/or production use.

- **Regression Test Suite** tests previously tested system features to determine if they continue to function correctly as corrections, tuning, and enhancements are added to the system during its maintenance phase—these additions can introduce new defects.

Specialized System-Level Tests

- **Benchmark Test Suite** tests system performance under varying conditions such as different hardware and software platforms and contrasting system loads. An automated benchmarking tool is an absolute must here. There are many products on the market that can implement automated benchmark tests. Trying to do these tests manually is not feasible given the resource requirements; if an automated tool is not available, the tests are simply not done.

- **Stress Testing Suite** tests the system under extreme conditions such as heavy system loads during peak usage times. These tests can also require an automated testing tool such as Mercury Interactive's Load-Runner or Rational TestManager. There are free performance testing tools available on the WWW—MS Web Analysis Stress Tool, for example. However, tools such as this have limited capacity to develop tests and usually are not sufficient for testing large client-server and Web applications. As is the case with benchmark tests, load and stress tests will not be done if there are no tools because they require too many resources.

Recording versus Programming Test Scripts

Recorded test scripts have their limitations and frequently must be edited before they work properly. Zambelich stated the disadvantages of recorded test scripts very clearly (10):

1. The scripts resulting from this method contain *hard-coded values*, which must change if anything at all changes in the application.
2. The costs associated with maintaining such scripts are astronomical and unacceptable.
3. These scripts are not reliable, even if the application has not changed, and they often fail on replay (pop-up windows, messages, and other things can happen that did not happen when the test was recorded).
4. If the tester makes an error entering data, etc., the test must be rerecorded.
5. If the application changes, the test must be rerecorded.
6. All that is being tested are things that *already work*. Areas that have errors are encountered in the recording process (which is manual testing, after all). These bugs are reported, but a script cannot be recorded until the software is corrected. So what are you testing?

As pointed out in number 3 above, recorded test scripts are not reliable. Many test conditions represent functional variations of a single test case. As a consequence, many variations of the same test script must be recorded. The problem here is that each test script includes both test procedure instructions and hard-coded test data values. In addition, each functional variant of a specific test requires a separate test script to be generated and executed. This is an awkward approach and one that results in a substantial amount of script maintenance later on. Every time the AUT's GUI changes or is enhanced, and every time the AUT's features are modified, recorded test scripts will fail. Ultimately, someone has to go back, open, and edit each script to modify the code and accommodate these changes. This means modifying and/or writing additional programming statements in the tool's scripting language.

A good rule to follow is this: to do any meaningful testing you must first become proficient in the test scripting language. According to Fuchs, many testers prefer to *write* test scripts rather than *record* them. Fuchs suggests creating test script template files that contain three types of data in common—header information, setup routines, and include files. The tester then can use them as a starting point for writing test scripts, keeping the portions of the template that are relevant and deleting the portions not required for a particular testing circumstance (2). The CSDDT approach discussed in Chapters 7 and 8 applies Fuchs's ideas pertaining to test script development and template use.

Of course, not everyone is a programmer; many testers are individuals who have domain experience, but not technical expertise. People who know the business make much better test designers than people who have technical expertise because they have different perspectives. Individuals with programming skills, in turn, are much better test scriptwriters. This is one reason there must be a division of labor within an automated testing framework (discussed in Chapter 3). Test *design* engineers do not need to be programmers, but test *implementation* engineers require a programming background.

Thus, a typical scenario for automated testing tool use should include a combination of activities on the part of the test implementation engineers. They must be able to write, from scratch, test scripts that can navigate the AUT and input the test data. They must also use the tool's recording facility to capture AUT properties that must be embedded in the test script (some automated tool suites capture AUT properties automatically and store them as application maps for the test scripts to reference during test execution). Basic test script templates can be developed in this manner.

Unfortunately, test scripts that have been recorded using a test tool's recording facility simply are not appropriate for testing an application's functionality. Creating functional variations of recorded tests is where we run into a roadblock. How can we do this? If you intend to test business objects and database objects, along with their associated rules, with your test tool, then simply recording test scripts and editing them will not suffice. Rule-based validations can occur at many levels, but they commonly involve GUI- and server-level validations (business rule validations). To test at either of these levels, you must first develop test data that exercises the application's ability to enforce these validation rules. However, to record all of the specific data input scenarios that may be required to perform the tests, you would have to sit at the computer for years, inputting data while running the test tool's macro recorder. The solution is to develop test data files and create specialized test script to input the data they contain. This type of test script cannot be recorded; it has to be written by a tester who is competent in the test tool scripting language.

To test application functionality with an automated test tool, we advocate using written script templates that are driven by control data values embedded in the test data that store functional variations of the tests as test data records. This approach has been generically dubbed *data-driven testing* (9), and it is extremely effective. This is the only way you can effectively test application functionality with an automated test tool.

A modular test script design technique known as *framework-based testing* has evolved as a complement to data-driven testing (3). Framework-based testing is really *structured programming* (8) for test script design and construction; however, it follows different rules than does structured programming and is not nearly as rigorous.

Zambelich's *functional decomposition* test script development methodology further enhances the framework-based testing concept. He defines his approach as follows:

> "Functional Decomposition" script development methodology is to reduce all test cases to their most fundamental tasks, and write *User-Defined Functions, Business Function Scripts,* and *"Sub-routine"* or *"Utility" Scripts* which perform these tasks *independently* of one another.(10)

Zambelich breaks the scripting tasks into these essential areas (10):

1. GUI screen navigation
2. Specific business functions
3. Data verification
4. Return navigation

The most fundamental concept concerning the development of test scripts is the separation of data from function. Zambelich says:

> In order to accomplish this, it is necessary to <u>separate</u> *Data* from *Function*. This allows an automated test script to be written for a *Business Function*, using <u>data-files</u> to provide both the input and the expected-results verification. A hierarchical architecture is employed, using a structured or modular design.(10)

According to Zambelich, the main level is the driver script, which is the engine of the test. It contains a series of calls to one or more test case scripts that contain the test case logic. The logic then calls the business function scripts necessary to perform the testing. Utility scripts and functions are called as needed by the driver, main, and business function scripts. Zambelich defines these scripts as (10):

- **Driver Scripts** perform initialization (if required), then call the Test Case Scripts in the desired order.
- **Test Case Scripts** perform the application test case logic using Business Function Scripts.
- **Business Function Scripts** perform specific Business Functions within the application.
- **Subroutine Scripts** perform application specific tasks required by two or more Business scripts.
- **User-Defined Functions** include General, Application-Specific, and Screen-Access Functions

Note that functions can be called from any of these script types. Zambelich's Test Plan Driven testing methodology is discussed in detail in Chapter 7.

Conclusion

Our approach to test automation—CSDDT—combines data-driven testing with modular test script design and adds control data values and keyword processing. It is discussed in detail in Chapters 7 and 8.

References

1. Adhikari, Richard. "Planning, Testing, Teamwork: A Recipe for Quality Apps." *Software Magazine* 14, no. 3, March 1994, pp. 41–47.

2. Fuchs, Steve. "Building Smart Testware." Microsoft Technet CD, Test Technical Notes, Vol. 4, Issue 2, February 1996.

3. Kaner, Cem. "Improving the Maintainability of Automated Test Suites." A paper presented at Quality Week '97, 10th International Software Quality Week, San Francisco, CA, May, 1997. Available at *www.kaner.com/lawst1.htm*

4. Maggio, Michael D. "Automated Software-Testing Scripts." *UNIX Review*, no. 13, December 1995, p. 43.

5. Mosley, Daniel J. *The Handbook of MIS Application Software Testing: Methods, Techniques, and Tools for Assuring Quality Through Testing.* Prentice-Hall Yourdon Press, Englewood Cliffs, NJ, 1993.

6. Mosley, Daniel J., and Bruce A. Posey. *Building and Executing Effective Real-World Test Scripts with Rational Suite TestStudio 2001.* Workbook from seminar offered by CSSTTechnologies, Inc., and Archer Group.

7. Myers, Glenford. *The Art of Software Testing.* Wiley-Interscience, New York, 1979.

8. Powers, Mike. "Styles for Making Test Automation Work." January 1997, Testers' Network, *www.veritest.com/testers'network*

9. Strang, Richard. "Data Driven Testing for Client/Server Applications." Fifth International Conference on Software Testing, Analysis and Reliability (STAR '96), pp. 395–400.

10. Zambelich, Keith. "Totally Data-Driven Automated Testing." Whitepaper published at *www.auto-sqa.com/articles.html*, the Automated Testing Specialists (ATS) Web site.

Automated Unit Testing 5

Introduction

Contrary to previous wisdom in the testing field, unit testing is a process that developers must complete. It is the developer's responsibility to prove that the software does what it is supposed to do and that there are no missing features. The purpose of unit testing is to: (6)

- Verify that the logic works
- Verify that all of the necessary logic is present

Hetzel published the following definition of unit testing.

> Testing individual units of logic as they are coded. What we are concerned with is testing logical pieces or units of work that arise naturally. These may be functions, subroutines, or just logically distinct parts of individual programs. (6)

Unit testing is also known as *testing in the small, program testing, module testing*, and *isolation testing*. Unit testing is the process of verifying that the code does what the system specifications say it will do.

Unit Testing Justification

Testing and fixing errors can be done at any phase of the development cycle. However, Boehm (2) has shown, and others have reiterated (7,8), that the cost of finding and fixing errors increases dramatically as development progresses. Defects are radically cheaper to fix when programmers find their own errors.

Developers are obligated to perform unit tests on their code. They cannot afford to pass buggy code to today's sophisticated software consumers. The units they create must pass unit tests with 100% accuracy before they can be placed in the build process. If any problems are detected by unit tests, developers must give them high priority and resolve them immediately, as the following axiom from *JavaWorld* states:

> A project's unit test suites should always execute successfully at 100 percent. Any failure in the unit tests instantly becomes a top priority for responsible developers.(9)

The cost and effort required to do unit testing causes many developers and even many development organizations to do only limited or no unit testing at all. Problems that are not found by unit testing, or problems that are ignored by the developer(s), will show up later at times when development resources are even more scarce than they are at the time developers should be unit testing. Problems that are found during unit tests must be repaired, and then they must be regression tested at the unit level.

The Unit Testing Process

Unit testing must be done in a repeatable manner. A documented unit testing process, along with management-level facilitation of training and enforcement of that process's implementation, will ensure that the testing is done properly and in a timely manner. The purchase and implementation of a unit testing tool does not ensure a repeatable process—*using* the tool does. Automated testing tools support specific testing activities; thus they require specific circumstances in order to operate properly. Furthermore, there is always some extra nonautomated setup and cleanup associated with them. Thus, it is often difficult to coax developers to use them.

A Rigorous Approach to Unit Testing

A rigorous unit testing approach (3) means that the design of the units is documented in a specification before coding even begins. It also means that the unit tests are designed from the specification for the unit, also preferably before coding begins. And finally, it means that the expected outcomes of unit test cases are specified in a unit test specification.

The Unit Test Specification

The unit test specification is a statement of the initial state of the unit; the starting point of each test case; the inputs to the unit, including the value of any external data read by the unit; what the test case actually tests, in terms of the functionality of the unit; and the analysis used in the design of the test case (e.g., which decisions within the unit are tested). The specification must include the expected outcome of the test case.

Unit Testing Tasks

Developers should implement the following steps when unit testing: (6)

1. Develop a statement of the program's required behavior from the Black Box perspective.
2. Identify requirements-based test cases.
3. Supplement with design-based test cases.
4. Add additional test cases from randomization or extraction (optional).
5. Organize the test cases into test procedures.
6. Review the test cases and test procedures.
7. Execute the tests against the program/module/unit.

Obviously, if you are a developer whose job is writing application code, you would look at these tasks with major disdain. It is well known, as well as a real-world fact, that developers do not do adequate unit testing because they see it as interfering with their application development work. They also feel that there is not enough time to do unit tests.

Implementating the Unit Testing Tasks

Developers should implement the unit testing tasks in the list above at the beginning of the development process. Before developers ever write a line of code, they should develop a unit test that will confirm a particular behavior, they need to fully understand what that component should do. The focus should be on capturing the intent of the component, not on the implementation, and on writing unit tests to confirm that behavior.

Next, the developer should code the component to the design specifications and execute the unit tests. If errors are present, the developer should rewrite code as necessary. When the tests pass, coding can stop. In addition, the programmer should consider other possible weaknesses for the component and write tests to defend against them.

When a defect is identified, it should be verified. The developer must write tests to confirm the problem, and a defect problem report must be created and entered into the defect tracking system. This is an area where developers fail miserably unless they have access to an automated defect reporting and problem resolution system. We have found that developers will not document defects on their own, but when a user-friendly tool is provided along with training in its use, they willingly enter and track unit test problems.

One final note, each time the developer changes the code, all tests must be rerun to make sure nothing is broken that was previously working. This is regression testing during unit testing. Software regression must occur at all levels of testing. Regression tests cry out for automation—they are the most successfully automated.

Rules of Thumb for Unit Testing_____

The following heuristic applies to unit testing. First, cultivate tests that focus on a particular piece of code. Second, monitor tests using debugging tools such as those available in popular integrated development environments (IDEs). Third, use techniques such as single stepping, variable inspection, and memory leak detection. Fourth, manipulate code and data so that all the functionality of a given piece of code is thoroughly tested.

Unit Testing Data

Sources for developing unit testing data include functional requirements specifications, high- and low-level design specifications, and so on. Some different test case types and the sources from which they can be developed are as follows: (6)

Test Case Categories	Test Case Sources
Requirements Based	Specifications
Design Based	Logical System
Code Based	Data Structures and Code
Randomized	Random Generator
Extracted	Existing Files
Extreme	Limits and Boundary Conditions

A Unit Testing Framework

As with all levels of software testing, unit testing requires that a supporting infrastructure be in place. The unit testing infrastructure must provide the information necessary to design unit tests and unit test data. It must also provide a repository where all unit testing artifacts (tests, test data, and test results) can be permanently stored. This infrastructure must also serve as a test harness for unit test execution, and it must capture and store the test results. ANSI/IEEE STD 1008-1987 defines unit testing and documents a formal unit testing approach (1).

Performing unit tests manually is time consuming and burdensome. This is why developers shy away from it. Of course, as with all endeavors, we develop shortcuts that allow us to do our work faster and better. This is true even for unit testing, which can be enhanced through the use of MS Excel and MS Word to document test data, etc. We have also seen Lotus Notes database used to document and store unit testing. The problem is the manual work required to update these databases, especially when doing unit-level regression testing. Overall, this leads to increased test data maintenance.

A more effective approach is to use tools that have been especially designed for unit testing. There are several commercially available products and several others that can be found free of charge on the Web. There are tools available that support commonly used programming environments such as Visual Basic, C, and Java. Many of the available tools instrument the source code and provide test coverage metrics.

Commercial tools vary in functionality. Some are extremely sophisticated. For instance, Rational Software's QualityArchitect can parse Java code and reverse engineer it into Rational Rose diagrams that it uses to construct test cases. This product also executes the test against the application and captures the results. On the other hand, there are tools that are very unsophisticated in terms of the features they provide, but yet are powerful tools. JUnit, which is freely distributed on the Web, is an excellent unit testing tool, but it places on the developer's shoulders the burden of designing, constructing, executing, and analyzing the tests. Once the initial test framework has been set up using JUnit, it does support unit-level regression testing. The difference between these two products is not in what they do as much as it is in the amount of effort required to implement them. The moral of the story is that you get what you pay for.

For Object-Oriented Development Using Java

Unit tests should be written from the developer's perspective and focus on particular methods of the class under test. When developing unit tests in an object-oriented environment, Canna has the following advice to offer: (3)

- Write the unit test before writing code for the class it tests.
- Capture code comments in unit tests.
- Test all the public methods that perform an "interesting" function (that is, not getters and setters, unless they do their getting and setting in some unique way).
- Put each test case in the same package as the class it's testing to gain access to package and protected members.
- Avoid using domain-specific objects in unit tests.

Conclusion _____

Automated unit testing is a necessity if developers are to meet the fast-paced development deadlines of today's software markets. More and more development organizations are following Microsoft Corporation's lead and implementing the *build-a-day* approach. In the past, build dates were set and builds occurred at specific intervals that were measured in days, weeks, or months. New development processes such as those associated with object-oriented development and languages like Java require more frequent software builds. For Java developers, a comprehensive unit testing tools listing can be found at *www.javaworld.com/javaworld/tools/jw-tools-testing.html*.

In addition, JUnit is a unit-level regression testing framework written by Erich Gamma and Kent Beck. It is intended for use by developers implementing unit tests in Java. JUnit is Open Source Software, released under the IBM Public License and hosted on SourceForge. It now has its own Web site at *www.junit.org*. We have downloaded the zipped JUnit source code and placed it at *www.phptr.com/mosley*, which supports this book.

In addition, the link for downloading Java programming testing tools for use with Windows XP is located at *www.xprogramming.com/software.htm*. Two tools of note are JUnitPerf and JDepend. From their author's own description (both tools were created by Mike Clark, Clarkware Consulting Inc. [4,5]), the purpose of JUnitPerf is "a collection of JUnit test decorators used to measure the performance and scalability of functionality contained within existing JUnit tests."(5) The download link and an overview and examples of test cases are located at *www.clarkware.com/software/JUnit-Perf.html*.

Clark summarizes JDepend this way: "JDepend traverses a set of Java class and source file directories and generates design quality metrics for each Java package. JDepend allows you to automatically measure the quality of a design in terms of its extensibility, reusability, and maintainability to effectively manage and control package dependencies."(2) The link to download JDepend and detailed information on JDepend and its use are located at *www.clarkware.com/software/JDepend.html*.

References

1. American National Standards Institute/Institute of Electrical and Electronics Engineers. *Software Unit Testing.* ANSI/IEEE Std 1008-1987.
2. Boehm, Barry. *Software Engineering Economics.* Prentice Hall, Englewood Cliffs, NJ, 1981.
3. Canna, Jeff. "Testing, fun? Really? Using unit and functional tests in the development process." *IBM developerWorks : Java technology.* Java technology articles available at *www-106.ibm.com/developerworks/library/j-test.html*.
4. Clark, Mike. JUnitDepend, *www.clarkware.com/software/JDepend.html*.
5. ———. JUnitPerf, *www.clarkware.com/software/JUnitPerf.html*.
6. Hetzel, William. *The Compete Guide to Software Testing.* 2d ed. QED Information Sciences, Wellesley, MA, 1988.

7. Mosley, Daniel J., and Bruce A. Posey."Building and Executing Effective Real-World Test Scripts with Rational Suite TestStudio 2001," Workbook from public seminar of the same name offered by CSST Technologies, Inc., and the Archer Group.

8. Myers, Glenford. *The Art of Software Testing.* Wiley-Interscience, New York, 1979.

9. Nygard, Michael T., and Karsjens Tracie. "Test Infect Your Enterprise Java-Beans™: Learn how to test your J2EE components live and in the wild." *Java-World* Web Page, 2001. *www.javaworld.com/javaworld/jw-05-2000/jw-0526-testinfect_p.html*

Automated Integration Testing

6

Introduction

Who does integration testing in your organization? Your answer will determine what types of tests should be executed and how they are automated. Is there a separate group, made up of people who are neither developers nor system testers, that tests the application immediately following the build process? In some departments, the developers create their own builds and test the integrated units. In other groups, a specialist—a build master—does some preliminary tests before the application is given to the system test group, who complete the build. Is integration testing really the build master's responsibility?

There is a second question: What is integration testing? This answer can be found by analyzing the answer to the first question. If the answers do not reflect a structured build and test process, the integration testing is a free-for-all ad hoc approach that may or may not be completed effectively. But how much control is needed?

To answer this question, we must recognize that this is one of the most problem-prone areas of development. An effective process supported by a good automated tool is required. Wherever we have consulted, we have seen two chronic problems: First, the build frequently does not install on the system test machines. Second, the fact that unit and integration testing has not been done previously forces the system test team to do tests that development should have already executed.

Integration testing, like unit testing, must be automated because otherwise it will not be done. The minimum automated tool set required for integration testing includes a defect tracking system, a problem reporting system, a capture/playback tool, and a configuration management tool. The tool set must be integrated in the sense that the builds and files in the configuration management (CM) repository can be associated with automated tests in the test repository and with the defects in the defect database.

Why is such tight integration needed? It is necessary because many applications require problem resolution across builds as well as across major and minor production releases. Tools such as Rational Software's ClearCase, ClearQuest, and Robot offer this type of control for integration testing.

What Is Integration Testing?

Integration testing is the testing of groups of units. The units can be modules, subsystems, or systems. These entities are traditionally defined along procedural boundaries and along system-to-system/subsystem-to-subsystem interfaces. In fact, integration testing has many names that originated in the early days of software development: *string* testing, *interface* testing, and so on. It is important not to confuse the use of the phrase *interface testing* as it is applied to integration testing with UI or GUI testing. The term, as it is used here, refers to the communications interface between and among groups of procedures, modules, subsystems, and systems. In particular, it applies to messages that are passed to and from objects in object-oriented applications. For languages such as Java, the unit can be logically and operationally defined at the level of the class or subclass. It could also be defined as the method(s) contained in the class.

The Daily Build Smoke Test

The primary purpose of a smoke test is to verify that the system's basic functions/features do what they are intended to do after the software system build is installed in the system test environment. A secondary purpose of the smoke test, one that helps it to achieve its primary goal, is to set up and configure environment variables and data. An automated build smoke test should accomplish both of these activities.

The build smoke test is important to the test group because application features that do not work cannot be tested. Furthermore, functions that do not operate properly cannot be regression tested. The build smoke test should also be thought of as a preview of the final installation test. Wallace, Ippolito, and Cuthill define installation testing as follows:

> The software installation test activity is the final step before launching full customer acceptance testing. The purpose of installation test is to demonstrate that the correct software has been delivered and that the software interfaces are correct relative to any interfaces at the installation site. (1)

From this definition, we can develop a formal definition of smoke testing.

> The smoke test activity is the final step before the software build enters the system test stage. With respect to post-release software builds, it is the final step before the software enters regression testing.

A smoke test must be performed for each new build that is turned over to the test group. This applies to new development, major and minor system releases, and customizations for specific customers. A basic build smoke test workflow is illustrated in Figure 6.1; it includes the test objectives listed in the next section, among other activities.

Build Smoke Test Objectives

- Verify that all components have been installed.
- Verify that nothing extra has been installed.
- Initialize database.
- Configure system variables and constants (e.g., configure table settings).
- Create and configure basic system-level metastructures that are required for system testing.
- Verify basic functionality for each feature/GUI screen.

The verification of the basic features may appear to be redundant with the unit testing having just been completed by developers. It does retrace those

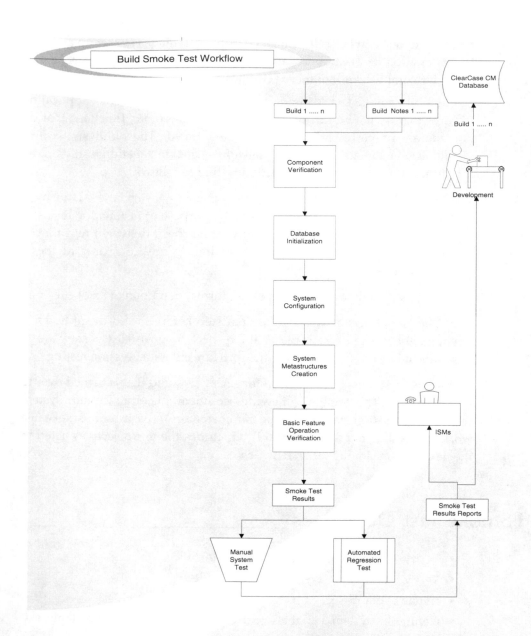

FIGURE 6.1
Build Smoke Test Work Flow

activities, but for different reasons. First, the unit testing is executed in isolation from other system components. Second, it is conducted on the developers' desktops in the development environment. Yes, integration testing is intended to test the components as a newly created system after unit testing and before system testing. Regression testing is frequently completed using test data developers designed and executed in a development environment (on development servers) rather than a test environment. The development server does not reflect the target production environment. The test server and its client are configured to emulate the production platform. It is acceptable to use the unit test data as part of the smoke test data set.

Automated Build Smoke Test Checklist _____

The following list describes the kind of information that the build notes should contain and can be used to verify that the information is present and correct.

- Does the build include the build notes?
- Do the build notes include a list of the features new to this build?
- Do the build notes include any special considerations that must be addressed before, during, or after installation?
- Do the build notes identify all of the defects that have been repaired in this build?
  - ✗ Are the correct components on the test machines after the initial install?
  - ✗ Are all of the components there that should have been installed?
  - ✗ Has the test database been initialized?
  - ✗ Have all pretest conditions been identified and addressed?
  - ✗ Have all application-specific variables and constants been initialized?
  - ✗ Have the necessary application metaentities been created?
  - ✗ Have automated tests for all GUI screens been created?
  - ✗ Have automated tests for all basic features been created?
  - ✗ Has feature-specific test data been constructed?
  - ✗ Is unit test data available for use during the smoke test?
- Is it included in the smoke test data set?
  - ✗ Is the installation documentation available?
- Is it up-to-date for the current build/release?

Conclusion

In today's world of Web development using language such as Java, integration testing is a step in an efficient software build process. No software release should be presented for system testing without first being integration tested. Open-source tools such as JUnit (discussed in the previous chapter) should be an integral component in setting up postbuild integration tests on the development side. Commercial tools such as Rational QualityArchitect can also be used in development environments where the software process is more formalized. Tools such as Rational TestStudio should be used for the final smoke tests, which are the final integration tests. The team that will also perform automated regression testing should conduct the smoke tests.

References

1. Wallace, Dolores R., Laura M. Ippolito, and Barbara Cuthill. "Reference Information for the Software Verification and Validation Process," NIST Special Publication 500-234, March 29, 1996. Available at *hissa.nist.gov/HHRFdata/Artifacts/ITLdoc/234/val-proc.html#APPEN*

Automated System/ Regression Testing Frameworks

7

The Data-Driven Approach

Kit defines three generations of automated software testing (1):

- The first generation is basically GUI testing. The use of capture/play-back tools to develop automated test scripts is limited to recording user actions at the level of the GUI, editing the resulting test scripts, and replaying the edited test scripts. The resulting test scripts are unstructured, undocumented, and not maintainable.

- In the second generation, the scriptwriters have developed the ability to "build well-structured, documented, robust, maintainable tests." The testing project becomes an engineering project at this level; test scripts include error capture and recovery logic, and a key characteristic is reusability of test script components.

- Kit characterizes the third generation of test automation as being in control of the test resources. At that level, test design and test automation are seen as separate activities.

The key to third-generation capture/playback use is in the nature and quantity of the test scripts and, in particular, the relationship between test scripts and test cases. First- and second-generation capture/playback users typically have one main script for each test case. This results in many scripts, all of which must be maintained. Third-generation users have discovered a way to use scripting in a different, novel way—a way that lets a single script process every test case.

What is the data-driven framework and where does it sit with the generations of capture/playback tool use? There are several opinions as to what constitutes data-driven testing. In fact, a heated and lengthy discussion appeared in the SQA users group (*www.dundee.net/sqa*) a couple of years ago. See Appendix B for the complete text of the discussion as it was captured by Nagle of SAS Institute, synthesized, and posted on the Web site (*groups.yahoo.com/group/RobotDDEUsers*) devoted to data-driven testing and the DDE approach. This approach is implemented in the SQABasic language that is the native language used in Rational Software's Robot product. For Mercury Interactive customers who use WinRunner, Keith Zambelich of Automated Testing Specialists (*www.auto-sqa.com*) has developed a toolkit for WinRunner that supports a data-driven testing framework implementation very similar to Nagle's DDE. These approaches, as well as the CSDDT framework, are discussed below.

So, what is data-driven testing? It is a commonly used term these days, but most think of data-driven testing as simply using external data as the source of input into the AUT; for example, cases in which data pools are used. Here is our definition:

> Data-driven testing is testing where data contained in an input test data file control the flow and actions performed by the automated test script.

An input test data record is read from an external file or spreadsheet and is developed independently from the test script program. This idea has been further enhanced and modified by the Archer Group and others. The methodology introduced here also employs the use of *control data* to determine what actions are taken and the order in which they occur.

Data-driven testing is the use of archived test data, usually in the form of simple CSV text files, to drive the automated testing process. Data-driven testing can be expanded to include control data as well as test data. The test data test both GUI and server-level data validation rules that represent an application's functionality. The control data drive the test script by directing it to the appropriate location in the application to execute the test and by indicating what type of test or action to execute.

The characteristics of data-driven test scripts include the following:

- They use simple input text files.
- They are highly maintainable.
- They are easier for nonprogrammers to use.
- They document the tests that are being executed.
- They allow dynamic data input via *placeholders*.
- They use input data to control the test execution.

The content of data-driven tests can include (18, 26):

1. Parameters that you can input to the program
2. Sequences of operations or commands that you use to make the program execute
3. Sequences of test data through which the program is driven
4. Placeholders that trigger the test script to create a dynamic data value at runtime
5. Documents that you have the program read and process

The test data should be designed using the techniques described in Chapter 3 in the section discussing Black Box (requirements-based) and White Box (code-based) approaches.

The advantages of data-driven test scripts are

1. It is not necessary to modify the test script when adding additional test data because the test data is appended to the existing text file.
2. It is easy to modify the data records.
3. Multiple test data records can be developed as functional variants.
4. Multiple input data files can be created and used when required.

One thing we can be sure of: Data-driven testing fits Kit's definition of third-generation capture/playback test tool use. It satisfies all of his criteria.

Framework-Driven (Structured) Test Scripts_____

Framework-driven testing isolates the AUT from the test scripts. It provides a set of functions in a shared function library. The functions are treated as if they were basic commands of the test tool's programming language. Framework-based test scripts can be programmed independently of the UI.

Framework-driven testing can occur at multiple levels (18):

- Menu/command level—executing simple commands
- Object level—performing actions on specific things
- Task level—taking care of specific, commonly repeated tasks

Developing Framework-Driven Test Scripts

The following hints will help you develop framework-based test scripts (26).

1. Write functions for all features of the application under test.
2. Write functions for custom controls.
3. Write wrapper functions around language-specific commands.
4. Write functions for tasks that are used frequently.
5. Write functions for large complex tasks that are used across test scripts.

The Archer Group Framework

The Archer Group has spent countless hours refining this methodology based on the needs of multiple test projects and clients over the last five years. Like any software process, it has evolved to accommodate many testing scenarios and has been utilized in real-world situations.

The goal has always been to *keep it simple*, *make it effective*, and, above all, *make it maintainable*. In this chapter and in the next, we will discuss a testing framework designed for use with data-driven testing. The framework scripts can be found at *www.phptr/mosley*, which supports this book. Although originally developed for use with Rational's Robot product, the templates should be readily adaptable to other test tools.

The three primary focus areas of Archer Group's efforts have been:

1. Developing a simple, easy-to-use, highly organized scripting framework
2. Utilizing external data as a way to control the test flow and provide input data to the application's GUI versus hard coding the data in test script files.
3. Developing a method for using dynamic input data by using keyword data substitution.

We have adopted the term Control Synchronized Data-Driven Testing to refer to this type of automated testing. Why control synchronized? In addition to the data being utilized as inputs to the AUT, control information is added to the front of each data record to specify the *where, how,* and *what-to-expect* information. CSDDT specifies

- Where to go in the AUT; navigation to the window, tab, dialog, etc.; the target of the testing action
- What to do when you get there, the action to be performed
- What to expect after the action is performed—whether to expect an error or normal condition
- The data to be used for input or selection criteria

The input test data records that are read by the Main test script should first contain information that provides record-level identity/control or how the record is to be processed after it is read from the input data file. It is very beneficial to have the ability to skip records because they may not work initially, but we don't want to remove them from the input file. For the process of debugging newly added code, it might be necessary to step through the script after it is read in the record (perform a breakpoint after the record is read). This allows you to substitute data dynamically, such as using keyword data substitution (e.g., substitute text DATE with the current date in the format 01/25/2002). Based on this information, the input data record type can be categorized as:

- Good input record; this may or may not cause an expected error.
- Skip this record; record data is bad or incomplete or is being used to comment following records.
- Breakpoint at this record (in Rational Robot, this causes a software breakpoint used for debug purposes).
- Perform special processing such as *keyword* substitution.
- Terminate the test before end of file (EOF) is reached.

In general, CSDDT directs test script navigation of the AUT, indicating what window/tab, child window, dialog box, etc., is to be activated or selected. The data also specifies what action is to be performed, for example:

Select/Display

Insert/Add

Update/Modify

Delete

Save

OK

Cancel

Apply

Furthermore, the data also describes the expected results, whether or not an error condition is expected, and the type of error. The CSDDT data record format also allows comments to be included, which makes the data records *self-documenting*.

Last, but not least, the data records include the test data values that will be input to the AUT. CSDDT allows a variable number of input data fields. For example, one record could have 0 data fields (a command to execute only, such as CANCEL), and the next could have 50 or more data fields. The size should be dynamic.

Visualize that each data record to be read and acted upon by the Main test script is one line in a text file. The first seven sections or fields (separated by double quotes and commas, similar to a CSV file) contain the control information, and the remaining fields are the data to be used as input to AUT.

We have separated the general tests into several groups according to test type. Each type corresponds to a unique automated test type and a specific class of automated test script drives. Some of these tests may use strictly record/playback types of test scripts, while the **Business Rules Test** utilizes the CSDDT approach.

- The **GUI Test**'s purpose is to test Windows/GUI component functionality.
- The **properties test** tests object properties of all windows, child windows, tabs, and objects.
- The **Special Features Test** (when needed) tests custom controls, features to be tested that do not readily fall into other categories, and may include special manual testing.
- The **Data Base Content/Initialization Test/Program**. This may not be a test but instead be utilized to either validate database content for testing or initialize a database with test-specific records.
- The **Business Rules Test** tests client and server business rules/edits via data input and data-controlled selections.
- **Performance and/or Load Test** (when needed).

Business Rules Test

This test type is the heart of the data-driven testing approach. It simulates user testing. It should not be intermixed with GUI and object property tests because this slows down test script execution. This test examines the heart of the business processing logic that drives the application features. It can include testing internal application logic, application components, stored procedures, etc. In some cases, testing of the AUT may require a large volume of input data to test all of the required combinations. The CSDDT approach is very well suited for this.

GUI Test

This test examines the standard GUI objects and controls. It looks at system menu controls, Min, Max, Restore, and Close; MDI/child window actions, sizing, moving, minimizing, and switching between child windows; the AUT's menu, toolbar, help system, common look and feel among child windows. This test is based on and is a refined and automated version of the tests illustrated in Figures 5.5A and 5.5B in (2).

Properties Test

This test type looks at the AUT's command buttons, data display objects, input data objects, etc. Common properties that are examined include

- The size and alignment of objects
- Which objects are enabled and disabled
- Which items have been added, removed, or changed (since the baseline capture)

Examining these properties helps to predetermine problems that may occur during the data tests. Using the same codes from the data test helps to identify the window/tab and object faster.

PROPERTIES TEST WARNING

If you are using Rational Suite TestStudio, this can be accomplished using any or all properties available that an object properties verification point can detect. The properties test is sensitive to data values and must be adjusted to ignore values like changing dates and other data or else the tester must ensure that the same data values will be present.

Input Data Test

This test type examines the capability of the AUT to accept valid data input, as well as its capacity to reject invalid data input (either create an error or mask out invalid values at the object level). This test can be combined with the business rule test type (which tests client- and server-level validations) or it can be developed independently. When constructed separately, it should test only GUI-level validations. It can also be used as a method for entering volume input during load/stress testing and reliability testing.

Formatting the Test Data File

The script is designed to read test data records from an external input file and then perform actions based on the data record contents. A sequential text file or data pools are the fastest input methods and thus are preferred; however, an MS Excel spreadsheet (slowest and may be code dependant) or an MS Access database can also be used. After the test is performed, verify the expected result. (For example, using Rational TestStudio, this would be accomplished through Robot's recorded verification points, windows existence test, etc.) If the expected result occurs, no error condition is generated. An expected error from the AUT is *not* a test error. If the expected result does *not* occur, a test error condition occurs and is logged. In the test script, control returns to the beginning of the test loop and the next record is read. The test continues until there are no more data records to process.

This loop is controlled via a

```
DO WHILE NOT EOF            (EOF= End Of File)
    -code inside of the loop
    -read and process records
LOOP
```

loop construct. As long as there are more records to read, the test continues, unless a critical error occurs.

Application-Level Errors

Unexpected application-level errors occur when an expected result does not occur, such as when incorrect data are detected, correct data are not found, a window or object is not found, or a major property has changed. Errors also happen when an unexpected result transpires such as the detection of an *Unexpected Active Window*, especially if it is an error display window. If you are a Rational user, a test verification point failure of any kind represents this type of error. These types of errors are deemed *test failures*.

A critical test script error occurs when

- The input file cannot be opened or read.
- Coded access to a database fails.
- A script command failure or runtime error occurs, usually a coding problem.

Critical errors are generally environment/programming errors and do not constitute a test failure.

Building the External Data Input File _____

External means that the input file is not part of the test scripts, but instead is a separate text file(s) that will contain the test data. To construct the input data file, begin by building a generic Excel spreadsheet and laying out the format of the data records. The format is:

- Each row in the spreadsheet will eventually become a data record in the input file.
- Each column will become a data field in a given record.

Conversion routines—such as those developed by Andy Tinkham of CWC, Inc., and modified by Archer Group for use with Rational Robot—can be utilized to read the Excel spreadsheet and write the data to rows in a sequential CSV file.

The difference between a generic CSV text file and an SQABasic sequential file is that values in a generic CSV file look like

```
value1,value2,value3
```

Before you can use the CSV file values, they may need to be converted to a format required by the test tool you are using. For instance, when using Rational Robot, the values must be formatted as an SQABasic sequential file, which looks like this:

```
"Value1","value2", "value3"
```

Note that the only difference in this example is that Robot requires quotes around the data values; otherwise it is still just a CSV file. This format allows for commas inside a field or value string. This file can be built with a simple text editor; however, data are easier to organize and much easier to read in a spreadsheet. Furthermore, it is not necessary to have a conversion program because the task can be accomplished in MS Excel. Conversion routines may be used to simplify the process.

In the CSDDT approach, the first seven columns contain the record's control information and comment field. This is the fixed portion of the data record. The test script code reads this portion of the record first. Its values are input into the script's internal string variables, and then they are examined to determine what the next step will be. The control field requirements below represent one possible convention. Others may be designed as needed.

The record format is:

```
"Rec_Type","WinCd","TabCd","ActCd","ErrCd","FldCnt","comment","data1","data2", etc.
```

The spreadsheet form is illustrated in Table 7.1. When converted from the spreadsheet form into input records for an input text file, these five records would look like this:

```
"G","User_Preference","Font","OK","none","1","Select a font style","Arial"
"G","Options","none","Apply","none","2","Enter numeric values into the first two edit
    boxes","123","456"
"H","Customer_Info","Billing_Address","Save","Required_fld_1","2","Test address field
    inputs","null","Apt.2b"
"K","Customer_Info","Billing_Address","Save","Required_fld_1","3","Test address field
    inputs","123 main st","null","Illinois"
"X","Customer_Info","Acct_Info","Cancel","none","0","Select the cancel button"
```

- Field 1—Rec_Type represents the record type. Normal values that we have implemented are as follows:
  - ✘ G represents a normal good record.
  - ✘ K represents a good record. Preprocess for keyword substitution.
  - ✘ H represents a header or comment record, which is to be read but not processed (or simply, skip this record).
  - ✘ B represents a breakpoint record. This instructs the code to pause so that the tester may step through the code at this point. It is used for debugging purposes.
  - ✘ X represents a terminate condition—stop processing records now, before the EOF is reached.

  Other codes can be added as desired for special purposes. The exception cases are coded for special processing, such as the K, H, B, and X codes. Everything else is simply considered a normal record, such as the G value.

- Field 2—WinCd represents the window selection code.

  This value or field is used to specify which window to select in the AUT. This is a code that you must design relative to your application.

TABLE 7.1
Fromatted Test Record Example

Column Name	Record Type	Window Selection Code	Tab Selection Code	Action Code	Error Code	Data Field Count	Comment Field	Data Field 1	Data Field 2	More Data Fields as needed
Shortcut	Rec_Type	WinCd	TabCd	ActCd	ErrCd	FldCnt	N/a	N/a	N/a	N/a
Function	Used by Main to help program flow	Used to identify the AUT's target window to be tested	Used to identify the AUT's target tab control to be tested	Identifies the action to be performed against the targeted window/tab	(Used only when an error is expected after an action is performed) Identifies an associated error processing routine	Identifies the number of data fields following the comment column, for this record	A place to document the record's purpose	A data value to be input to AUT	A data value to be input to AUT	A data value to be input to AUT
Example Record 1	G	User_Preference	Font	OK	none	1	Select a font style	Arial		
Example Record 2	G	Options	none	Apply	none	2	Enter numeric values into the first two edit boxes	123	456	
Example Record 3	H	Customer_Info	Billing_Address	Save	Required_fld_1	2	Test address field inputs	null	Apt.2b	
Example Record 4	K	Customer_Info	Billing_Address	Save	Required_fld_1	3	Test address field inputs	123 main st	null	Illinois
Example Record 5	X	Customer_Info	Acct_Info	Cancel	none	0	Select the cancel button			

We use a code constructed of the shortcuts of the menu commands and buttons that can be used to select the window. For example:

F for File, then O for Open. A code of FO would then represent the menu action of File→Open.

TA might represent Tools→AutoCorrect, etc.

Each additional letter or number in the code may represent an additional level in the menu or a sublevel child window. For example:

A code of KHL might specify this: Select the menu item that has a shortcut of K. Then select the submenu item with the shortcut of H. Then select the submenu item with the shortcut of L.

The letters and/or numbers you select for the code can be anything as long as you use that same code in the input data and inside your script. It could be, for example, User_Preferences or Options—whatever works for you.

- Field 3—TabCd represents the tab selection code.

This code is used to select a specific tab and/or subtab in a given window in the same fashion as the window selection. If there is no tab or subtab in a window, simply leave the data value blank or null, but make sure to include the double quotes as a placeholder ("G","WinCd","","ErrCd"…) or use a keyword such as None to indicate that it was specifically left blank so that the code can detect it.

- Field 4—ActCd represents the action code.

We typically use this code to represent an action to be performed. Such actions include

- ✗ Insert
- ✗ Delete
- ✗ Update
- ✗ Display
- ✗ Select
- ✗ OK
- ✗ Cancel
- ✗ Whatever is needed for your AUT

- Field 5—ErrCd represents error code (expected results).

This value is used as an error detection code. If the value is blank or set to ErrCd or None, then no special error window/message or indicator is expected. If a specific code is utilized here such as Err1, then the code should look for a window, message box, or micro help/status line or other indicator that is relative to this error. If the code were to equal Err1, then we would look for the specific condition that matches this error.

Testing for error conditions is very necessary to verify data values that should not be allowed or are not valid. This is just as important as testing for values that are valid.

- Field 6—FldCnt represents field count.

This field specifies how many data fields beyond the next comment field are to be read. This allows for a variable number of input data fields, so that all of the lines or records in the input text file do not have to be the same length. The count may be a value of 0 to n. The code should interpret this as a numerical value.

- Field 7 is the comment field.

This field is inserted as one of the normal input fields. It allows for self-documenting data files. No processing is performed on this field—it is used for human interpretation and documentation only and is read and discarded. It has to be read by the program so that the internal file pointers end up pointing at the first input data field as the next item to be read. In Rational TestStudio this comment can be passed through to the test log for documentation and reporting purposes.

- Fields 8 through n are the data input fields.

These data fields are used as direct input into the AUT in place of the typed-in values or list selections a user might make. If you are in a Rational environment, the usual method is to substitute the value recorded via the SQABasic command

```
'InputKeys "x"
```

where "x" is the recorded value that you would have typed, with the variable name and/or the string variable array index, where the data values are read from the input file.

Data being read from an external source has to go somewhere. When read, the values are placed into *variables*. These variables can then be utilized throughout the program and examined for content. Their content can then be used to make decisions as to how to control the flow of the program.

```
If a variable equals value x then
   do this
otherwise
   do something else
```

Data File Summary

To summarize, once the data have been created in the Excel spreadsheet, we convert it to an SQABasic sequential text file or a file suitable for your test tool environment. This is done for speed purposes and to simplify the test script code. These files can be further edited with a standard text editor such as Notepad, provided they do not become too large. You should build several different files, perhaps one for each major feature set to be tested. Each time you run the test, you can specify a different input file to use. Keep in mind that the input test data files can be built independently from the test scripts, provided that the control codes used in input data and the values used in the scripts that will act on those codes match exactly.

Code Construction for the Business Rules Test

This section explains how the scripts are built for implementing the CSDDT only. It does not cover scripts for building a GUI or properties test. For more information refer to the scripting examples set forth in Chapter 8. The test script components we employ include

- Shell script
- Main script/procedure
- Window selection script/procedure
- Tab selection script/procedure
- Action selection script/procedure
- Error detection script/procedure
- Other supporting functions and include files

The Shell Script

The optional shell script is usually used to set up input conditions for the Main script, such as calling scripts that would initialize a database prior to testing or other setup-type functions. The shell script is also the location to prompt the tester for the name and path of the input file to be processed. This allows the test script to process multiple test scenarios one at a time as specified by the tester at runtime. The acquisition of the input file to be processed can be handled any number of ways depending on the tool you are using. The Main script in the next section invokes the windows file browser to acquire the input text file.

The Main Script

The Main script or procedure is kept in a script file named DDMain and is used to

1. Open and read data from the input data file
2. Control the primary processing loop
3. Examine the control fields
4. Call the appropriate procedures and functions that perform the various processes, procedures such as:
   a. Selecting the window (window selection procedure is kept in a script file named DDWindow_Select)
   b. Selecting the tab or subwindow (tab selection procedure is kept in a script file named DDTab_Select)
   c. Performing the specified actions (perform action procedure is kept in a script file named DDPerform_Action)
   d. Testing for the expected result (error handling procedure for detecting expected errors is kept in a script file named DDProcess_Error)

   The Main procedure process has the following steps:

Acquire the path and filename of the input file to be read.

Open the file.

Enter the primary processing loop.

Read the first seven fields of the data record.

The Rec_Type code is examined first to determine if it is a normal or special record. If it is a special record, perform the special processing

Otherwise

Perform normal input processing as follows.

(The next section describes the program flow from this point.)

Read the remaining data fields into an internal string array, named DFld()

If necessary…

Call the DDWindow_Select procedure

If necessary…

Call the DDTab_Select procedure

If necessary…

Call the DDProcess_Error procedure

Return to the beginning of the loop and read the next record. If there are no more records to read, then DDMain is finished.

After the Data Are Read

The next step is to select the window that is specified in WinCd (window code) by calling the DDWindow_Select procedure. The WinCd value is made available to this procedure. Once the window has been selected and validated by the window selection procedure, the DDTab_Select procedure is called. It uses the TabCd (tab code), much like the window selection procedure used the WinCd, to select a targeted tab on the window. Realize that not all windows have tabs; therefore, the tab code is not used in all records. When there is no tab code, this procedure is simply skipped. The Main procedure should keep track of what window and/or tab is open so that, when the next record is read, if the window and/or tab called for are the same as the previous ones, a new selection is not necessary.

Now that the test script has navigated to the targeted window/tab, it is ready to perform an action against that window. Just as you would have had to create your own window and tab codes, you will need to create your own action codes. This will depend upon what actions can be performed on the window. Usually there are limited sets of actions that can be performed, such as inputting text; selecting check boxes, radio buttons, or items in drop-down lists (DDLs); or selecting items in a grid. Selecting these GUI objects should not be considered the actions, but rather the data inputs that translate into object selections. Actions are what occur either prior to or after the data input is performed. Using a simple example, the script might perform the data input and then execute a command, like clicking on the OK button, a Save button, or even the Cancel button. Design this script segment so that it inputs data to all controls (using null values for those that do not require any interaction) and then perform the final action such as clicking on the OK button.

Now that the action has been performed, the script has to determine if it should look for a normal response or an error response from the application. It must have previously determined if an error condition is expected (because the tester intentionally used bad input data to force an error). To do this, while still in the Perform_Action procedure, it preexamines the value of the ErrCd (error code).

If the error code is blank (null) or is equal to "none," then it should continue processing as if it expected a normal response from the application.

Looking for an indicator that the normal action occurred is dependent upon the AUT. The script might receive an indicator (for example, a status bar message) that a Save operation completed normally, or normal completion might be indicated by the fact that a window closed and a new record was added to a grid. It may also be something as benign as nothing happening. If no error message was displayed, then the action completed normally. Whatever happens, it must script the existence of that indicator. If nothing happens, then there is nothing to script. The test error will occur when you expect nothing to happen, and you get an error message instead. In Rational Robot, an unexpected error window is detected and the script can then be set up to cause the test to fail (you just caught a bug!). If the action performed completes normally, then the Perform_Action procedure returns to the Main procedure.

Now, if the error code is not blank or not equal to "none" then the script is expecting an error to occur. At this point the Perform_Action procedure returns to the Main procedure.

After returning to the Main procedure, the ErrCd (error code) is examined once again by the Main procedure. If the error code is not blank or not equal to "none" then the Process_Error procedure is called; otherwise, Main is finished processing this record, and it returns to the beginning of the loop and the next record is read and processed.

In the Process_Error procedure, the code is used to select a code segment that will check and verify the existence of the predetermined error indication. This may be a message box displaying the error text or some other indication that the AUT uses to show the user that an error has occurred. Once the error processing is finished, it returns to Main. Main then returns to the beginning of the loop and the next record is read and processed.

Each of the four procedures other than Main is designed in precisely the same manner. The design objective here is to keep it simple!

The code for the Main procedure template file follows.

Note: The apostrophe in the scripts is used for comment fields except where '$ is used for compiler directives.

```
'$Include: "Global.sbh"        'storage for global variables
'$Include: "DataDriven.sbh"    'storage for global variables specific to the Data-Driven
                                procedures

    Declare Function ReadFields BasicLib "Global" (File_Num, Fld_Cnt, GFlds())
    Declare Function Key_Word_Sub  BasicLib "DDKeyWord_Sub" (Fld_Cnt)

Dim Rec_Type                        'Record Type
```

```
    Dim Fld_Cnt                        'Data Field count
    Dim Comment As String
    Dim Child_Open As String
    Dim record_counter

Option Compare text                    'allows LIKE to be case insensitive
Sub Main                               'program starts here
    Dim Result As Integer
    On Error GoTo Error_Handler1
    Child_Open="No"
    current_win=""
    current_tab=""
    record_counter=0

'other ways to initialize the InfileName variable
  'InFileName="c:\sqatemplates\testdata\testdata1.txt"
  'InFileName=InputBox$("Enter the name of the input file to process.","Data Driven
                        testing",InFileName)

    CallScript "OpenFile_txt" 'open a text file for test input data this script opens a file
                        browser window
    InFileName=txt_filename 'from the openfile_txt routine

    If InFileName="" then
        Exit Sub        'the test is canceled no filename was supplied
    End if
    Open InFileName For Input As #1
    Do while Not EOF(1)    'Main process loop. Read and Process input records until there are
                        none left.
''''''''''''''''''''''''''''''
'read input test data file
''''''''''''''''''''''''''''''
        Input #1,Rec_Type,WinCd,TabCd,ActCd,ErrCd,Fld_Cnt,Comment
        if Fld_Cnt<> 0 then

            ReDim DFld(Fld_Cnt) 'set the appropriate size of the array for the number of
                        'data fields in this record

            Result=ReadFields(1, Fld_Cnt, DFld())    'pass file number, fld_cnt, address of
                        DFld
            if Result=0 then
                MsgBox "ReadFields function failed. Program terminating"
                Close #1  'close the open file
                Exit Sub
            end if
        end if

'''''''''''''''''''''''''''''''''''''''''''''''
'log which record we are processing
'''''''''''''''''''''''''''''''''''''''''''''''

        record_counter=record_counter+1
        SQALogMessage sqaPass, "last record read ="&Cstr(record_counter), ""

''''''''''''''''''''''''''''''''''''''''''''''''''''''''''''
'Determine the record type
'
' H=header record, skip this do not process
' B=Breakpoint stop for program debugging
```

```
' X=Terminate prior to the end of the input data file
' G=Good record. Process normally
' K=Good record. Pre-Process for Keyword substitution,
'   then process normally
'''''''''''''''''''''''''''''''''''''''''''''''''''''''''
        if Rec_Type LIKE "H" then
            goto NoProcess
        elseif Rec_Type LIKE "B" then
            stop                'data breakpoint
        elseif Rec_Type LIKE "X" then 'terminate the program
            Close #1
            Exit Sub
        elseif Rec_Type LIKE "G" then
            Goto Start                    'good record
        elseif Rec_Type LIKE "K" then
            key_word_sub(Fld_Cnt)        'this call is used when keywords are used in the data
                          such as 'AutoDate"
        else
            MsgBox "The record type is invalid. The program is terminating"
            Close #1
            Exit Sub
        end if

Start:              'this is a label
'''''''''''''''''''''''''''''''''''''''''''''''''''''''''
'Determine if we need to open a new window or not
'''''''''''''''''''''''''''''''''''''''''''''''''''''''''
        if Child_Open="No" then
            'Result = Window_Select(WinCd) 'go open the selected window. This is executed at
                          first pass only.
            CallScript "DDWindow_Select"
            if Gen_Return_Code=0 then
            'if Result=0 then
                close #1
                exit sub
            end if

            Current_Win=WinCd    'update and save the current window selection
            Child_Open="Yes"     'we have now opened a window
        else
            if Current_Win<>WinCd then
                CallScript "DDWindow_Select"
                if Gen_Return_Code=0 then
                    close #1
                    exit sub
                end if
                Current_Win=WinCd    'update and save the current window selection
                Child_Open="Yes"     'we have now opened a window
            end if
        end if

'tab select
'''''''''''''''''''''''''''''''''''''''''''''''''''''''''
'Determine if we need to open a new tab or not
'''''''''''''''''''''''''''''''''''''''''''''''''''''''''
            if TabCd <> "" and TabCd <> "none" and TabCd <> "TabCd" and Current_Tab<>TabCd
                          then
                CallScript "DDTab_Select"
                if Gen_Return_Code=0 then
```

```
                close #1
                exit sub
            end if
            Current_Tab=TabCd
        end if

''''''''''''''''''''''''''''''''''''''
'Perform the specified Action
''''''''''''''''''''''''''''''''''''''
        CallScript "DDPerform_Action"
        if Gen_Return_Code=0 then
           MsgBox "Specified Action Could Not be Performed"
           close #1
           exit sub
        end if


''''''''''''''''''''''''''''''''''''''
'Process the Error Code
''''''''''''''''''''''''''''''''''''''
        if ErrCd="" or ErrCd="none" or ErrCd="ErrCd" then 'Error is not expected
           goto NoProcess
        else
           CallScript "DDProcess_Error"
           if Gen_Return_Code=0 then
              MsgBox "Specified Error Processing Could Not be Performed"
              close #1
              exit sub
           end if
        end if

NoProcess:        'this is a label
    Loop 'end of main loop

    'End of File has been reached, close any open child window
    Exit Sub

Error_Handler1:
    MsgBox "Error number "&Cstr(Err)& " occurred at line: "&Erl &" -- "&Error$
    Exit Sub
End Sub
```

Window Select and Tab Select Procedures

This is the actual code for the Window_Select template script with some
example placeholder information.

```
'$Include: "DataDriven.sbh"
Declare Function Window_Select(WinCd)
Sub Main
    Gen_Return_Code = Window_Select(WinCd)
End Sub
''''''''''''''''''''''''''''''''''''''''''''''''''''''''''''''''''''''''''''''''
Function Window_Select(WinCd)
Window_Select=1
Select Case WinCd
    Case "w1"
```

```
         msgbox "w1 selected"
     Case "w2"
         msgbox "w2 selected"
     Case "w3"
         msgbox "w3 selected"
     Case Else
         Msgbox "Window Select not found for WinCd: "&Cstr(WinCd)&" Terminating"
         Window_Select=0  ''return value FAIL
         SQALogMessage sqaFail, "Window Select not found for: "&Cstr(WinCd)&"", ""
     End Select
End Function
```

The line from the front of the file:

```
'$Include: "DataDriven.sbh"
```

tells the compiler to include or use variables defined in the Header file named datadriven.sbh below.

The following takes this piece of code that was originally written in Rational Robot's SQABasic and modifies it slightly for discussion purposes. Let's assume for example that it will be coded to select one of three windows—the User Preference window, the Options window, and the Customer Information window. We would have decided to use the window selection codes of

User_Preference

Options

Customer_ Info

These window selection codes would then be utilized in the input data file and in the Select Case statement as indicated here.

```
'$Include: "DataDriven.sbh"
Declare Function Window_Select(WinCd)
Sub Main
    Gen_Return_Code = Window_Select(WinCd)
End Sub

'''''''''''''''''''''''''''''''''''''''''''''''''''''''''''''''''''''''''''''''''''
Function Window_Select(WinCd)
Window_Select=1    'this is the return code for this function indicating success. It is
                         preset here
                   'below in the case else statement it is changed to indicate an error
                         because the WinCd
                   'could not be found.

Select Case WinCd

    Case "User_Preferences"
        Record here, performing the actions necessary to select the User_Pref window
```

```
            It is very important to insert code here that verifies that the window opens and is
                              in the expected state.
            The test fails here if the window does not open as expected.

        Case "Options"
            Record here, performing the actions necessary to select the Options window
            It is very important to insert code here that verifies that the window opens and is
                              in the expected state.
            The test fails here if the window does not open as expected.

        Case "Customer_Info"
            Record here, performing the actions necessary to select the Customer Information
                              window
            It is very important to insert code here that verifies that the window opens and is
                              in the expected state.
            The test fails here if the window does not open as expected.

    Case ... add additional cases as needed.

    Case Else
        Msgbox "Window Select not found for WinCd: "&Cstr(WinCd)&" Terminating"
        Window_Select=0   ''return value FAIL
        SQALogMessage sqaFail, "Window Select not found for: "&Cstr(WinCd)&"", ""
    End Select
End Function
```

Verifying that the selection took place properly is very important here. When using Rational Robot, always insert a window existence verification point at the end of the selection code. For other test tool environments, develop similar window verification tests using the capabilities unique to your tool of choice.

If the window is present and in the proper state (enabled, maximized, etc.) and ready to accept an action, then this section of the test passes, else a test case failure occurs, which should terminate the test.

Keep Your Code Clean and Robust

Your code should be fairly robust, meaning that it should account for the unexpected and always allow for orderly termination when errors do occur. Notice the Select Case statement in our example in the previous section. These three lines of simple code alert the tester that an unknown window code was read either because a new case statement has not yet been added to accommodate it or because a bad code found its way into the test data.

When using called procedures and functions, always construct it so that a *return code* is made available to the caller. This alerts the caller that either the function/procedure was successful, or failed, and allows for proper action to be taken.

Now that the window is selected, it follows that the tab or subwindow as specified in TabCd (tab code) is selected. Use the same type of Select Case construct as was used for the Window_Select code.

```
'$Include: "DataDriven.sbh"
Declare Function Tab_Select(TabCd)

Sub Main
    Dim Result As Integer
    Gen_Return_Code = Tab_Select(TabCd)
End Sub

''''''''''''''''''''''''''''''''''''''''''''''''''''''''''''''''''
Function Tab_Select(TabCd)
tab_Select=1                                'initially set the return code to "Success"

    Select Case tabCd

        Case "t1"
            msgbox "t1 selected"

        Case "t2"
            msgbox "t2 selected"

        Case "t3"
            msgbox "t3 selected"

        Case Else
            Msgbox "Tab Select not found for TabCd: "&Cstr(TabCd)&" Terminating"
            Tab_Select=0                    'return value FAIL
            SQALogMessage sqaFail, "Tab Select not found fortab code: "&Cstr(tabCd)&"", ""
    End Select
End Function
```

Notice that this procedure is constructed in exactly the same way as the window select procedure. The only difference is that in this procedure we are working with the Tab_Select code instead of the Windows_Select code. Sticking with our example, let's say that on the Customer Information window there are two tabs, one for Billing Information and one for Account Information. Therefore, we need Tab_Select codes for both. Let's use Acct_Info and Billing_Info. Our newly modified tab selection procedure may now look something like this.

```
'$Include: "DataDriven.sbh"
Declare Function Tab_Select(TabCd)

Sub Main
    Dim Result As Integer
    Gen_Return_Code = Tab_Select(TabCd)
End Sub

''''''''''''''''''''''''''''''''''''''''''''''''''''''''''''''''''
Function Tab_Select(TabCd)
```

```
tab_Select=1                        'initially set the return code to "Success"

    Select Case tabCd

        Case "Acct_Info"
            Record selection of the account information tab here
            Validate the tab was selected and is now in focus

        Case "Billing_Info"
            Record selection of the billing information tab here
            Validate the tab was selected and is now in focus

        Case ......-
            Add additional cases for as needed

        Case Else
            Msgbox "Tab Select not found for TabCd: "&Cstr(TabCd)&" Terminating"
            Tab_Select=0  ''return value FAIL
            SQALogMessage sqaFail, "Tab Select not found fortab code: "&Cstr(tabCd)&"", ""
        End Select
End Function
```

Now that the tab or subwindow is selected, it is time to perform the action as specified in ActCd (action code), and subsequently to perform error processing based on the content of the ErrCd (error code) value. As with the window and tab selection codes, the Perform_Action code and Process_Action code should also be kept in a separate script or procedure file. This helps keep the code in the Main procedure small. We can use identical Select Case constructs for the action selection and error processing as we did with window and tab selection. The code for these routines is in Chapter 8.

Since the actions being performed in each window or tab are not the same from window to window, unique action codes relative to each window and/or tab must be used. For example, if there is an OK button on multiple screens, use a code that is a combination of the window name and the OK button such as "User_Pref_OK" and "Options_OK"—this will help to eliminate confusion among all of the various command buttons, which are on different screens.

We can usually record (using the *insert-at-cursor* record/playback feature that accompanies Robot) the window and tab selections directly into the Window_Select Tab_Select functions because the amount of code required to perform these actions is fairly small, and it is easy to set the cursor and insert these recorded excerpts into the function code. The same holds true for the Process_Errors function. In the Perform_Action procedure, this does not hold true, as you will usually be required to enter/record a significant amount of code. If that becomes the case, then simply construct a separate script/procedure to hold that code. The scripts can then be called from within the primary Perform_Action procedure. Use a good naming convention to assist in keeping the filenames straight—for example, PA_Options and PA_User_Pref.

Here is the code for the DDPerform_Action procedure template, followed by the same code demonstrating calling subprocedures such as our example, PA_User_Pref.

```
'$Include: "DataDriven.sbh"
Declare Function Perform_Action(ActCd)

Sub Main
    Dim Result As Integer
    Gen_Return_Code = Perform_Action(ActCd)
End Sub
'''''''''''''''''''''''''''''''''''''''''''''''''''''''''''''''''''''''''''''''''''''''''''''''
Function Perform_Action(ActCd)
    Perform_Action=1

    Select Case ActCd

        Case "a1"
            msgbox "a1 selected"

        Case "a2"
            msgbox "a2 selected"

        Case "a3"
            msgbox "a3 selected"

        Case Else
            Msgbox "Action Selection not found for ActCd: "&Cstr(ActCd)&" Terminating"
            Perform_Action=0   ''return value FAIL
            SQALogMessage sqaFail, "Action Selection not found for: "&Cstr(ActCd)&"", ""
    End Select
End Function
'''''''''''''''''''''''''''''''''''''''''''''''''''''''''''''''''''''''''''''''''''''''''''''''
```

Here is the same code with an inserted procedure call.

```
'$Include: "DataDriven.sbh"
Declare Function Perform_Action(ActCd)

Sub Main
    Dim Result As Integer
    Gen_Return_Code = Perform_Action(ActCd)
End Sub
'''''''''''''''''''''''''''''''''''''''''''''''''''''''''''''''''''''''''''''''''''''''''''''''
Function Perform_Action(ActCd)
    Perform_Action=1

    Select Case ActCd

        Case "User_Pref_OK"              'processing for selecting the OK button on the User
                                         Preference window.
```

```
        CallScript "DDTab_Select"    'instead or recording in-line here, we will call a
                                     different script where
                                     'the recording/code entries were made

    Case "a2"
        msgbox "a2 selected"

    Case "a3"
        msgbox "a3 selected"

    Case Else
        Msgbox "Action Selection not found for ActCd: "&Cstr(ActCd)&" Terminating"
        Perform_Action=0  ''return value FAIL
        SQALogMessage sqaFail, "Action Selection not found for: "&Cstr(ActCd)&"", ""
  End Select
End Function
```

Think about how you would verify that a new data value or record was entered into your AUT. Here are some possible scenarios:

- Access the database directly, outside of the AUT, to verify that the record was entered.
- Look for an expected message box or status indicator that states that the record/data was entered and saved.
- Look for an expected new window.
- Close the window/tab and, in the next data record, perform a selection or display type of action using the same data that was used for the insert or add action to verify that it was entered.

The ability to delete the newly inserted record without error on a subsequent input record is another possible method. Or simply assume that the lack of an error message indicates that the insert was successful, but this is the least desirable method. Why? The verification code should be included directly after the action performance code (e.g., inputting data or selecting a record). A verification failure here constitutes a test failure and should terminate the test.

Data input is performed and recorded in the portion of the code where the action selection procedure takes place. This occurs in conjunction with an Insert, Add or New, Delete, Update, Select, Display, etc., type of action where data input to the AUT is necessary to satisfy these conditions.

Assume for a moment that we wish to input data into a window/tab that has already been selected, enabled, and is in focus. Also assume that this window/tab has only three input fields into which data can be input. We would record (using the insert-at-cursor method) the selection of each of these fields, preferably using the Tab order.

If not using the Tab order, we should record the selection utilizing the normal order that a user would employ. As each field is selected, assuming for the moment that it is an input data field, we will type in a value. Start by typing a 1; then tab or double-click to/on the next input field; then type a 2, and so on. This will help us to easily identify the selected fields in the code.

Note that double-clicking on a data input field is preferable to tabbing and is usually necessary. Double-clicking on an input data field generally selects all of the data in that field so that it can be replaced. A single-click operation may merely position the cursor in the input control where it would normally put you into insert mode. Not good! The data is not replaced with the new value.

Our small piece of recorded code may look like this:

```
Window SetContext, "Caption=Window Name", ""
EditBox DblClick, "Label=Label name:", "Coords=x,y"
InputKeys  "1"
EditBox DblClick, "Label=Label name:", "Coords=x,y"
InputKeys  "2"
EditBox DblClick, "Label=Label name:", "Coords=x,y"
InputKeys  "3"
PushButton Click, "Text=OK"
```

We will substitute the data values in the InputKeys command with the names of the variables that contain the data read from our external source. Suppose we choose to read our data into a string array named DFld( )—we might then substitute the recorded, typed-in value with the variable name DFld(x), where x represents the index into the array, as follows:

DFld(1) is the first data value read

DFld (2) is the second data value read

DFld(3) is the third data value read

and so on; it is continued as necessary to enter all of the required values.

Our small piece of recorded code may now look like:

```
Window SetContext, "Caption=Window Name", ""
EditBox DblClick, "Label=Label name:", "Coords=x,y"
InputKeys DFld(1)
EditBox DblClick, "Label=Label name:", "Coords=x,y"
InputKeys DFld(2)
EditBox DblClick, "Label=Label name:", "Coords=x,y"
InputKeys DFld(3)
PushButton Click, "Text=OK"
```

Notice the text in italics. Instead of x it is now DFld(x).

At this point our script is entering values from our data file versus using data that was originally input. Our goal at this point is to substitute data and/or selections that were made manually during a recording session with values or data from our input file

Now that the data has been entered, we typically have to perform a subsequent action such as

Add

Save

Delete

Update the database

and so on. This is usually accomplished by selecting a control button or menu selection such as File→Save. This type of common action should be recorded into a subroutine, which can be called throughout the code. Then, if changes are made, there is only one place to fix.

CAUTION:

Stay away from using toolbar buttons when menu selections can perform the same actions.

Now that the action is finished, we are ready to check the ErrCd (error code) value to determine if we should look for an error condition—an error message or other identifiable error condition. We can build a Select Case construct using the same procedure we used for the window/tab selection. Again, separate this code into procedure or the library file to help keep Main small and manageable.

Typical coding in the error processing section might look like this:

```
Select Case ErrCd
    Case "Err1"
        Verify the existence of the appropriate error msg, etc. before proceeding!
    Case "Err2"
        Verify the existence of the appropriate error msg, etc. before proceeding!
    Case Else
        Msgbox "The Error code in ErrCD code does not exist. Terminating"
        SQALogMessage sqaFail, "Error Code not found for "&Cstr(ErrCd)&"", ""
End Select
```

If the expected error condition is found, the processing of this record is complete and is successful. Main continues processing by reading the next data record, provided we are not at the end of the input file and more records are available to be read. If the expected error condition is not found, a test failure occurs (usually a test case). The test can be terminated and the result entered into the test log, or Main can log the result and continue processing as long as the test data records represent independent tests.

The test log should indicate what the last recorded read contained and the record number. This allows for fast debugging and problem isolation. This can be accomplished in Main with very little code.

Archer Group Summary

CSDDT consists of a group of routines, libraries, or procedures that will allow the use of data from an input file to perform selections; CSDDT also allows data input versus what we typed in as input or clicked on as selections. If we change the data in our input file, the selections and actions as well as the data that are to be input into the AUT can be modified or altered without changing the script.

This is the real benefit of a Data Driven testing framework. Once the mechanics of making the selections are in place, the test code is set up to operate on the input data, and we can modify each test scenario using different data, not different test scripts, to create functional variants. This is because the test data file contains codes that specify where to go in the AUT, what action to perform, what to expect, how many data fields to use, a comment (documentation), and what data to use (input into the AUT).

Carl Nagle's DDE Framework_____

Nagle's approach moves test automation to the third level as it uses a nontechnical front end (a table-driven approach that is implemented in MS Excel format) that describes the tests to be performed, lays out the test scenarios, and implements the steps to be executed. When the tables are parsed by the DDE, the DDE executes automated tests without the user needing to write test script code.

DDE Overview

Carl Nagle of SAS Institute developed this framework for SAS (SAS Institute owns the intellectual property rights to the DDE), but also released it to the public domain as is indicated in the following copyright information:

Copyright (2001) SAS Institute Inc. All rights reserved.
NOTICE: Permission to use, copy, modify and distribute this code and

its documentation, if any, for any purpose and without fee is hereby granted, subject to the following conditions:

Note: This copyright permission notice must appear in all copies of the code and in any related documentation.

The DDE concept is another alternative to the capture/playback approach. The main reason for test automation implementation failures is the maintenance burden associated with the capture/playback method. Automated test script development is application development, and a set of automated test scripts constitutes a software system to test another software system. As the application software tested by the scripts evolves, the scripts themselves require maintenance to keep them working.

The level of the maintenance effort depends on the implementation approach. Capture/playback test scripts require the most maintenance because they contain both test procedure commands and test data; everything is hard coded in the test script. The keys to maintenance reduction are to remove the test data from the script and use that data to drive the test script, as well as to develop reusable subroutines and functions that can be shared across automated testing projects.

The Archer Group approach (discussed in the previous section) does this using CSV files containing two types of data: The first data type functions to direct the test script's navigation in the AUT and to direct the actions it performs against the AUT. The second data type is the actual test data used by the script to implement specific tests of the AUT. The script control data and the test data are developed in Excel spreadsheets and exported to CSV files in the format Rational Robot requires.

The DDE method is very similar, but it has been enhanced so that non-technical testers can also develop test data. Test data development involves construction of a hierarchical set of tables in MS Excel that drives the tests of the application. These tables include three types of driver tables—Cycle Driver tables, Suite Driver tables, and Step Driver tables. The Cycle Driver table is the highest level and the farthest removed from the actual test. Figure 7.1 illustrates the DDE automation framework structure.

The DDE method is best described in Nagle's own words:

> …the framework itself is really defined by the *Core Data Driven Engine*, the *Component Functions*, and the *Support Libraries*. While the *Support Libraries* provide generic routines useful even outside the context of a keyword driven framework, the core engine and *Component Functions* are highly dependent on the existence of all three elements.

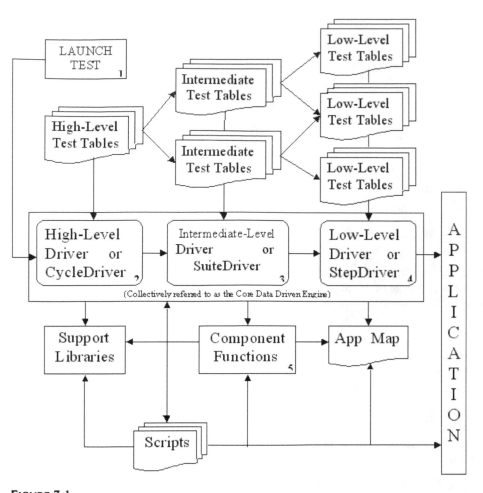

FIGURE 7.1

The DDE Automation Framework (Reprinted by permission).
Figure 5 from: Nagle, Carl. "Test Automation Frameworks." *groups.yahoo.com/group/RobotDDEUsers/files/Doc/
FRAMESDataDrivenTestAutomationFrameworks.htm.*

The test execution starts with the LAUNCH TEST script. This script invokes the *Core Data Driven Engine* by providing one or more *High-Level Test Tables* to *CycleDriver*. *CycleDriver* processes these test tables invoking the *SuiteDriver* for each *Intermediate-Level Test Table* it encounters. *SuiteDriver* processes these intermediate-level tables invoking *StepDriver* for each *Low-Level Test Table* it encounters. As *StepDriver* processes these low-level tables it attempts to keep the application in synch with the test. When *StepDriver* encounters a low-level command for a specific component, it determines what Type of component is involved and invokes the corresponding *Component Function* module to handle the task.(3)

The major advantage to this approach is that the information in the Cycle Driver tables can be entered by anyone with a working knowledge of the AUT and an idea of what should be tested. This means that the cycle and suite driver tables can be developed by test designers prior to system testing efforts and provided to the automation team, which subsequently develops the Step Driver tables. The effort required for the test designers to build their test tables can be minimized through the use of Nagle's VB (VisualBasic) Test Generator utility that allows the designers to enter the table values via a GUI rather than by typing them directly into the tables.

NOTE:

Most often test designers can develop the Suite-level test tables. Thus a nontechnical designer may be able to do both Cycle- *and* Suite-level development. However, the lowest-level step tables definitely seem to be the realm of the technical automator.

The DDE is already implemented. It just needs setup and installation, and then it is complete and ready to use—no local customizations are required to commence using it. Users need only to develop their test data to begin using the DDE. Only in cases where existing DDE functionality does not adequately provide solutions to given problems will users need to implement custom scripts, and these are not part of the DDE, but can be called by the DDE as necessary.

In the Archer Group methodology, the control data was included in the test scripts. In DDE, however, control data are placed in an application map containing GUI object recognition strings as well as other data. Action words invoke component functions, which are subroutines that act against the AUT. Test record type indicators are used that are similar to the Archer Group method. The application map is similar in function to the maps created by commercial automated tools such as Rational Software's TestFactory and Mercury Interactive's WinRunner. Nagle's framework includes an application mapping tool, the Process Container utility that comes with the DDE code.

The following are examples of DDE record types:

b = BLOCKID (defines the start of a named block within the input file) c = DRIVER COMMAND (driver performs utility function other than test)

s = SKIPPED TEST (a test that is temporarily disabled [and logged as such]).

t = TEST (a test to perform; might be navigation, changing values, or verifying data)

The driver forwards the data record to the appropriate test script routine based on the record type.

Test data can be entered in the tables or contained in CSV files that the tables direct the test script routine to read and process. The Suite Driver test case example directs the DDE to process an application login via Step Driver with specific credentials:

```
T,  Login, ^id=myuserid, ^pw=mypassword
```

The Step Driver then processes the Login test table data to complete the operation:

```
t, LoginWin, UserIDBox, SetTextValue, ^id
t, LoginWin, PasswordBox, SetTextValue, ^pw
```

As you can see, no technical expertise is required to develop these tests. They are keyword based. Each record directs the test scripts to a specific location and tells it what action to take depending on the keywords it contains.

DDE Development Effort

The DDE setup reference document is located at *groups.yahoo.com/group/ RobotDDEUsers/files/Doc/sqabasic2000/DDEngineSetup.htm*. This document is a must-read prior to installing the DDE and performing a pilot project. The pilot project requires a sustained effort, perhaps as much as 90 days. The project should be implemented specifically on a select subset of AUT features. At the end of the pilot period, the effort should be evaluated, and identified problem areas should be addressed.

Following the pilot, the remaining AUT feature tests should be automated, constituting a complete regression test suite. The actual time to develop the test suites should be estimated on the number of features and the number of test cases per feature for each AUT version.

Keith Zambelich's Test Plan Driven Testing Framework for Mercury Interactive Users

Zambelich describes his *ToolKit for WinRunner,* available at *www.auto-sqa. com/toolkit.html,* as being

> basically composed of User-Defined Functions and Utility scripts which give the tester more control of the WinRunner® test tool. These functions and utilities facilitate the tester's ability to use the tool in whatever method or manner is dictated by specific testing requirements, rather than being subjected to the inherent limitations of the test tool.(3)

This tool kit contains functions that are the basic infrastructure of Zambelich's "Test Plan Driven (Key Word Driven)" automated testing methodology. His approach uses the test case documentation that testers have developed in a spreadsheet containing special "Key-Words." To quote Zambelich, "In this method, the entire process is *data-driven,* including functionality. *The Key Words control the processing.*"(4)

Zambelich's tool kit currently contains the following categories of utility scripts (4):

- "Generic" Windows utilities: used for testing any object-oriented application
- "Language-Specific" utilities: used for testing object-oriented applications developed under a specific language
- "Terminal Emulator" utilities: used for testing AS\400, ACP/TPF, and other mainframe applications via terminal emulation
- "Application-Specific" or "customized" utilities: may also need to be developed for the specific Application Under Test

The WinRunner® ToolKit allows the tester and the script developer to accomplish the following (4):

- Quickly generate Automated Tests without an extensive knowledge of WinRunner or TSL (Test Script Language).
- Develop scripts that are "robust," in that they will not stop running due to an application error, a WinRunner error, or a test script error (allows "*unattended* testing").
- Develop Automated Test Scripts for more than one application (tests can be developed for *any number of applications of different types* without having to "reinvent" the script development process).

- Easily develop "customized" functions and utilities using the ToolKit as a framework (if familiar with using the TSL *Test Script Language*).
- Create customized "Test Reports" for each test and "Summary Reports" for each scenario or series of tests.
- Assume total control of the test tool and essentially make it do whatever is required to test an application.

Zambelich Approach Summary

Zambelich summarizes his approach as follows (4):

The Spreadsheet (which may be one of many contained in a workbook) is saved as a "tab-delimited" file. Tab-delimited rather than comma-delimited is used because data often contains commas (e.g., Last_Name, First_Name) that will confuse the processing.

This file is read by a *Controller script* and processed. When a *Key Word* is encountered, a list is created using data from the remaining columns. This continues until a "null" (blank) in column-2 and column-3 is encountered (this is why we use a blank or null line between Key-Word sections).

The Controller script then calls a *Utility script* associated with the Key Word, which passes the "list" created as an *input parameter*. The Utility script processes this list, which contains the specific actions to take, data to enter or verify, etc.

The Utility script processes the column-2 (parameter) and column-3 data for each row, in much the same way as the Controller script processes the column-1 (Key-Word) data. The Utility script may call User-Defined functions to perform specific actions or may just use the standard TSL functionality to accomplish this.

This continues until an "end-of-list" condition is reached or until a fatal-error occurs. The Utility script then returns control back to the Controller script, which continues processing the tab-delimited file until an "end-of-file" condition is reached or until a "fatal-error" return-code is received from the Utility script.

In order to process a number of scripts, the Controller script is called by a *Driver script*. The Driver script contains the names of all of the Test Cases to run, and calls the Controller script for each test, passing to it the name of each Test Case (saved tab-delimited file).

This architecture is very flexible, as the Driver script is not limited to calling the Controller script to process the Key-Word driven Test Case. It can also call Business Function type scripts, or even Recorded scripts. All methods of automated testing can be supported by this architecture.

TABLE 7.2
Example of a Spreadsheet Containing Key Words (Using Zambelich's ToolKit for WinRunner Methodology)

COLUMN 1 Key Word	COLUMN 2 Field/Screen Name	COLUMN 3 Input/Verification Data	COLUMN 4 Comment	COLUMN 5 Pass/Fail
Start_Test:	Screen	Main Menu	Verify Starting Point	
Enter:	Selection	3	Select Payment Option	
Action:	Press_Key	F4	Access Payment Screen	
Verify:	Screen	Payment Posting	Verify Screen Accessed	
Enter:	Payment Amount	125.87	Enter Payment Data	
	Payment Method	Check		
Action:	Press_Key	F9	Process Payment	
Verify:	Screen	Payment Screen	Verify Screen Remains	
Verify_Data:	Payment Amount	$ 125.87	Verify Updated Data	
	Current Balance	$1,309.77		
	Status Message	Payment Posted		
Action:	Press_Key	F12	Return to Main Menu	
Verify:	Screen	Main Menu	Verify Return to Menu	

"Test Plan Driven" Method Architecture _____

- Driver Script
  - ✗ Performs initialization (if required)
  - ✗ Calls the Application-Specific "Controller" Script, passing to it the file-names of the Test Cases (which have been saved from the spreadsheets as "tab-delimited" files)
- The "Controller" Script
  - ✗ Reads and processes the file-name received from Driver
  - ✗ Matches on "Key Words" contained in the input-file
  - ✗ Builds a *parameter-list* from the records that follow
  - ✗ Calls "Utility" scripts associated with the "Key Words," passing the created parameter-list
- Utility Scripts
  - ✗ Process input parameter-list received from the "Controller" script
  - ✗ Perform specific tasks (e.g., press a key or button, enter data, verify data, etc.), calling "User Defined Functions" if required
  - ✗ Report any errors to a Test Report for the test case
  - ✗ Return to "Controller" script
- User Defined Functions
  - ✗ General and Application-Specific functions may be called by any of the above script-types in order to perform specific tasks (4)

Using TestDirector to Drive the Test Suite

If TestDirector is being used to drive the Test Suite, then the architecture changes somewhat, as TestDirector does not have the capacity to pass a parameter to a called script. Consequently, TestDirector cannot be used to call the Controller script. We handle this by creating a **Test Case Driver** script to act as an intermediary between Test Director and the Controller. The Test Case driver is called by Test Director, and it subsequently calls the Controller script passing to it the required tab-delimited file name. Note that this means that there must be one Test Case Driver per Test Case. The actual code contained within these is exactly the same, but each must have the name of the Test Case.

TestDirector

- Calls Initialization script if required

- Calls the "Test Case Driver" script for each Test Case

Test Case Driver

- Performs initialization (calls Initialization scripts) if required
- Calls the application-specific "Controller" script, passing to it the file-names of the Test Cases (which have been saved from the spreadsheet as "tab-delimited" files)

From this point, the architecture is the same as for using a Driver script to drive the Test Suite. Refer to Figure 7.2.

The following is an example TSL driver script outline.

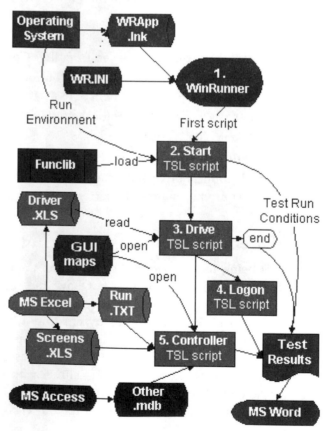

FIGURE 7.2

Data-Driven Test Execution Flow Using TestDirector

Having filled out the spreadsheet as in Table 7.2, the following would then be done:

1. Save the Workbook file.

2. Save the Spreadsheet as a "tab-delimited" text file. Use the name of the Test Case as the filename (if Test Case = TC0001A, text file = tc0001a.txt.

3. Add the Test Case to the list of cases to be run in the Driver script.

When the **Driver** script is executed, the following would be done:

- Call **Controller** script, passing Test Case name: ret_code = call "Controller"("TC0001A")
- **Controller:**
  - ✗ Opens file TC0001A.txt and reads each record
  - ✗ On "**Test_Description**" writes the Test Description to the Test Report
  - ✗ On "**Start_Test**", calls *Application-Specific* Utility script **Start_Up** (Screen~Main Screen)
  - ✗ **Start_Up:**
    - Writes data to the Test Report re: start of test, time, date, etc.
    - Verifies we are positioned at the Main Screen
    - Returns to **Controller**
- **Controller:**
  - ✗ On "**Test_Step**" writes the Test Step Number and Description to the Test Report
  - ✗ On "**Enter**", calls *Generic* Utility script **Enter** (Selection~1)
  - ✗ **Enter:**
    - Verifies field "Selection" exists
    - Enters "1" in Selection
    - Returns to **Controller**
- **Controller:**
  - ✗ On "**Action**", calls *Generic* Utility script **Action** (Press_Key~Enter)
  - ✗ **Action:**
    - Verifies "Enter" is a valid key name
    - Calls WinRunner function to press the "Enter" key
    - Returns to **Controller**

- **Controller:**
  - ✗ On "**Verify**", calls *Generic* Utility script **Verify** (Screen~Payment Screen)
  - ✗ **Verify:**
    - Calls WinRunner function to set the Screen (logical name) in the GUI_file
    - Note: this verifies that the Screen is displayed and active
    - Returns to **Controller**
- **Controller:**
  - ✗ On "**Test_Step**" writes the Test Step Number and Description to the Test Report
  - ✗ On "**Enter**", calls Utility script **Enter** (Payment Amount~125.87 | Payment Method~Check)
  - ✗ **Enter:**
    - Verifies field "Payment Amount" exists
    - Enters "125.87" in Payment Amount
    - Verifies field "Payment Method" exists
    - Enters "Check" in Payment Method
    - Returns to **Controller**
- **Controller:**
  - ✗ On "**Action**", calls Utility script **Action** (Press_Key~F9)
  - ✗ **Action:**
    - Verifies "F9" is a valid key name
    - Calls WinRunner function to press the "F9" key
    - Returns to **Controller**
- **Controller:**
  - ✗ On "**Verify**", calls Utility script **Verify** (Screen~Payment Screen)
  - ✗ **Verify:**
    - Calls WinRunner function to set the Screen (logical name) in the GUI_file
    - Note: In this step, we are verifying that the screen has *not* changed
    - Returns to **Controller**

- **Controller:**
  - ✗ On "**Test_Step**" writes the Test Step Number and Description to the Test Report
  - ✗ On "**Verify_Data**", calls Utility script **Ver_data** (Payment Amount~$ 125.87 | Current Balance ~$1,309.77 | Status Message~Payment processed.)
  - ✗ **Ver_data:**
    - Verifies field "Payment Amount" exists
    - Extracts the contents of Payment Amount & compares with data entered
    - If data doesn't match, reports an error-msg to the Test Report showing Expected versus Actual results
    - Verifies field "Current_Balance" exists
    - Extracts the contents of Current_Balance & compares with data entered
    - If data doesn't match, reports an error-msg to the Test Report
    - Verifies field "Status Message" exists
    - Extracts the contents of Status Message & compares with data entered
    - If data doesn't match, reports an error-msg to the Test Report
    - Returns to **Controller**
- **Controller:**
  - ✗ On "**End_Test**", calls the *Application-Specific* Utility script **End_Test** (Press_Key~F3 | Screen~Main Screen)
  - ✗ **End_Test:**
    - Performs End-Of-Test functions, and includes some of the same parameters as the Action and Verify Utilities. Will ordinarily contain additional functions as required by the **Application Under Test.**
    - Verifies "F3" is a valid key-name
    - Calls WinRunner function to press the "F3" key
    - Calls WinRunner function to set the Screen (logical name) in the GUI_file
    - Note: In this step, we must minimally verify that we have returned to the *Starting Position* ("Main Screen").
    - Returns to **Controller**

- **Controller:**
  - ✗ Performs End-Of-Test functions:
  - ✗ Verifies that additional GUI_files opened during the test are closed
  - ✗ Verifies that we have returned to the *Starting Position* ("Main Screen") in the event that the End_Test routine was not run (due to a fatal error encountered).
  - ✗ Calls an application-specific "ReturnToBaseState()" function to ensure we are at the Starting Position.
  - ✗ Returns to **Driver**

The Driver script tests the Return Code from the Controller and writes a "pass/fail" message to the Summary Report. It also determines what test to run next, and calls the Controller script, passing the next Test Case name to it. The Driver continues to the tests until there are no more to run except if an error forces the routine to end.

The different types of keyword files roughly correspond to the Excel tables that Nagle's DDE used to drive testing (see Tables 7.3, 7.4, and 7.5).

Zambelich's tool kit also provides a set of "generic" functions used by the controller script. They include functions in three Toolkit Function libraries (Main_TK1, Main_TK2, and Main_TK3). These compiled modules are extracted from "ToolKit.zip" and are then installed in WinRunner's Func-

TABLE 7.3
Test Administration Keywords

Utility Keyword	Client/Server Usage	Web Usage	Note
START_TEST:	Start_Up	Start_Up (Application-Specific)	
TEST_DESCRIPTION:	N/A - See 'Start_Test'		
TEST_STEP:	N/A - See 'Start_Test'		
END_TEST:	End_Test (Application-Specific)		

TABLE 7.4
Data Manipulation Keywords

Utility Keyword	(Gen_Util)	(Web_Util)	Note
ACTION:	Action	Web_Action	
DO_IF: / ELSE:			
SELECT_LIST_ITEM:	Sel_List		

TABLE 7.4
Data Manipulation Keywords (Continued)

Utility Keyword	(Gen_Util)	(Web_Util)	Note
ENTER:	Enter	Web_Enter	
UPDATE_IF_NULL:	Enter		
APPEND:	——		
EXTRACT_DATA:	Sav_Data	Web_Save_Data	
EXTRACT_TABLE_DATA:	——	Web_Save_Table	
GENERATE_DATA:	Gen_Data		
GENERATE_INPUT:			
CALCULATE:	Calculate (Gen_Util)		
CALCULATE_DATE:	Gen_Data	Calc_Date (Gen_Util)	
SET_CONDITION:	Set_Cond	Web_Set_Cond (Gen_Util)	
SET_DATE:	Set_Date	Web_Set_Date	

TABLE 7.5
Verification Keywords

Utility Keyword	Client/Server Usage	Web Usage	Note
MATCH_DATA:	Ver_Data	Web_Verify_Data	
VERIFY_DATA:			
VERIFY_TEXT:	Ver_Text	Web_Verify_Text	
VERIFY_TEXT_LINKS:	——	Verify_Text_Links	
VERIFY_IMAGE	Ver_Bitmap	Web_Verify_Image	
VERIFY_ATTRIBUTES:	Ver_Attr	Web_Verify_Prop	
VERIFY_ENABLED:	Ver_Enbl	Web_Verify_Enbl?	
VERIFY_VALUE:	Ver_Value	Web_Ver_Value	
VERIFY_NUMERIC_VALUE:	Ver_Value	Ver_Value (Gen_Util)	
VERIFY:	Verify	Web_Verify	

TABLE 7.5
Verification Keywords (Continued)

Utility Keyword	Client/Server Usage	Web Usage	Note
VERIFY_LIST_ITEMS:	Ver_List (Gen_Util)		
VERIFY_TREEVIEW_ITEM:	Ver_Tree	—	

tion Generator category **ATS ToolKit Functions** by script AUT_INIT in the APP_Init folder. The utility scripts fall into the categories below.

The Just Enough Software Test Automation FTP site (*www.phptr/mosley*) contains documentation explaining Zambelich's data-driven automation framework. He has provided an overview document that fully describes the Functions and Utility scripts and his slide presentation, as well as some excellent example spreadsheets (see Figure 7.4).

Automated Testing Specialists offers the toolkit and an associated consuting program for a fee. If you are using WinRunner and want to obtain the tookkit and implement this framework, you should contact Keith Zambelich directly (at Automated Testing Specialists, Inc., P.O. Box 65564, Los Angeles, CA 90065, email: *keithz@auto-sqa.com*) to obtain the TooKit for WinRunner.

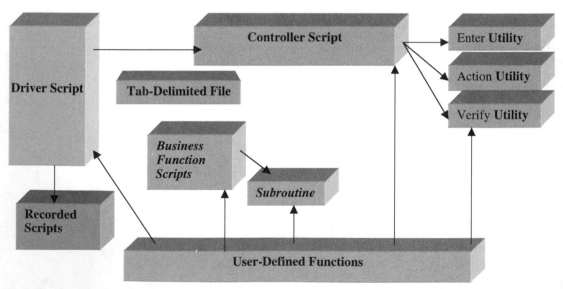

FIGURE 7.3
ToolKit for WinRunner Architecture

Conclusion

The data-driven testing frameworks discussed in this chapter are generic scaffolds for automating the testing of application software that have moved beyond the limitations of the capture/playback paradigm representing the first generation of automated testing. They are designed to allow for the execution of a large number of functional variations of the test data using a small number of test scripts and subroutines/functions.

References

1. Kit, Edward. "Integrated Effective Test Design and Automation." *Software Development* 7, no. 2, February 1999.

2. Mosley, Daniel J. *Client-Server Software Testing on the Desktop and the Web.* Prentice Hall PTR, Upper Saddle River, NJ, 1999.

3. Nagle, Carl. "Test Automation Frameworks." *groups.yahoo.com/group/Robot-DDEUsers/files/Doc/FRAMESDataDrivenTestAutomationFrameworks.htm*

4. Zambelich, Keith. "Totally Data-Driven Automated Testing, Using Key-Word Input to Drive the Automated Testing Process." Whitepaper, Automated Testing Specialists (ATS), *www.auto-sqa.com*

The Control Synchronized Data-Driven Testing Framework in Depth

An individual educated in testing methods, who understands the needs of the targeted users and has an in-depth knowledge of the application to be tested, is the best by far at performing software testing. This person would perform these tests in a manual fashion observing every nuance of the system as it is put through its paces.

This level of manual testing is very time consuming and thus very expensive. Unfortunately, in today's rapid application development (RAD) environments, time and expense are the critical factors. Automated testing, although no faster and definitely more expensive to develop up front than manual testing, pays off in the speed of execution with repeated regression testing. Using CSDDT methodology can benefit this situation in that it helps to reduce the up-front time required to put together an effective automated testing suite.

Creating Data-Driven Test Scripts

Once again it is important to note that CSDDT is an implementation of an organized testing framework. *The key to how effective your testing is going to be lies in the test data that are created and utilized.* Remember that this framework performs no validation or object verification on its own. It merely holds the code that interacts with your AUT's windows and objects. The input records determine how the interaction occurs as the framework code parses it and acts upon its contents. It is similar to you and your car. The car provides the mechanics to take you from one place to another, but it can do nothing on its own. You, the driver, are like the input data. You control how the trip takes place—starting, accelerating, turning, stopping, and finally shutting down after you arrive at your destination.

One of the benefits in implementing CSDDT is that the data can be designed at the same time or prior to constructing the framework scripts, allowing for a concurrent process of building your test environment. In more than one situation, Dan has worked on developing the input test data while Bruce implemented the test scripts. This helps to reduce the time required to start running our tests. In addition, the entire set of tests does not have to be finished before you start using it. As soon as all of the components are in place to provide interaction with the first set of requirements to be tested, one tester can start executing the tests, while a second tester continues building new or additional test data, and a third can be implementing/building the new code to interact with the next set of windows and objects. This concurrent development can then provide for useful testing earlier than using only capture/playback methods to build your automated test suite.

Implementing the CSDDT Approach _____

The main concept of data-driven testing is literally to read data records from an input file that controls the program flow in a test script and that provides the input data. Simple applications can be completely controlled by recorded events; however, they are difficult to modify and may become very large, even if a limited number of functional variations of input data are tested. In the Rational Robot world, input keystrokes from the keyboard are recorded as *InputKeys* script commands. The recorded InputKeys command records a series of keystrokes with one or more commands. The following example shows how keystrokes might be recorded when entering an address in a window, using the tab character to move from input field to input field. The typed data are inside the double quotes.

```
InputKeys "123 main street,{BACKSPACE}{TAB}{TAB}Columbia{TAB}Il{TAB}6226{LEFT}3"
```

Can you easily determine what the final result is? {BACKSPACE} is used to erase the comma after the word *street* and {LEFT}3 is used to insert the number 3 before the last 6. Yes, all of the keystrokes were recorded, including the corrections. This is referred to as recording input noise.

Frequently when a large number of keystrokes are recorded, they are spread across several InputKeys commands. When these commands are interspersed among many other commands, such as edit box clicks, you can imagine how difficult it would be to edit a script later to correct an error. If you have several screens in which you need to input data to numerous controls, you can very easily end up with hundreds of lines of script commands. This may work well at playback time; however, the test you accomplish may only be limited. What if you need to enter 20 different sets of data in a GUI screen with only 10 to 15 input objects, and then you need to perform recorded events that verify that all of that input data were saved correctly? You can begin to imagine how massive the scripts can become. In order to keep them manageable, you determine that you have to record limited functionality per script and that you have to record a lot of scripts to provide proper test coverage. If you have an application with more than a dozen different screens to test, you would then end up with an enormous quantity of test procedures with an enormous number of recorded test cases.

The problem is in managing the stages the scripts are in—whether they are completed, in progress, or in need of updating—as well as how many testers and administrators are required to stay on top of the test suite. How do you begin to modify these scripts for the next prerelease build of the application, when the developers have made changes to the screen's functionality or have moved, added, or removed objects that your test was interacting with? Your company decides that, on the next release some months down the road, the application will have different types of input controls, such as data grids versus edit boxes of various types. Can you reuse the tests you've put together? Not likely.

It has been our experience (and that of others, judging from their published experiences) that the number one cause for project-level test automation failure and abandonment is *the eventual inability to properly maintain the automated test scripts.* This is especially true on large-scale AUTs, where changes are made and new or additional functionality is incorporated on a frequent basis.

Common Problems and Solutions

Problem: Data Input

You need to test multiple data combinations to verify the business rules, edit rules, etc. If you have to type in all of these combinations while recording with Rational Robot, you had better be a perfect typist and have the patience of a saint. In addition, all data that have been typed and recorded are now hard-coded data. To alter or repair this data, the scripts must be edited or rerecorded.

Solution: Utilize Input Data Text Files

1. The immediate benefit is that, if you need additional data, you can simply add more records; there is no need to modify the test script.

2. If you need to modify the data records, simply do it in your original Excel spreadsheet or modify the text file with a text editor (it is better to register text files from a modified spreadsheet; this keeps the test data in synch with the test requirements); there is no need to modify the test script.

3. You can create multiple input data files if needed or desired for different scenarios; there is no need to modify the test script.

Problem: Program Flow Changes

After the script is recorded, you discover that you need to test different screens in a variety of orders based upon input to one screen affecting the data in another.

Solution: Let the Input Data Do the Driving

Build a simple set of codes that represent the various windows and tabs in the destination window where the data will be input, selected, deleted, etc. Next, build a set of codes, or keywords, that represent an action, such as Insert, Delete Select, Update—whatever you need. You will probably find yourself adding to the list as you determine new actions needed. Plan on building a set of codes that represents a corresponding set of expected error responses. You will probably have to do this on the fly as you determine what the error responses are.

These codes are included at the beginning of each record to specify where to go, what to do when you get there, and what response to look for. The remainder of the record is used as the data to be input or found/selected.

The script is designed to read the codes and then perform the appropriate actions. You will have to prerecord a small section of script commands that will be used in response to the data file codes. For example, we record the menu selections necessary to get to a specific window and/or the tab control clicks needed to get to a specific location in the application. These code snippets are separated into Select Case statements that perform very limited, but reusable and manageable functions. Refer to the section on Select/Case statements in the *SQABasic Language Reference* book, which is available online to registered Rational SuiteTest Studio users at *www.rational.com/docs/v2002/sqabasic.pdf* (2).

Problem: Managing Application Changes

A different button, menu selection, tab click, etc., is required to go to a specific location, or an object or control on a screen is changed.

Solution: Rerecord or Modify a Very Small Section of Code

If something changes in the application and now a different set of menu selections and tab clicks are required to go to a specific location, you have to rerecord only this small piece. This piece will be very easy to identify and find in your script because of the way it is separated into small case statements. This same scenario holds true with the code snippets that control the actions and responses.

NOTE:

It is very important to construct the code so that any given AUT object or control is interacted with in only **one** location within the test scripts—**one** location to interact with the control, **one** place to fix when it changes!

Setting Up Common Startup and Ending Test Conditions

As with any set of recorded test scripts, it is necessary to always start and terminate at a common point. This ensures that the AUT is in the same state as it was when the initial recording took place. An example would be where the AUT is open and maximized and there are no leftover open child windows or leftover data values from previous manual or automated testing.

Without this return to home state, the tests are not repeatable. Therefore, you must always clean up your AUT prior to stating the automated test scripts. Of course there are situations where you will rely on leftover data or conditions that are present (persistent applications) because you are testing for them. You will also run into situations where date stamps and other data are automatically updated from one run of the test to the next. The test's sensitivity to these items should be removed so subsequent runs of your tests do not fail.

Modifying Recorded Code to Accept Input Data _____

The key ingredient to modifying your recorded code/script is understanding what to modify in order to utilize the external file data in place of what was typed in during your recording session.

Typically the code that will interact with objects and data input controls of the AUT's windows/tabs is placed in the Perform_Action script or in scripts that are called from within the Perform_Action script. Refer to Chapter 7 for the high-level program flow and description.

Let's assume for a moment that we want to input data to a window and that the window has already been selected and enabled, and is in focus. Let's also assume for discussion's sake that this window/tab has only three input fields where data can be typed in. Using Rational Robot, we would record the selection of each of these fields, in turn, preferably using the tab order (assuming that it is already properly set). If not using the tab order, we should record the selection utilizing the normal order that a user would choose. As each input data field is selected, we will type in a value. Start by typing a **1**, then tab to or double-click on the next input field and type **2**, and so on. This will help us easily identify the selected fields in the code, which will be modified shortly.

Very Important Practices_____

In most cases, double-clicking on a data input field is the preferable method of selection; furthermore, it is usually necessary versus a single mouse click on the object. Double-clicking selects all of the data in that field so that it can be replaced with new data. A single-click operation may only place the cursor in the input control, selecting none of the existing data, and normally activates the insert mode. Not good. The existing data is not replaced with the new value. In some applications where multiple words or values separated by spaces can live in a single edit box, we have found that even double-clicking may not get all of the text selected and ready for replacement. In this case, the method that consistently ensures that all of the data is selected is this: Navigate to the control via the keyboard control, such as tabbing, right arrow, or mouse click. Once the cursor is placed into the control, record these keystrokes:

- Home
- Shift+End
- Delete

This selects all of the existing data and then deletes it, which allows for complete replacement.

As we previously have demonstrated in Chapter 7, our small piece of recorded code, inside of the Perform_Action script, may look like this:

```
Window SetContext, "Caption=Window Name", ""
EditBox DblClick, "Label=Label name:", "Coords=x,y"
InputKeys "1"
EditBox DblClick, "Label=Label name:", "Coords=x,y"
InputKeys "2"
EditBox DblClick, "Label=Label name:", "Coords=x,y"
InputKeys "3"
PushButton Click, "Text=OK"
```

Note the placement of the values in bold type—1, 2, and 3. We will substitute the data values in the InputKeys command with the variable names we have utilized that contain the data read from our external source file. Suppose we choose to read our data into a string array named DFld( ). We might then substitute the recorded, typed-in value with the variable name DFld(x) where x represents the index into the array. Although string arrays typically start with index 0 and not 1, in order to make it a little easier for the new programmer, we will start with index value 1 instead of index 0. Remember from our previous discussions that the first seven fields of each data record are read first and are placed into individual unique string variables. One of these values tells the program how many data values are to be read. Based on that value, we set the size of the array, Dfld(), to match. After we perform a small program loop that reads the remainder of the input record's data fields

DFld(1) contains the first data value read

DFld(2) contains the second data value read

DFld(3) contains the third data value read

and so on, it continues as is necessary for us to read and acquire all of the data fields.

Now we will edit our small piece of recorded code to utilize the data in the array instead of the hard-coded values we recorded. Our recorded code may now look like this:

```
Window SetContext, "Caption=Window Name", ""
EditBox DblClick, "Label=Label name:", "Coords=x,y"
InputKeys DFld(1)
EditBox DblClick, "Label=Label name:", "Coords=x,y"
InputKeys DFld(2)
EditBox DblClick, "Label=Label name:", "Coords=x,y"
InputKeys DFld(3)
PushButton Click, "Text=OK"
```

Notice the text in bold. These are the data fields DFld(1), DFld(2), and Dfld(3) instead of the literal hard-coded values of 1, 2, and 3 that we recorded originally.

At this point, when we play back our script, it will enter those values that originated in our data file that were subsequently read into our string array Dfld(); what we won't get is the data that were typed in originally. This means that, every time we change the data in the input file that will be loaded into the array and subsequently play back this script segment, we can input and use different values. This should then be the only location in the entire set of scripts used for CSDDT where we will interact with these controls. If one of them changes, we have to fix in only one place—here.

Obviously edit boxes are not the only controls and objects with which we have to interact—there are many others. Among controls, there are Drop-down lists (DDLs):

- Combo boxes
- Check boxes
- Radio buttons
- Command buttons
- Grids
- Menu bars

You must determine which part of the recorded code can be modified/replaced with data values in order to provide for proper selection or interaction. Sometimes we must predetermine the state of the control, as we must for check boxes, so that we can determine if we need to change it by clicking on it or not. The input data may be used to indicate what state is desired (i.e., checked or unchecked). We would programmatically test the state of the control and then determine if it matches that specified by the data. If they are the same (both indicating checked), then we would not click on the check box. If they are different, we would click on the check box to set it to the new state. Frequently we cannot incorporate the data value directly into our recorded code, just as in the example with the check boxes.

Now we'll examine another control example—radio buttons. Radio buttons are, by the nature of their use, grouped together in groups of at least two or more. We will have to record clicking on each one of the radio buttons in turn so that we will have the option of selecting any one of these buttons. We will then modify the code so that the input data will specify which radio button out of the group will be selected. Below is an example of how this might be accomplished, in an If/Else construct. Note the information in bold type. Dfld(1) contains the data we're testing to see which button will be selected. We simply use the names RadioButton_1 and RadioButton_2 for the selection code. This should give you a good idea about how to perform selections based on the data values when the data values are not input directly into the GUI but are used to determine what to do or which piece of library code to execute.

```
if Dfld(1)="RadioButton_1" then
    Window SetContext, "Name=main window name", ""
    Window SetContext, "Name=child window name;ChildWindow", ""
    RadioButton Click, "Name=rb_name1"
    Window SetTestContext, "Name= main window name ", ""
    Window SetTestContext, "Name= child window name;ChildWindow", ""
    Result = GroupBoxVP (CompareProperties, "Name=gb_mybutton_group",
        CaseID=RadioButtonProp1")
    Window ResetTestContext, "", ""
elseif Dfld(1)="RadioButton_2" then
    Window SetContext, "Name=main window name", ""
    Window SetContext, "Name=child window name;ChildWindow", ""
    RadioButton Click, "Name=rb_name2"
    Window SetTestContext, "Name= main window name ", ""
    Window SetTestContext, "Name= child window name;ChildWindow", ""
    Result = GroupBoxVP (CompareProperties, "Name=gb_mybutton_group",
        CaseID=RadioButtonProp2")
    Window ResetTestContext, "", ""
end if
```

Note that, after we performed the selection, we recorded a verification point that captures the properties of the radio button group, confirming that we did in fact select the radio button desired and that the state is the same as when we recorded the script. This type of after-the-action cross-check is necessary to consistently verify that the action took place as expected. Anywhere you perform an action in your scripts, you must confirm the result of that action; otherwise you are not performing a valid test! Sometimes you have nothing to verify except the absence of an error.

In Rational Robot, when a verification point is initially recorded, say, for object properties, the properties are saved in the test tool's data repository as baseline data. Later during playback when the verification is replayed, the tool once again acquires the properties of the object being tested and compares the results against the previously saved baseline data. This is a valuable tool; however, don't make the mistake of assuming that the initially recorded values were correct! It is rare, but on occasion the initial values captured reflect the fact that one or more properties are not as they should be. It is up to you, the tester, to verify, when you are initially creating the script, that the values are correct at that time. It can become very confusing when you play back a script and determine that your baseline data was incorrect.

> It is very important to remember this: Before you automate anything, you must verify manually or with the aid of the test tools that what you are testing works properly!

It is somewhat incorrect to say that the verification point confirms that what we selected was proper. In reality, replaying the verification point confirms only that our originally recorded data and properties captured are still the same as that baseline data.

If what we were doing in the Perform_Action script was inputting data or combinations of inputting data, selecting radio buttons, and so on, we typically have to perform a subsequent action such as

Add

Save

Delete

Update the database

OK

To perform one of these actions, select a control button or menu selection such as File→Save. Once the final action has been executed, we have to either look for an expected normal result/response from the AUT or look for an error condition, if we are expecting one. Typically when we hit the OK button or the Save button, some sort of indicator usually tells the user that the action has performed as expected, but not always. When there is an indicator, capture it in your test tool so that during playback you can rely on a positive confirmation that the result was correct. Of course, there isn't always something to capture and the confirmation lies in the fact that an error did not occur. Depending on how critical the operation is, you may decide to perform a process to go behind the GUI to determine if the action was performed correctly. In cases where it would be appropriate, you may be able to accomplish this by accessing the associated database, acquiring the appropriate data, and then comparing it with what was entered. This could be a significant task, so you must decide if the effort required to build these additional routines or functions is worthwhile and whether it provides a good return on your investment of time. We have provided on the FTP site the ones we developed. There is much information written about this subject. One such author is James Bach of Satisfice Inc. This information is available on the Internet.

CAUTION:

Stay away from using toolbar buttons when menu selections or pop-up menus can perform the same actions. Menu selections are more reliable (less frequently changed) in recorded scripts.

Creating Functions for Common Operations— Isolating Command Objects

If your AUT has any common command buttons to interact with—e.g., those that exist on toolbars—or menu actions to perform, record their selection/ utilization inside of functions that can be called from anywhere in the set of test scripts. The grief that this will save you when a change is made to the object in question is well worth any extra effort it may take to isolate interaction with it. Once again, it is the process of ensuring that you have only one place in the code to repair when changes are made relative to these items.

Continuing with the Program Flow

Now that the action has been performed, we are ready to check the error code value to determine if we should look for an error condition, such as an error message or other identifiable error condition. We will build a Select Case construct in the same manner as we did for the window/tab selection. We have separated this code off into a script to help keep the Main script procedure small and manageable. Once again, referring back to Chapter 7, we will use a script framework just like the Window_Select, Tab_Select, and Perform_Action.

Code the error processing template script as follows:

```
'$Include: "DataDriven.sbh"
    Declare Function Process_Error(ErrCd)
Sub Main
    Dim Result As Integer
    Gen_Return_Code=Process_Error(ErrCd)
End Sub

''''''''''''''''''''''''''''''''''''''''''''''''''''''''''''''''''''''''''''''''''

Function Process_Error(ErrCd)
    Process_Error=1

    Select Case ErrCd

        Case "ERR1"
        'Process or detect error code 01 here
            MsgBox "ERR1 code"

        Case "ERR2"
        'Process or detect error code 02 here
            MsgBox "ERR2 code"

        Case "ERR3"
        'Process or detect error code 03 here
            MsgBox "ERR3 code"

        Case Else
            Msgbox "Error Code not found for ErrCd: "&Cstr(ErrCd)&" Terminating"
            Process_Error=0  ''return value FAIL
            SQALogMessage sqaFail, "Error Code not found for: "&Cstr(ErrCd)&"", ""
    End Select
End Function
```

If the expected error condition is found, then the processing of this record is complete and successful. Main continues processing by reading the next data record, provided we are not at the end of the input file and more records are available to be read.

If the expected error condition is not found, a test failure has occurred (usually a verification point recorded by the test tool). Thus the test should terminate. The test log should indicate what the last record read contained and the record number. This allows for fast debugging and problem isolation. This can be accomplished in Main with very little code. Let's take a look at some sample Perform_Action code that has input some data into a screen; select the OK button and look to see if an error was expected; then exit and let the Process_Error script handle the error.

```
'$Include: "DataDriven.sbh"
Declare Function Perform_Action(ActCd)

Sub Main
```

```
    Dim Result As Integer
    Gen_Return_Code = Perform_Action(ActCd)
End Sub

' ' ' ' ' ' ' ' ' ' ' ' ' ' ' ' ' ' ' ' ' ' ' ' ' ' ' ' ' ' ' ' ' ' ' ' ' ' ' ' ' ' ' ' ' ' ' ' ' ' ' ' ' ' ' ' ' ' ' ' '

Function Perform_Action(ActCd)
    Perform_Action=1

    Select Case ActCd

        Case "User_Pref_OK"                'processing for selecting the OK button on the User
                            Preference window.
            Window SetContext, "Caption=Window Name", ""
            EditBox DblClick, "Label=Label name:", "Coords=x,y"
            InputKeys DFld(1)
            EditBox DblClick, "Label=Label name:", "Coords=x,y"
            InputKeys DFld(2)
            EditBox DblClick, "Label=Label name:", "Coords=x,y"
            InputKeys DFld(3)
            PushButton Click, "Text=OK"
            If ErrCd ="none" then            (ErrCd equal to text "none")

            (If we are not expecting an error then record whatever the normal ending
                        status
            would be after selecting OK here, otherwise if we expect an error
            we would not process this code and we would rely on the DDProcess_Error  to
            handle it.)
            End if

        Case Else
            Msgbox "Action Selection not found for ActCd: "&Cstr(ActCd)&" Terminating"
            Perform_Action=0  ''return value FAIL
            SQALogMessage sqaFail, "Action Selection not found for: "&Cstr(ActCd)&"", ""
    End Select
End Function
```

We have returned to Main at this point. Main then also examines the ErrCD variable and, detecting that it was neither equal to none nor blank, it would determine that an error was expected and then call the DDProcess_Error procedure. Let's assume that in our data file and error processing code we decided that we would expect a Data Error message box to occur with text that explained what the error was. Once we detect the error window, we can then select the OK button to close it. We expected an error and we got it, so the test case passes.

```
'$Include: "DataDriven.sbh"
    Declare Function Process_Error(ErrCd)

Sub Main
    Dim Result As Integer
    Gen_Return_Code=Process_Error(ErrCd)
End Sub
```

' '

```
Function Process_Error(ErrCd)
    Process_Error=1

    Select Case ErrCd

        Case "User_Pref_Data_Error"
            Result = WindowVP (Exists, "Caption=Data Error", _
                         "VP=Window Existence ")
            Window SetContext, "Caption= Data Error ", ""
            PushButton Click, "Text=OK"

        Case Else
            Msgbox "Error Code not found for ErrCd: "&Cstr(ErrCd)&" Terminating"
            Process_Error=0  ''return value FAIL
            SQALogMessage sqaFail, "Error Code not found for: "&Cstr(ErrCd)&"", ""
    End Select
End Function
```

At this point we have finished the loop in processing a record.

Using Multiple Input Records to Create a Test Scenario

You may have noticed that there is no special area in the framework for closing windows or tabs. This is because, in our experience in testing a variety of applications, we have come across a multitude of ways to close windows and tabs. Sometimes they are closed using a Cancel command or by selecting either the OK or Finish button. Frequently there is a Close button. And there are others—the system close X button, File→Exit menu item, to name two. There are more methods for closing windows and tabs than there usually are for opening them. So, if you need to programmatically close a window or tab for your test scenario, simply create an additional action code to cause the close action to take place. Just as you would have created a small segment of code in the Window_Select and Tab_Select scripts to open it, create a small code segment in the Perform_Action script to close it. Because of this, however, you must also realize that frequently you will need to create multiple records in your input data file to complete a full test scenario with a given window. For example, you may need to create one record to open a window and test its initial state or content before you ever input any new data or interact with it. You may need another record to input new information into that same window or tab, selecting the Apply button to submit the changes to the server but leaving the window open. You may then wish to utilize yet another record to invoke a subroutine that will access the application's database to verify that the Apply action from the previous record did in fact cause the correct information to be saved. Finally, last but not least, you may choose to add a record that simply causes the window to be closed.

This being said, hopefully you now realize that, when testing most test cases, you will need to create and organize a series of input records to perform all of the necessary actions.

Utilizing Dynamic Data Input—Keyword Substitution

One of the challenges we have faced in working with data-driven testing and manual testing is having to handle data that has *aged* to the point that it is no longer usable. A prime example is where date values become out of date. One application on which we worked had a business rule that required, when entering certain transactions, the date entry field to be within 7 days from the current system date. This meant that, whether we were using hard-coded scripts or data from external files, the date values had to be modified on a regular basis to comply with this business rule. It rapidly became evident that we needed another method for handling this type of problem. The solution was to use a data substitution routine. In our input data file, we placed a special keyword that, when detected by the script that reads the data, would automatically substitute it with a replacement value. This would occur in much the same way as word processors such as MS Word perform autocorrect operations. This routine turned out to be very beneficial because it led the way for the substitution of other values.

While working with a client server application that utilized a copy of production data in the associated database, this same company would regularly replace the data with a newer copy of the production data. This presented a whole new set of problems in that the data values we were using for testing purposes were being replaced with new ones. This forced us to search out the database for new acceptable values to utilize for testing and then replace the data in our data-driven input files with the new information. Again we needed a way to automatically update or substitute our test data. Since we had already created a method of changing the date value automatically, it was a natural evolution to do the same for data relative to the existing database content. We would use keywords to cause the script to query the database to find an acceptable record to use with the current test. In doing so the tests became dynamic in nature and were no longer as sensitive to the database content. The challenge became how to implement this new code. Ultimately we used a two-dimensional string array (like two columns in a spreadsheet with multiple rows). The first dimension (or column) contains the keyword we wish to match from the input data file. The second dimension (or column from the same index or row) contains a call to a function to acquire the desired data. The new data value is then loaded into the DFld() array in place of the keyword that was read from the input data file.

The keyword substitution routine is called only when the record type value of the newly read data record is equal to K, so that we don't call the routine every time we read a new record. The K record type indicates to the Main script that a keyword has been placed in the input data record. Each data field of the new record is examined to see if it matches any of the predefined substitution values. When a match occurs, the substitution routines are then invoked. This means that you define the keywords and that you will have to build the routines/functions to acquire the substitution data. We have provided some examples for you to use and to pattern yours after.

Using Library or Include Files (*.sbh and *.sbl Files in Rational Robot)

You should have noticed by now that at the beginning of each of our scripts there is a line that looks like '$Include: "DataDriven.sbh" or '$Include: "global.sbh" or sometimes a combination of two or more. There is fairly detailed information in the SQABasic help files (from Rational) regarding the use of include files. The $Include value is a metacommand. The SQABasic help files in Rational Suite Test Studio state that a metacommand is a command that gives the compiler instructions on how to build the program. In SQABasic, metacommands are specified in comments that begin with a dollar sign ($). The apostrophe (') indicates a comment, so '$ specifies a metacommand. '$Include then specifies that the named file—for example, DataDriven.sbh or global.sbh or *.sbl—is in fact supposed to be used as include files.

Include files typically come in two flavors—**header** type and **library** type. The primary difference is that header files contain the definition of variables that can be used or referenced by all script files that include them and library files may contain codelike functions or program routines that can be called by the scripts that include them. Library files contain code that can be compiled and executed, while header files do not; they contain only variables that can be referenced.

In Rational's test products, the scripting language is SQABasic (after the original builders, SQA). Therefore SQABasic header files are *.sbh files and SQABasic library files are *.sbl files.

Note that you may not record events inside of the Rational *.sbl files. You can create these files only by using an editor. Many programming languages, including Microprocessor assembler and C programming, utilize these types of files. Therefore, we utilize these file types in our scripting procedures.

For more detailed information about the use of include files, reference your test tool's scripting language help files.

If you create and use these file types, then follow this rule. Files commonly named *global* are just that. They should contain those values that all procedures or scripts can use. If you wish to define variables, constants, etc., for a specific test set, then use a name that is appropriate for it. For example, we use the names DataDriven.sbh and a DataDriven.sbl.

Due to some of the programming constraints in Rational's SQABasic language we utilize the *.sbh files extensively to provide global access to these variables, such as the WinCd, ActCd, ErrCd, and FldCnt code variables.

This is the global.sbh file. It contains a variable for keyword date substitution values.

```
'SQABasic Header File
'Global Values
    Global Today As String
    Global Today2K As String
    Global Tomorrow As String
    Global UKToday As String
    Global NextWeek As String
    Global LastWeek As String
    Global NextMonth As String
    Global LastMonth As String
    Global NextYear As String
    Global LastYear As String
    Global Dates_Have_Been_Set as String
    Global Substitutes_initialized as String
    Global txt_filename As String
    Global xls_FileName As String
    Global index_last_selected_Db as integer
    Global global_query As String
```

The DataDriven.sbh file is as follows:

```
'Global definitions for the Data Driven Main, Window Select, Tab Select, Perform Action
'  and Process Error functions
    Global Dfld()
    Global WinCd As String
```

```
Global TabCd As String
Global ActCd As String
Global ErrCd As String
Global Current_Win As String
Global Current_Tab As String
Global InFileName As String
Global Gen_Return_Code As Integer
Global Gen_Return_String As String
Global Key_word_list(9,1) as String      'this defines the current size of the keyword
                                         'substitution two dimensional array.
```

This is the DataDriven.sbl file where the function for keyword substitution is kept.

```
'DDKeyword_Sub.sbl  version 2.0

'$Include: "DataDriven.sbh"
'$Include: "global.sbh"

Option Compare text        'allows the LIKE to be case insensitive

Declare Function DateSet BasicLib "Global"  (Fld_Value)

Declare Function Key_Word_Sub (Fld_Cnt)
Declare Function Key_Word_Init()
Dim x,j as Integer

Function Key_Word_Sub (Fld_Cnt)
    Key_Word_Sub=1 'return a good value unless keyword not found
    if Substitutes_initialized<>"YES" then
        Key_Word_Init
    end if
    For x=1 to Fld_Cnt
        For j=0 to KWListSize-1
            if DFld(x) LIKE Key_word_list(j,0) then
                DFld(x)=Key_word_list(j,1)
                exit for
            end if
        Next j
    Next x
End Function

'''''''''''''''''''''''''''''''''''''''''''''''''''''''''''''''''''''''''''''''''''''''''
Function Key_Word_Init()
    ' if the size of the keyword array needs to be changed the size is dimmed in
                        DataDriven.sbh

    Key_word_list(0,0)="Today"          'this is the keyword to be matched up with input from
                        the data file.

    Key_word_list(0,1)=DateSet("Today")    'this function call gets today's date which will
                                        'replace the keyword in the Dfld() array

    Key_word_list(1,0)="Tomorrow"
    Key_word_list(1,1)=DateSet("Tomorrow")

    Key_word_list(2,0)="NextWeek"
```

```
    Key_word_list(2,1)=DateSet("NextWeek")

    Key_word_list(3,0)="LastWeek"
    Key_word_list(3,1)=DateSet("LastWeek")

    Key_word_list(4,0)="NextYear"
    Key_word_list(4,1)=DateSet("NextYear")

    Key_word_list(5,0)="LastYear"
    Key_word_list(5,1)=DateSet("LastYear")

    Key_word_list(6,0)="null"
    Key_word_list(6,1)=""

    Key_word_list(7,0)="6spaces"
    Key_word_list(7,1)="      "

    Key_word_list(8,0)="8spaces"
    Key_word_list(8,1)="        "

    Key_word_list(9,0)="keyword-a"
    Key_word_list(9,1)="substitute-a"
    Substitutes_initialized="YES"
End Function
```

This Openfile.sbh file is used in conjunction with the Openfile.txt and Openfile.xls scripts. It is fashioned after the Windows operating system (OS) for the open file browser. You can find these and other files on the FTP site for this book.

```
Type OPENFILENAME
        lStructSize As Long
        hwndOwner As Long
        hInstance As Long
        lpstrFilter As Long
        lpstrCustomFilter As Long
        nMaxCustFilter As Long
        nFilterIndex As Long
        lpstrFile As Long
        nMaxFile As Long
        lpstrFileTitle As Long
        nMaxFileTitle As Long
        lpstrInitialDir As Long
        lpstrTitle As Long
        Flags As Long
        nFileOffset As Integer
        nFileExtension As Integer
        lpstrDefExt As Long
        lCustData As Long
        LpfnHook As Long
        lpTemplateName As Long
    End Type

Declare Function lstrcpy Lib "kernel32" Alias "lstrcpyA" (ByVal lpString1 As String, ByVal
                    lpString2 As String) As Long
```

```
Declare Function GetOpenFileName Lib "comdlg32.dll" Alias "GetOpenFileNameA" (pOpenfilename
                    As OPENFILENAME) As Long
Declare Function FindWindow    Lib "user32" Alias "FindWindowA" (ByVal lpClassName As
                    String, ByVal lpWindowName As Any) As Long  'Last parameter used
                    to be As String
Declare Function CommDlgExtendedError Lib "comdlg32.dll" () As Long

    Global Const OFN_READONLY = &H1
    Global Const OFN_OVERWRITEPROMPT = &H2
    Global Const OFN_HIDEREADONLY = &H4
    Global Const OFN_NOCHANGEDIR = &H8
    Global Const OFN_SHOWHELP = &H10
    Global Const OFN_ENABLEHOOK = &H20
    Global Const OFN_ENABLETEMPLATE = &H40
    Global Const OFN_ENABLETEMPLATEHANDLE = &H80
    Global Const OFN_NOVALIDATE = &H100
    Global Const OFN_ALLOWMULTISELECT = &H200
    Global Const OFN_EXTENSIONDIFFERENT = &H400
    Global Const OFN_PATHMUSTEXIST = &H800
    Global Const OFN_FILEMUSTEXIST = &H1000
    Global Const OFN_CREATEPROMPT = &H2000
    Global Const OFN_SHAREAWARE = &H4000
    Global Const OFN_NOREADONLYRETURN = &H8000
    Global Const OFN_NOTESTFILECREATE = &H10000
    Global Const OFN_SHAREFALLTHROUGH = 2
    Global Const OFN_SHARENOWARN = 1
    Global Const OFN_SHAREWARN = 0
```

Utility Scripts

As stated earlier in this book, Andy Tinkham developed and we utilized a utility script that converts the contents of an Excel spreadsheet to an SQABasic sequential text file. For those of you not utilizing Rational Robot, this script will not be of much use except that you may be able to see how Andy Tinkham, the original developer of the Excel access routines, built his portion of the code. For those of you who are using Rational Robot, the Convert script demonstrates not only how to access an Excel spreadsheet but also how to build and use the very powerful dialog box functions supported by SQABasic.

The Convert procedure allows you to select the pathname of the input .xls file. Notice the built-in browser buttons on the dialog box when you run it. It also allows you to specify the output text file (*.txt). Next you need to specify the starting column (where you have the column for Record Type) and the maximum or last column used (the last data field of the longest record), as well as the starting row (the row of the first input record) and which Excel spreadsheet to use, e.g., 1 through 6. It determines when to stop when it encounters an empty row. This procedure is customized to work with the seven control fields that CSDDT utilizes, looking at the sixth field to determine how many data records to read on that given row. The data is read from the spreadsheet and converted into the CSDDT format explained earlier in this book.

Debugging Your Scripts—When the Test(s) Uncover a Defect

It's great to plan and design your test scripts. Building them can be very enjoyable; at least this is when we had the most fun. You will learn a lot in the process, especially about the tool you are using and its restrictions and strong points. Figuring out how to overcome specific problems can be very rewarding. *However*, utilizing them in everyday practice can become a whole other ball game. In the Main script, we've included a record counter. As each record is read, write the record counter value into the Robot's log file. This is a significant aid in determining which input data record caused the error. You can imagine how difficult it would be to read through several hundred lines of log information to determine which record caused the error. Although we did not include a line number as part of the format of the CSDDT input records, most good text editors, including the editor in Robot, do indicate the line number. If you have taken the time to include comments where they are provided for in the seventh control field of each input data record, it should then be an easy matter to determine what the test was doing and where the failure occurred (especially if the comment text has been included in the text log).

Implementing the CSDDT Template Scripts

CAUTION:

If you have already implemented a global.sbh file, do not copy over it. Instead, open the included global.sbh file with a text editor, click on Select All in the Edit menu, Copy, and then Paste it to the end of your existing global.sbh file.

Only after you have read and fully digested this note of caution should you begin to implement your scripts.

Step 1. Copy the *.sbh and *.sbl files to your default sqabas32 folder. Under Rational 2001, this should be the default path. For example :

```
C:\your repository folder.....\TestDatastore\DefaultTestScriptDatastore\TMS_Scripts\SQABas32
```

Step 2. Copy the *.rec files to your default script folder. Under Rational 2001, this should be the default path unless the administrator has changed it. For example:

```
C:\your repository folder.....\TestDatastore\DefaultTestScriptDatastore\TMS_Scripts
```

Step 3. After the script files have been copied, Robot will not be aware of these files. You must open Robot and then select New Script. Type in the name of the script file exactly the same as the name of the file(s) that was copied over. When you click OK, the file should be displayed, already populated with the script commands.

The *.sbh, *.sbl, and *.rec files can be opened and edited with a standard text editor like MS Notepad.

After all the files have been created and then closed, go to Robot's File menu and select Compile All. Provided all files have been copied to the proper location, the scripts should be able to be run at this point.

The DDScripts

The following template files are included on the CD-ROM.

```
'DDMain Template Version 2.0

'This is a template file updated May 24, 2001
'updated May 25, 2001  added the openfile browser for selecting the input file
'updated May 31, 2001  change call function window_select to CallScript DDWindow_Select.
                       Added Global Genral_Return_Code in DataDriven.sbh
'updated June 6,2001  change call function perform action and process error

'$Include: "global.sbh"
'$Include: "DataDriven.sbh"

    Declare Function ReadFields BasicLib "global" (File_Num, Fld_Cnt, GFlds())
    Declare Function Key_Word_Sub  BasicLib "DDKeyWord_Sub" (Fld_Cnt)

    Dim Rec_Type                    'Record Type
    Dim Fld_Cnt                     'Data Field count
    Dim Comment As String
    Dim Child_Open As String
    Dim record_counter

Option Compare text                      'allows LIKE to be case insensitive

Sub Main
    Dim Result As Integer

    On Error GoTo Error_Handler1
```

```
    Child_Open="No"
    current_win=""
    current_tab=""
    record_counter=0

'other ways to initialize the InfileName variable
    'InFileName="c:\sqatemplates\testdata\testdata1.txt"
    'InFileName=InputBox$("Enter the name of the input file to process.","Data Driven_
    'Testing",InFileName)

    If txt_filename="" then
        CallScript "OpenFile_Txt"
         'open a text file for test input data this script opens a file browser window
    End if

    InFileName=txt_filename                          'from the Openfile_Txt routine

    If InFileName="" then
        Exit Sub      'the test is canceled no filename was supplied
    End if

    Open InFileName For Input As #1
    txt_filename="" 'clear the name for the next time the script is started

    Do while Not EOF(1)    'Main process loop. Read and Process input records
                                    ' .until there are none left.

'''''''''''''''''''''''''''''''
'Read input test data file
'''''''''''''''''''''''''''''''
        Input #1,Rec_Type,WinCd,TabCd,ActCd,ErrCd,Fld_Cnt,Comment

        if Fld_Cnt<> 0 then

            ReDim DFld(Fld_Cnt)   'set the appropriate size of the array for the number of
                                  'data fields in this record

            'pass file number, fld_cnt, address of DFld
            Result=ReadFields(1, Fld_Cnt, DFld())
            if Result=0 then
                MsgBox "ReadFields function failed. Program terminating"
                Close #1  'close the open file
                Exit Sub
            end if
        end if

''''''''''''''''''''''''''''''''''''''''''''''''''
'Log which record we are processing
''''''''''''''''''''''''''''''''''''''''''''''''''
        record_counter=record_counter+1
        SQALogMessage sqaPass, "last record read ="&Cstr(record_counter), ""

''''''''''''''''''''''''''''''''''''''''''''''''''''''''''''''''''''''''
'Determine the record type
'
' H=header record, skip this record do not process
' B=Breakpoint stop for program debugging
' X=Terminate prior to the end of the input data file
' G=Good record. Process normally
```

```
' K=Good record. Pre-Process for Keyword substitution,
'   then process normally
''''''''''''''''''''''''''''''''''''''''''''''''''''''
        if Rec_Type LIKE "H" then
            goto NoProcess
        elseif Rec_Type LIKE "B" then
            stop            'data breakpoint
        elseif Rec_Type LIKE "X" then 'terminate the program
            Close #1
            Exit Sub
        elseif Rec_Type LIKE "G" then
            Goto Start                  'good record
        elseif Rec_Type LIKE "K" then
            key_word_sub(Fld_Cnt)
            'this call is used when keywords are used in the data such as 'AutoDate"
        else
            MsgBox "The record type is invalid. The program is terminating"
            Close #1
            Exit Sub
        end if

Start:
''''''''''''''''''''''''''''''''''''''''''''''''''''
'Determine if we need to open a new window or not
''''''''''''''''''''''''''''''''''''''''''''''''''''
        if Child_Open="No" then
            'go open the selected window. This is executed at first pass only.
            CallScript "DDWindow_Select"
            if Gen_Return_Code=0 then
                close #1
                exit sub
            end if

            Current_Win=WinCd       'update and save the current window selection
            Child_Open="Yes"            'we have now opened a window
        else
            if Current_Win<>WinCd then
                CallScript "DDWindow_Select"
                if Gen_Return_Code=0 then
                    close #1
                    exit sub
                end if
                Current_Win=WinCd   'update and save the current window selection
                Child_Open="Yes"        'we have now opened a window
            end if
        end if

'TAB SELECT
''''''''''''''''''''''''''''''''''''''''''''''''''''
'Determine if we need to open a new tab or not
''''''''''''''''''''''''''''''''''''''''''''''''''''
            if TabCd <> "" and TabCd <> "none" and TabCd <>_
                "TabCd" and Current_Tab<>TabCd then

                CallScript "DDTab_Select"
                if Gen_Return_Code=0 then
                    close #1
                    exit sub
                end if
```

```
              Current_Tab=TabCd
           end if
''''''''''''''''''''''''''''''''''''''''
'Perform the specified Action
''''''''''''''''''''''''''''''''''''''''
       CallScript "DDPerform_Action"
       if Gen_Return_Code=0 then
          MsgBox "Specified Action Could Not be Performed"
          close #1
          exit sub
       end if

'''''''''''''''''''''''''''''''''''''''''''
'Process the Error Code
'''''''''''''''''''''''''''''''''''''''''
       if ErrCd="" or ErrCd="none" or ErrCd="ErrCd" then 'Error is not expected
          goto NoProcess
       else
          CallScript "DDProcess_Error"
          if Gen_Return_Code=0 then
             MsgBox "Specified Error Processing Could Not be Performed"
             close #1
             exit sub
          end if
       end if

NoProcess:
    Loop 'end of main loop
    Exit Sub

Error_Handler1:
    MsgBox "Error number "&Cstr(Err)& " occurred at line: "&Erl &" -- "&Error$
    Exit Sub
End Sub

''''''''''''''''''''''''''''''''''''''''''''''''''''''''''
'Error code  Error Text as defined in SQABasic for runtime errors
'        5    Illegal function call
'        6    Overflow
'        7    Out of memory
'        9    Subscript out of range
'       10    Duplicate definition
'       11    Division by zero
'       13    Type Mismatch
'       14    Out of string space
'       19    No Resume
'       20    Resume without error
'       28    Out of stack space
'       35    Sub or Function not defined
'       48    Error in loading DLL
'       52    Bad file name or number
'       53    File not found
'       54    Bad file mode
'       55    File already open
'       58    File already exists
'       61    Disk full
'       62    Input past end of file
```

```
'    63   Bad record number
'    64   Bad file name
'    68   Device unavailable
'    70   Permission denied
'    71   Disk not ready
'    74   Can't rename with different drive
'    75   Path/File access error
'    76   Path not found
'    91   Object variable set to Nothing
'    93   Invalid pattern
'    94   Illegal use of NULL
'   102   Command failed
'   429   Object creation failed
'   438   No such property or method
'   439   Argument type mismatch
'   440   Object error
'   901   Input buffer would be larger than 64K
'   902   Operating system error
'   903   External procedure not found
'   904   Global variable type mismatch
'   905   User-defined type mismatch
'   906   External procedure interface mismatch
'   907   Pushbutton required
'   908   Module has no MAIN
'   910   Dialog box not declared
```

Notes about this example copy of DDPerform_Action:

First, remember that an apostrophe marks the start of a comment.

Line continuation is underscore, space, then newline (_).

The ampersand character (&) is used as a concatenation character.

The basic format of this version of DDPerform_Action is a procedure—Sub Main through End sub—followed by a function—Function Perform_Action(ActCd) through End Function—followed by yet another function—Function Execute_Pref_Command through End Function. This offers a benefit in performing debugging of your code without having to have it called from DDMain.

In Robot, since this is a procedure/script, it can be executed in a stand-alone mode. In normal operation, DDMain would call it, where DDMain would have acquired all the information needed for DDPerform_Action before it was called. For debug purposes we can initialize some of the needed values for the Perform_Action function prior to calling it from the local sub main. Take note of the line Debug code area—although the subsequent lines are currently commented out, if uncommented they would become executable code. They would initialize the ActCd and TabCd variables, resize the dfld() array, and then initialize it with values, simulating what might have come in from an external-files input data record. I could then *step* through the code relative to the ActCd and TabCd values and ensure that the dfld() values did what they were supposed to. When I am finished debugging, I can then simply comment out the debug code lines until I need to use them again with different values for the purpose of testing a different case.

A little background about the target window in the AUT: As you might guess, the window was simply called "Preferences" which was invoked from the menu bar. It contained several (7) different tabs upon each of which resided a variety of controls. Since this was a copy of production code that was being worked on at a client's location, all labels, comments, and real tab names have been changed so that it could be included here.

Notice that, in this particular instance, the tab code was used to determine which piece of code should be executed first (based on what tab had been selected); then the data was entered and the desired objects selected on that targeted tab. On this window are three common buttons: Apply, Cancel. and OK. Since these buttons are common to all seven tabs on the window, it made more sense to put the code to execute for all of the possible actions—PREF_APPLY, PREF_CANCEL, PREF_OK, and a do-nothing-but-enter-data action (PREF_DataEntryOnly)—in a separate function that would be called after the data was entered. In order to have the ability to not interact with any specific tab but to simply execute a command, we also provided for a TabCd code of Command_Only (see the last case statement).

```
-----------------------------------------------------------------------------
'DDPerform_Action Version 2.0

'Copyright Archer Group, 2001 All Rights Reserved

'This is a template file updated May 24, 2001
'updated June 2001

'$Include: "DataDriven.sbh"
'project specific include files

'$Include: "MyApp_global.sbh"

Option Compare text                          'allows LIKE to be case insensitive

Declare Function Perform_Action(ActCd)
Declare Function Execute_Pref_Command

Dim Result as Integer

Sub Main
    Dim Result As Integer

    'Initially Recorded: 6/5/2001  1:26:55 PM
    'Script Name: DDPerform_Action
```

```
'Debug code area

'     ActCd="PREF_DataEntryOnly"
'     TabCd="TAB-1"
'     redim dfld(14)
'     dfld(1)="<None>"
'     dfld(2)="Open"
'     dfld(3)="Some Value"
'     dfld(4)="Other Data"
'     dfld(5)="5 little bytes"
'     dfld(6)="6 little bytes "
'     dfld(7)="7 little bytes "
'     dfld(8)="8 little bytes "
'     dfld(9)="9 little bytes "
'     dfld(10)="10 little bytes "
'     dfld(11)="11 little bytes "
'     dfld(12)="12 little bytes "
'     dfld(13)="13 little bytes "
'     dfld(14)="14 little bytes "

    Gen_Return_Code = Perform_Action(ActCd)
End Sub

''''''''''''''''''''''''''''''''''''''''''''''''''''''''''''''''''''''''''''''''''''''''''''''
''''''''''''''''''''''''''''''''''''''''''''''''''''''''''''''''''''''''''''''''''''''''''''''
Function Perform_Action(ActCd)

    Perform_Action=1  'set the initial return value from this function to PASS

    Select Case (TabCd)

        Case "TAB-1"

            'Input test data

            Window SetContext, "Caption=Preferences", ""

            'first control
            if (dfld(1)="1" and ShowTime="False") or (dfld(1)="0" and _
                                         ShowTime="True") then
                CheckBox Click, "Text=Time"
            end if

            if (dfld(2)="1" and ShowDate="False") or (dfld(2)="0" and _
                                          ShowDate="True") then
                CheckBox Click, "Text=Date"
            end if

            if (dfld(3)="1" and ShowKeyboard="False") or (dfld(3)="0" and _
                                          ShowKeyboard="True") then
                CheckBoxClick, "Text=Keyboard Indicators"
            end if

            if (dfld(4)="1" and ShowRecCount="False") or (dfld(4)="0" and _
                                          ShowRecCount="True") then
                CheckBox Click, "Text=Selected Record Count"
            end if

            '5th control                ComboBox Click, "ObjectIndex=1", "Coords=196,7"
```

```
    ComboListBox Click, "ObjectIndex=1", "Text="&Cstr(Dfld(5))

    '6th control
    EditBox dblClick, "Label=control 6", "Coords=16,10"
    InputKeys Dfld(6)

    'Execute the command
    Execute_Pref_Command

Case  "TAB-2"

    '1st control

    Window SetContext, "Caption=Preferences", ""
    EditBox DblClick, "Label=control 1:", ""
    InputKeys Dfld(1)

    '2nd control
    ComboBox Click, "Label=Control 2:", "Coords=204,9"
    ComboListBox Click, "Label=Control 2:", "Text="&Cstr(Dfld(2))

    '3rd control
    ComboBox Click, "Label= Control 3:", "Coords=204,11"
    ComboListBox Click, "Label= Control 3:", "Text="&Cstr(Dfld(3))

    '4th control
    EditBox DblClick, "Label=Control 4:", ""
    InputKeys "{HOME}+{END}"
    InputKeys Dfld(4)

    '5th control
    EditBox DblClick, "Label=Control 5:", ""
    InputKeys "{HOME}+{END}"
    InputKeys Dfld(5)

    '6th control
    EditBox DblClick, "ObjectIndex=10", ""
    InputKeys "{HOME}+{END}"
    InputKeys Dfld(6)

    '7th control
    EditBox DblClick, "Label=Control7:", ""
    InputKeys "{HOME}+{END}"
    InputKeys Dfld(7)

    '8th control
    EditBox DblClick, "ObjectIndex=8", ""
    InputKeys "{HOME}+{END}"
    InputKeys Dfld(8)

    '9th control
    EditBox DblClick, "Label=Control 9:", ""
    InputKeys "{HOME}+{END}"
    InputKeys Dfld(9)

    '10th comtrol
    EditBox DblClick, "Label=Control 10:", ""
    InputKeys "{HOME}+{END}"
    InputKeys Dfld(10)
```

```
'11th Control
EditBox DblClick, "Label=Control 11:", ""
InputKeys "{HOME}+{END}"
InputKeys Dfld(11)

'x
EditBox DblClick, "Label=XXXXXXXX:", ""
InputKeys "{HOME}+{END}"
InputKeys Dfld(12)

'y
EditBox DblClick, "ObjectIndex=3", ""
InputKeys "{HOME}+{END}"
InputKeys Dfld(13)

'z
EditBox DblClick, "ObjectIndex=2", ""
InputKeys "{HOME}+{END}"
InputKeys Dfld(14)
Execute_Pref_Command

Case "TAB-3"

    Window SetContext, "Caption=Preferences", ""
    'A
    EditBox DblClick, "Label=A:", "Coords=18,8"
    InputKeys Dfld(1)
    'B
    EditBox DblClick, "Label=B:", "Coords=19,4"
    InputKeys Dfld(2)
    'C
    EditBox DblClick, "Label=C", "Coords=19,10"
    InputKeys Dfld(3)
    'D
    EditBox DblClick, "Label=D:", "Coords=21,7"
    InputKeys Dfld(4)
    'E
    EditBox DblClick, "Label=E:", "Coords=46,9"
    InputKeys Dfld(5)
    'F
    InputKeys "{TAB}"
    InputKeys "{HOME}+{END}"
    InputKeys Dfld(6)
    'G
    EditBox DblClick, "Label=Width:", "Coords=42,6"
    InputKeys "{HOME}+{END}"
    InputKeys Dfld(7)
    'H
    InputKeys "{TAB}"
    InputKeys "{HOME}+{END}"
    InputKeys Dfld(8)
    'comments
    InputKeys "{TAB}"
    InputKeys "{HOME}+{END}"
    InputKeys Dfld(9)

    Execute_Pref_Command
```

```
    Case "TAB-4"

        'Tab 4 stuff

        Window SetContext, "Caption=Preferences", ""
        EditBox DblClick, "Label=DP M:", "Coords=52,10"
        InputKeys Dfld(1)
        '
        ComboBox Click, "Label=D S M:", "Coords=168,9"
        ComboListBox Click, "Label=D S M:", "Text="&Cstr(Dfld(2))
        'Default Selection
        ComboBox Click, "Label=Default Decision:", "Coords=164,12"
        ComboListBox Click, "Label=Default Decision:", "Text="&Cstr(Dfld(3))
        '
        InputKeys "{TAB}"
        InputKeys Dfld(4)
        Execute_Pref_Command

    Case "TAB-5"
        Window SetContext, "Caption=Preferences", ""
        'Sxx
        EditBox DblClick, "Label=Sxx:", "Coords=42,8"
        InputKeys Dfld(1)
        'Dyy
        ComboBox Click, "Label=Dyy:", "Coords=168,9"
        ComboListBox Click, "Label=Dyy:", "Text="&Cstr(Dfld(2))
        'Z12
        ComboBox Click, "Label= Z12:", "Coords=165,13"
        ComboListBox Click, "Label= Z12:", "Text="&Cstr(Dfld(3))
        'Default Decision
        InputKeys "{TAB}"
        InputKeys Dfld(4)
        Execute_Pref_Command

    Case "TAB-6"
        Window SetContext, "Caption=Preferences", ""
        TabControl DblClick, "ObjectIndex=1;\;ItemText=TAB-6", ""
        TabControl Click, "ObjectIndex=1;\;ItemText=TAB-6", ""
        InputKeys "{TAB}"
        InputKeys "{HOME}+{END}{DELETE}"
        InputKeys Dfld(1)
        Execute_Pref_Command

    Case "TAB-7"
        Window SetContext, "Caption=Preferences", ""
        TabControl Click, "ObjectIndex=1;\;ItemText=TAB-7", ""

        InputKeys "{TAB}"
        Inputkeys Dfld(1)
        Execute_Pref_Command

    Case "Command_Only"
        Execute_Pref_Command

    Case Else
        Msgbox "Action Selection not found for ActCd: "&Cstr(ActCd)&" Terminating"
        Perform_Action=0  ''return value FAIL
        SQALogMessage sqaFail, "Action Selection not found for: "&Cstr(ActCd)&"", ""
End Select
```

CHAPTER 8 ▸ THE CONTROL SYNCHRONIZED DATA-DRIVEN TESTING FRAMEWORK

```
End Function

-----------------------------------------------------------------------------------
Function Execute_Pref_Command
            If ActCd="PREF_OK" then
                Window SetContext, "Caption=Preferences", ""
                PushButton Click, "Text=OK"

                if ErrCd LIKE "none" then
                    Result = WindowVP (DoesNotExist, "Caption=Preferences",_
                                "VP=Window Existence;Wait=2,30;Status=NORMAL")
                    Current_Win="none"
                    Current_Tab="none"
                end if
            elseif ActCd="PREF_APPLY" then
                Window SetContext, "Caption=Preferences", ""
                PushButton Click, "Text=Apply"
                if ErrCd LIKE "none" then
                    Result = WindowVP (Exists, "Caption=Preferences",_
                                "VP=Window Existence;Wait=2,30;Status=NORMAL")
                end if
            elseif ActCd="PREF_CANCEL" then
                Window SetContext, "Caption=Preferences", ""
                PushButton Click, "Text=Cancel"
                if ErrCd LIKE "none" then
                    Result = WindowVP (DoesNotExist, "Caption=Preferences",_
                                "VP=Window Existence;Wait=2,30;Status=NORMAL")
                    Current_Win="none"
                    Current_Tab="none"
                end if
            elseif ActCd="PREF_DataEntryOnly" then
                'do nothing
            end if
End function
```

In instances where it may be desirable, you can also select cases on combinations of values like the following code segment.

```
Function Perform_Action(ActCd)
    Perform_Action=1
    Select Case (ActCd & TabCd)
        Case "PREF_OK"&"TAB-1"

-----------------------------------------------------------------------------------
'DDProcess_Error  Version 2.0

'This is a template file updated May 24, 2001
'updated June 2001

'$Include: "DataDriven.sbh"

    Declare Function Process_Error(ErrCd)

Sub Main
    Dim Result As Integer

    'Initially Recorded: 6/5/2001  1:53:10 PM
```

```
    'Script Name: DDProcess_Error
    Gen_Return_Code=Process_Error(ErrCd)
End Sub

----------------------------------------------------------------------------------------
----------------------------------------------------------------------------------------
Function Process_Error(ErrCd)

    Process_Error=1

    Select Case ErrCd

        Case "PREF_GEN_ERR"
            Result = WindowVP (Exists, "Caption=Validation Errors", "VP=Window_
                            Existence;Wait=2,30;Status=NORMAL")
            Window SetTestContext, "Caption=Validation Errors", ""
            Result = LabelVP (CompareText, "ObjectIndex=1", _
                        "VP=Alphanumeric;Wait=2,30;Type=CaseSensitive")
            Window ResetTestContext, "", ""
            Window SetContext, "Caption=Validation Errors", ""
            PushButton Click, "Text=OK"

        Case "x"                ' a place holder for the next case to be inserted

        Case Else
            Msgbox "Error Code not found for ErrCd: "&Cstr(ErrCd)&" Terminating"
            Process_Error=0  ''return value FAIL
            SQALogMessage sqaFail, "Error Code not found for: "&Cstr(ErrCd)&"", ""
    End Select
End Function

'DDTab_Select  Version 2.0

'This is a template file updated May 24, 2001
'updated June 2001

'$Include: "DataDriven.sbh"

Declare Function Tab_Select(TabCd)
Dim Result

Sub Main
    Dim Result As Integer
    'Initially Recorded: 6/5/2001  1:16:14 PM
    'Script Name: DDTab_Select
    Gen_Return_Code = Tab_Select(TabCd)
End Sub

----------------------------------------------------------------------------------------
----------------------------------------------------------------------------------------
Function Tab_Select(TabCd)
    tab_Select=1 'initially set the return code to "Success"
    Select Case TabCd

'preferences tabs

        Case "TAB-1"
            Window SetContext, "Caption=Preferences", ""
            TabControl Click, "ObjectIndex=1;\;ItemText=TAB-1", ""
```

```
            Result = TabControlVP (CompareProperties, "ObjectIndex=1", "VP=OP TAB-
                         1;Wait=2,30")
            Window ResetTestContext, "", ""

       Case "TAB-2"
            Window SetContext, "Caption=Preferences", ""
            TabControl Click, "ObjectIndex=1;\;ItemText=TAB-2", ""
            Result = TabControlVP (CompareProperties, "ObjectIndex=1", "VP=OP
                         YTD;Wait=2,30")
            Window ResetTestContext, "", ""

       Case "TAB-3"
            Window SetContext, "Caption=Preferences", ""
            TabControl Click, "ObjectIndex=1;\;ItemText=TAB-3", ""
            Result = TabControlVP (CompareProperties, "ObjectIndex=1", _
                         "VP=OP NSI;Wait=2,30")
            Window ResetTestContext, "", ""

       Case "TAB-4"
            Window SetContext, "Caption=Preferences", ""
            TabControl Click, "ObjectIndex=1;\;ItemText=TAB-4", ""
            Result = TabControlVP (CompareProperties, "ObjectIndex=1",_
                         "VP=OP NFD;Wait=2,30")
            Window ResetTestContext, "", ""

       Case "TAB-5"
            Window SetContext, "Caption=Preferences", ""
            TabControl Click, "ObjectIndex=1;\;ItemText=TAB-5", ""
            Result = TabControlVP (CompareProperties, "ObjectIndex=1", _
                         "VP=OP ICB;Wait=2,30")
            Window ResetTestContext, "", ""

       Case "TAB-6"
            Window SetContext, "Caption=Preferences", ""
            TabControl Click, "ObjectIndex=1;\;ItemText=TAB-6", ""
            Result = TabControlVP (CompareProperties, "ObjectIndex=1",_
                         "VP=OP TAB-A;Wait=2,30")
            Window ResetTestContext, "", ""

       Case "TAB-7"
            Window SetContext, "Caption=Preferences", ""
            TabControl Click, "ObjectIndex=1;\;ItemText=TAB-7", ""
            Result = TabControlVP (CompareProperties, "ObjectIndex=1",_
                         "VP=OP MAP;Wait=2,30")
            Window ResetTestContext, "", ""
'add new set tabs

       Case "set information"
            Window SetContext, "Caption=MyApp Shell", ""
            Window SetContext, "Caption=Add Set;ChildWindow", ""
            TabControl Click, "ObjectIndex=1;\;ItemText=Set Information", ""
            Window SetTestContext, "Caption=MyApp Shell", ""
            Window SetTestContext, "Caption=Add  Set;ChildWindow", ""
            Result = TabControlVP (CompareProperties, "ObjectIndex=1",_
                         "VP=OP Set Info;Wait=2,30")
            Window ResetTestContext, "", ""

       Case "optional information"
            Window SetContext, "Caption=MyApp Shell", ""
```

```
            Window SetContext, "Caption=Add Set;ChildWindow", ""
            TabControl Click, "ObjectIndex=1;\;ItemText=Optional Information", ""
            Window SetTestContext, "Caption=MyApp Shell", ""
            Window SetTestContext, "Caption=Add Set;ChildWindow", ""
            Result = TabControlVP (CompareProperties, "ObjectIndex=1",_
                        "VP=OP Optional Info;Wait=2,30")
            Window ResetTestContext, "", ""

        Case Else
            Msgbox "Tab Select not found for TabCd: "&Cstr(TabCd)&" Terminating"
            Tab_Select=0  ''return value FAIL
            LogMessage sqaFail, "Tab Select not found for tab code: "&Cstr(tabCd)&"", ""
    End Select
End Function

'-------------------------------------------------------------------------------------------------
'DDWindow_Select   Version 2.0

'$Include: "DataDriven.sbh"

    Declare Function Window_Select(WinCd)
    Dim result as integer

Sub Main
    'Initially Recorded: 5/31/2001  1:49:50 PM
    'Script Name: DDWindow_Select
    Gen_Return_Code = Window_Select(WinCd)
End Sub

'-------------------------------------------------------------------------------------------------
'-------------------------------------------------------------------------------------------------
Function Window_Select(WinCd)
    Window_Select=1
    Select Case WinCd

        Case "preferences"
            Window SetContext, "Caption={MyApp*}", ""
            MenuSelect "Tools→Preferences..."
            Result = WindowVP (Exists, "Caption=Preferences", "VP=Window
                        Existence;Wait=2,30;Status=NORMAL")
            Window SetContext, "Caption=Preferences", ""
            Window MoveTo, "", "Coords=0,0"

        Case "CPWS_N"
            Window SetContext, "Caption={MyApp*}", ""
            MenuSelect "Action→Create PlanningWorkSheet→N"
            Window SetTestContext, "Caption={MyApp*}", ""
            Result = WindowVP (Exists, "Caption={N PWS*};ChildWindow", "VP=Window
                        Existence;Wait=2,30;Status=NORMAL")
            Window ResetTestContext, "", ""
            Window SetContext, "Caption={Ny PWS*};ChildWindow", ""
            Window WMaximize, "", ""

        Case "CPWS_Y"
            Window SetContext, "Caption={MyApp*}", ""
            MenuSelect "Action→Create PlanningWorkSheet→Y"
            Window SetTestContext, "Caption={MyApp*}", ""
            Result = WindowVP (Exists, "Caption={Yield PWS*};ChildWindow", "VP=Window
                        Existence;Wait=2,30;Status=NORMAL")
```

```
            Window ResetTestContext, "", ""
            Window SetContext, "Caption={Y PWS*};ChildWindow", ""
            Window WMaximize, "", ""

        Case "AddNSet"
            Window SetContext, "Caption={MyApp*}", ""
            Window SetContext, "Caption={N PWS*};ChildWindow", ""
            Window WMaximize, "", ""
            Window SetContext, "Caption={{MyApp*}", ""
            MenuSelect "PWS→Add N Set..."
            Window SetTestContext, "Caption={MyApp*}", ""
            Result = WindowVP (Exists, "Caption=Add N Set;ChildWindow",_
                        "VP=Window Existence;Wait=2,30;Status=MAXIMIZED")
            Window ResetTestContext, "", ""

        Case "AddYSet"
            Window SetContext, "Caption={MyApp*}", ""
            Window SetContext, "Caption={Y PWS*};ChildWindow", ""
            Window WMaximize, "", ""
            Window SetContext, "Caption={MyApp*}", ""
            MenuSelect "PWS→Add Y Set..."
            Window SetTestContext, "Caption={MyApp*}", ""
            Result = WindowVP (Exists, "Caption=Add Yield Trial Set;ChildWindow",_
                        "VP=Window Existence;Wait=2,30;Status=MAXIMIZED")
            Window ResetTestContext, "", ""

        Case ""

        Case Else
            Msgbox "Window Select not found for WinCd: "&Cstr(WinCd)&" Terminating"
            Window_Select=0  ''return value FAIL
            SQALogMessage sqaFail, "Window Select not found for: "&Cstr(WinCd)&"", ""
    End Select
End Function
```

SQABasic32 Include Files

```
DataDriven.sbh   version 2.0

'Global definitions for the Data Driven Main, Window Select, Tab Select, Perform Action and
                            Process Error functions

'This is a template file created May 24, 2001

    Global Dfld()
    Global WinCd        As String
    Global TabCd        As String
    Global ActCd        As String
    Global ErrCd        As String
    Global Current_Win As String
    Global Current_Tab As String
    Global InFileName  As String
    Global Gen_Return_Code As Integer
    Global Gen_Return_String As String
```

```
Global Key_word_list(9,1) as String   'the size of this list should match the number of
                              keywords defined
CONST KWListSize = 9

DBase_Util.sbl version 2.0

'update the DB_Num constant as database connections are added
Const DB_Num = 4

Global Available_Databases(4) as String
Global Available_Connect_Strings(4) as String

Sub DB_Util
'For each additional database bump from Available_Databases(1) to Available_Databases(2),
                              etc. supply a name and a connect string

Available_Databases(0)="(none)"
Available_Connect_Strings(0)="none"

Available_Databases(1)="Local MS Access Test Database"

Available_Connect_Strings(1)="DSN=TestData;DBQ=C:\Local_Repo\TestData\testdata.mdb;DriverId=
                              281;FIL=MS
                              Access;MaxBufferSize=2048;PageTimeout=5;PWD=saturn51;UID=admin;"

Available_Databases(2)="MYAPP xrem" 'description only

Available_Connect_Strings(2)="DSN=xREM;UID=baposey;PWD=xxxxx;DBQ=mrem.abccompany.com;DBA=W;A
                              PA=T;FEN=T;FRC=10;FDL=10;LOB=T;RST=T;FRL=F;PFC=10;TLO=0;"
Available_Databases(3)="XREM - MyApp" 'description only

Available_Connect_Strings(3)="DSN=DREM;UID=meeeeeee;PWD=xxxxx;DBQ=xrem.abccompany.com;DBA=W;
                              APA=T;FEN=T;FRC=10;FDL=10;LOB=T;RST=T;FRL=F;PFC=10;TLO=0;"
Available_Databases(3)="MSDE Local - MyApp" 'description only
Available_Connect_Strings(3)="DSN=MyAppMSDE;Description=MyApp
                              local;UID=ZXZXZXZ;PWD=zxzxzx;APP=Rational Test;WSID=MYAPP02"
End Sub

-------------------------------------------------------------------------------------------
excel.sbh    version 2.0

Declare Function ReadExcelDataSingle BasicLib "excel" (sFileName As String, sCell As String)
                              As String
Declare Function ReadExcelDataMulti BasicLib "excel" (sFileName As String, sCells As String,
                              sData() As String) As Integer
Declare Sub WriteExcelData BasicLib "excel" (sFileName As String, sCell As String, vValue As
                              Variant)

'excel.sbl v3.0--Andy Tinkham, CWC Inc.
'Permission to redistribute has been granted to Dan Mosley of CSST Technologies, Inc., and
                              Bruce Posey of Archer Group.

'*****************************************************************************************
'* ReadExcelDataSingle
'*
'* Retrieves the value from a cell on the first sheet in a specified Excel
'* workbook and returns it as a string.
'*
```

```
'* Parameters:
'*      sFileName -- full path and filename of the spreadsheet to open
'*      sCell -- cell column/row designator (e.g., "A1")
'*      vSheet -- optional parameter.  Use this to specify either an integer
'*          sheet number (where first sheet is numbered 1 not 0) or a string
'*          sheet name in order to reference the sheet to retrieve data from
'*
'* Note:  This will error if the specified sheet of a workbook is not a data sheet
'*
'******************************************************************************
Function ReadExcelDataSingle(sFileName As String, sCell As String, _
    Optional vSheet As Variant) As String

    'Dimension the needed variables
    Dim objExcel As Object
    Dim objWorkBook As Object
    Dim objWorkSheet As Object
    Dim sData As String

    'Open up Excel
    Set objExcel = CreateObject("Excel.Application")

    'Open the workbook
    Set objWorkBook = objExcel.Workbooks.Open(FileName:=sFileName)

    'See if a sheet was referenced in the call.  If not, default to the first sheet
    If IsMissing(vSheet) Then
        vSheet = 1
    End If

    'Set up a reference to the sheet in the workbook
    Set objWorkSheet = objWorkBook.WorkSheets(vSheet)

    'Make everything uppercase to ease comparision
    sCell = UCase(sCell)

    'Retrieve the value from the cell
    sData = objWorkSheet.Range(sCell).Value

    'Close the workbook
    objWorkBook.Close

    'Exit Excel
    objExcel.Quit

    'Clear all the references to the objects
    Set objWorkBook = Nothing
    Set objWorkSheet = Nothing
    Set objExcel = Nothing

    'Return the cell value
    ReadExcelDataSingle = sData
End Function

'******************************************************************************
'* ReadExcelData
'*
'* Retrieves the values from a cell or group of cells on a sheet in a specified
'* Excel workbook.  This function fills in an array that is passed in as an
```

```
'*  argument.  The return value is TRUE or FALSE and should be checked before the
'*  array is accessed to make sure that the data was correctly loaded.
'*
'*  Parameters:
'*       sFileName -- full path and filename of the spreadsheet to open
'*       sData -- array to hold the values of the cells.  Should be an undimensioned
'*           dynamic array (e.g., one declared like Dim arrExcelValues() As String)
'*       vSheet -- optional sheet name to retrieve data from.  If omitted, the first
'*           sheet of the workbook is used
'*       vRange -- optional range column/row designator (e.g., "A1:B16").  If omitted,
'*           the first table of data is returned (passing a range of "all" also will
'*           return this same table).  A table of data is defined as the
'*           block of cells contiguous to a cell without encountering any blank rows
'*           or columns (blank cells are ok).  The cell used for contiguousness is A1
'*           unless a cell is specified in the sCell parameter
'*       vCell -- optional parameter used to specify the cell used to determine the
'*           contiguous table.  Ignored if sRange is not omitted or set to "all".  This
'*           parameter must refer to a cell that is in the contiguous range you want
'*           to retrieve, but it can be any cell in that contiguous range
'*
'*  Note:  This will error if the specified sheet of a workbook is not a data sheet
'*
'*****************************************************************************
Function ReadExcelData(sFileName As String, sData() As String, Optional vSheet _
    As Variant, Optional vRange As Variant, Optional vCell As Variant) As Integer

    'Dimension the needed variables
    Dim objExcel As Object
    Dim objWorkBook As Object
    Dim objWorkSheet As Object
    Dim objRange As Object
    Dim i As Integer
    Dim j As Integer

    'Deal with the optional parameters first
    If IsMissing (vSheet) Then
        vSheet = 1
    End If

    If IsMissing (vRange) Then
        vRange = "all"
    End If

    If IsMissing (vCell) Then
        vCell = "A1"
    End If

    'Open up Excel
    Set objExcel = CreateObject("Excel.Application")

    'Open the workbook
    Set objWorkBook = objExcel.Workbooks.Open(FileName:=sFileName)

    'Set up a reference to the first sheet in the workbook
    Set objWorkSheet = objWorkBook.WorkSheets(vSheet)

    'Set a reference to the specified or default Range of data
    If LCase(vRange) = "all" Then
        Set objRange = objWorkSheet.Range(vCell).CurrentRegion
```

```vb
    Else
        Set objRange = objWorkSheet.Range(vRange)
    End If

    'Redimension the array to hold the data
    ReDim sData(1 to objRange.Rows.Count, 1 to objRange.Columns.Count) As String

    'Read in the data cell by cell (since SQA won't accept an array as a return value)
    For i = 1 to objRange.Rows.Count
        For j = 1 to objRange.Columns.Count
            sData(i,j) = objRange.Rows(i).Columns(j).Value
        Next j
    Next i

    'Close the workbook
    objWorkBook.Close

    'Exit Excel
    objExcel.Quit

    'Clear all the references to the objects
    Set objWorkBook = Nothing
    Set objWorkSheet = Nothing
    Set objExcel = Nothing

    'Return TRUE to indicate things worked correctly
    ReadExcelData = TRUE
End Function

'*****************************************************************************
'* WriteExcelDataSingle
'*
'* Writes a value to a cell on a specified sheet in a specified Excel
'* workbook.
'*
'* Parameters:
'*      sFileName -- full path and filename of the spreadsheet to open
'*      sCell -- cell column/row designator (e.g., "A1")
'*      vValue -- value to write out
'*      vSheet -- optional parameter used to specify the sheet to write
'*          to.  Can either be an integer specifying the sheet's index or
'*          a string specifying the sheet's name
'*
'* Note:  This will error if the specified sheet of a cell is not a data sheet
'*
'*****************************************************************************
Sub WriteExcelDataSingle(sFileName As String, sCell As String, vValue As Variant, _
    Optional vSheet As Variant)

    'Dimension the needed variables
    Dim objExcel As Object
    Dim objWorkBook As Object
    Dim objWorkSheet As Object

    'Deal with the optional parameters
    If IsMissing(vSheet) Then
        vSheet = 1
    End If
```

```
    'Open up Excel
    Set objExcel = CreateObject("Excel.Application")

    'Open the workbook
    Set objWorkBook = objExcel.Workbooks.Open(FileName:=sFileName)

    'Set up a reference to the first sheet in the workbook
    Set objWorkSheet = objWorkBook.WorkSheets(vSheet)

    'Write the value to the cell
    objWorkSheet.Range(sCell).Value = vValue

    'Save the changes
    objWorkBook.Save

    'Close the workbook
    objWorkBook.Close

    'Exit Excel
    objExcel.Quit

    'Clear all the references to the objects
    Set objWorkBook = Nothing
    Set objWorkSheet = Nothing
    Set objExcel = Nothing
End Sub
'*****************************************************************************
'* WriteExcelData
'*
'* Writes an array of values to a range on a specified sheet in a specified
'* Excel workbook.
'*
'* Parameters:
'*      sFileName -- full path and filename of the spreadsheet to open
'*      sCell -- cell column/row designator (e.g., "A1").  This should be
'*          the upperleftmost cell of the range you want to write out.  Values
'*          will then be written out in the order they are in in the array.
'*      vValues -- values to write out.  Must be a variant two-dimensional array
'*      vSheet -- optional parameter used to specify the sheet to write
'*          to.  Can either be an integer specifying the sheet's index or
'*          a string specifying the sheet's name
'*
'* Note:  This will error if the specified sheet of a cell is not a data sheet
'*
'*****************************************************************************
Sub WriteExcelData(sFileName As String, sCell As String, vValues() As Variant, _
    Optional vSheet As Variant)

    'Dimension the needed variables
    Dim objExcel As Object
    Dim objWorkBook As Object
    Dim objWorkSheet As Object
    Dim objRange As Object
    Dim i As Integer
    Dim j As Integer

    'Deal with the optional parameters
    If IsMissing(vSheet) Then
```

```
        vSheet = 1
    End If

    'Open up Excel
    Set objExcel = CreateObject("Excel.Application")

    'Open the workbook
    Set objWorkBook = objExcel.Workbooks.Open(FileName:=sFileName)

    'Set up a reference to the first sheet in the workbook
    Set objWorkSheet = objWorkBook.WorkSheets(vSheet)

    'Set a reference to a range the right size to hold the array values
    Set objRange = objWorkSheet.Range(sCell).Resize(UBound(vValues, 1) - _
        LBound(vValues, 1) + 1, UBound(vValues, 2) - LBound(vValues, 2) + 1)

    'Write the values out cell by cell
    For i = 1 to objRange.Rows.Count
        For j = 1 to objRange.Columns.Count
            objRange.Rows(i).Columns(j).Value = vValues(i, j)
        Next j
    Next i

    'Save the changes
    objWorkBook.Save

    'Close the workbook
    objWorkBook.Close

    'Exit Excel
    objExcel.Quit

    'Clear all the references to the objects
    Set objWorkBook = Nothing
    Set objWorkSheet = Nothing
    Set objExcel = Nothing
End Sub

global.sbh    version 2.0

'SQABasic Header File
'Global Values

'This is a template file created May 24, 2001

    Global Today As String
    Global Today2K As String
    Global Tomorrow As String
    Global UKToday As String
    Global NextWeek As String
    Global LastWeek As String
    Global NextMonth As String
    Global LastMonth As String
    Global NextYear As String
    Global LastYear As String
    Global Dates_Have_Been_Set as String
    Global Substitutes_initialized as String
    Global txt_filename As String
    Global xls_FileName As String
```

```
    Global index_last_selected_Db as integer
    Global global_query As String

global.sbl version 2.0

'SQABasic Source File: global.sbl
'Test Procedure Source File
'Originally Created 7/9/98 B. Posey  Common functions and sub-routines
'$Include: "global.sbh"

Declare Function ReadFields( File_Num, NumFlds, GFlds())  'passed in: File_number to read
                              from
Declare Sub AutodateSet
Declare Function DateSet(Fld_Value)
-------------------------------------------------------------------------------------------
Function ReadFields(File_Num, NumFlds, GFlds())

    Dim Index as integer

    ReadFields=1  ''return value PASS

    If NumFlds=0 then
        ReadFields=0  ''return value FAIL
        SQALogMessage sqaFail, "global.sbl function 'ReadFields' passed 0 numflds", ""
        Exit Function
    Else
        For Index=1 To NumFlds
            Input #File_Num,GFlds(Index)
        Next Index
    End If
 End Function

-------------------------------------------------------------------------------------------
Function DateSet(Fld_Value)

    if Dates_Have_Been_Set<>"YES" then
        Call AutodateSet
    end if

    if(Fld_Value)="AutoDate" or (Fld_Value)="Today" then
        Fld_Value=Today
    elseif (Fld_Value)="Today2K" then
        Fld_Value=Today2k
    elseif (Fld_Value)="UKToday" then
        Fld_Value=UKToday
    elseif (Fld_Value)="Tomorrow" then
        Fld_Value=Tomorrow
    elseif (Fld_Value)="LastWeek" then
        Fld_Value=LastWeek
    elseif (Fld_Value)="NextWeek" then
        Fld_Value=NextWeek
    elseif (Fld_Value)="NextMonth" then
        Fld_Value=NextMonth
    elseif (Fld_Value)="LastMonth" then
        Fld_Value=LastMonth
    elseif (Fld_Value)="LastYear" then
        Fld_Value=LastYear
    elseif (Fld_Value)="NextYear" then
```

```
            Fld_Value=NextYear
        end if
    DateSet=Fld_Value
    End Function

    ------------------------------------------------------------------------------------------

    Sub AutoDateSet

        Today=Date
        Today=Format$(Today,"mm/dd/yyyy")

        Today2K=Date
        Today2K=Format$(Today,"mm/dd/2000")

        Tomorrow=Date+1
        Tomorrow=Format$(Tomorrow,"mm/dd/yyyy")

        UKToday=Date
        UKToday=Format$(UKToday,"dd/mm/yyyy")

        NextWeek=Date+7
        NextWeek=Format$(NextWeek,"mm/dd/yyyy")

        LastWeek=Date-7
        LastWeek=Format$(LastWeek,"mm/dd/yyyy")

        LastMonth=Date-30
        LastMonth=Format$(LastMonth,"mm/dd/yyyy")

        NextMonth=Date+30
        NextMonth=Format$(NextMonth,"mm/dd/yyyy")

        LastYear=Date-365
        LastYear=Format$(LastYear,"mm/dd/yyyy")

        NextYear=Date+365
        NextYear=Format$(NextYear,"mm/dd/yyyy")

        Dates_Have_Been_Set="YES"
    End Sub

    Ini_access.sbh

    Declare Function GetPrivateProfileString   Lib "kernel32" Alias "GetPrivateProfileStringA"
                            (ByVal lpAppName As String, ByVal lpKeyName As String, ByVal
                            lpDefault As String, ByVal lpReturnedString as String, ByVal
                            nSize as Long, ByVal lpFileName as String) As Long
    Declare Function WritePrivateProfileString Lib "kernel32" Alias "WritePrivateProfileStringA"
                            (ByVal lpAppName As String, ByVal lpKeyName As String, ByVal
                            lpString As String, ByVal lpFileName as String) As Long

    Openfile.sbh

    Type OPENFILENAME
            lStructSize As Long
            hwndOwner As Long
            hInstance As Long
            lpstrFilter As Long
            lpstrCustomFilter As Long
```

```
        nMaxCustFilter As Long
        nFilterIndex As Long
        lpstrFile As Long
        nMaxFile As Long
        lpstrFileTitle As Long
        nMaxFileTitle As Long
        lpstrInitialDir As Long
        lpstrTitle As Long
        Flags As Long
        nFileOffset As Integer
        nFileExtension As Integer
        lpstrDefExt As Long
        lCustData As Long
        LpfnHook As Long
        lpTemplateName As Long
    End Type

Declare Function lstrcpy Lib "kernel32" Alias "lstrcpyA" (ByVal lpString1 As String, ByVal
                        lpString2 As String) As Long
Declare Function GetOpenFileName Lib "comdlg32.dll" Alias "GetOpenFileNameA" (pOpenfilename
                        As OPENFILENAME) As Long
Declare Function FindWindow     Lib "user32" Alias "FindWindowA" (ByVal lpClassName As
                        String, ByVal lpWindowName As Any) As Long   'Last parameter used
                        to be As String
Declare Function CommDlgExtendedError Lib "comdlg32.dll" () As Long

    Global Const OFN_READONLY = &H1
    Global Const OFN_OVERWRITEPROMPT = &H2
    Global Const OFN_HIDEREADONLY = &H4
    Global Const OFN_NOCHANGEDIR = &H8
    Global Const OFN_SHOWHELP = &H10
    Global Const OFN_ENABLEHOOK = &H20
    Global Const OFN_ENABLETEMPLATE = &H40
    Global Const OFN_ENABLETEMPLATEHANDLE = &H80
    Global Const OFN_NOVALIDATE = &H100
    Global Const OFN_ALLOWMULTISELECT = &H200
    Global Const OFN_EXTENSIONDIFFERENT = &H400
    Global Const OFN_PATHMUSTEXIST = &H800
    Global Const OFN_FILEMUSTEXIST = &H1000
    Global Const OFN_CREATEPROMPT = &H2000
    Global Const OFN_SHAREAWARE = &H4000
    Global Const OFN_NOREADONLYRETURN = &H8000
    Global Const OFN_NOTESTFILECREATE = &H10000
    Global Const OFN_SHAREFALLTHROUGH = 2
    Global Const OFN_SHARENOWARN = 1
    Global Const OFN_SHAREWARN = 0
```

Utility Scripts

```
OpenFile_Txt Version 2.0

'$include: "Openfile.sbh"
'$Include: "global.sbh"

sub main
    Dim OpenFile As OPENFILENAME
    Dim lReturn As Long
```

```
        Dim longerror as long
        Dim Title as string
        '
        Dim FileTitle as string
        Dim Filter as String 'new bp
        OpenFile.lStructSize = Len(OpenFile)

        'do the title
        Title = "Select input file to process for DataDriven Testing" & Chr$(0)
        Openfile.lpstrTitle = lstrcpy(Title,Title)

        'Do the file
        '* Allocate string space for the returned strings.
        txt_FileName = Chr$(0) & Space$(255) & Chr$(0)

        FileTitle = Space$(255) & Chr$(0)
        Openfile.lpstrFile = lstrcpy(txt_FileName, txt_FileName)
        Openfile.nMaxFile = Len(txt_FileName)

        'Do the filetitle
        Openfile.lpstrFileTitle = lstrcpy(FileTitle, FileTitle)
        Openfile.nMaxFileTitle = Len(FileTitle)
        'temp
        Filter ="Text Files"&Chr$(0)&"*.txt"&Chr$(0)&Chr$(0)
        Openfile.lpstrFilter = lstrcpy(Filter, Filter)
        'temp
        lReturn = GetOpenFileName(OpenFile)

        If lReturn = 0 Then
            longerror = CommDlgExtendedError
            'MsgBox longerror
            txt_FileName=""
        Else
            'msgbox FileName
            ' msgbox Filetitle
        End If
End Sub

Openfile_Xls   Version 2.0

'This is a template file updated May 24, 2001
'updated June 2001

'$include: "Openfile.sbh"
'$Include: "global.sbh"

sub main
    Dim OpenFile As OPENFILENAME
    Dim lReturn As Long
    Dim longerror as long
    Dim Title as string
    '
    Dim FileTitle as string
    Dim Filter as String 'new bp
    OpenFile.lStructSize = Len(OpenFile)

    'do the title
    Title = "Select *.xls, Excel Workbook" & Chr$(0)
    Openfile.lpstrTitle = lstrcpy(Title,Title)
```

```
'Do the file
'* Allocate string space for the returned strings.
xls_FileName = Chr$(0) & Space$(255) & Chr$(0)

FileTitle = Space$(255) & Chr$(0)
Openfile.lpstrFile = lstrcpy(xls_FileName, xls_FileName)
Openfile.nMaxFile = Len(xls_FileName)

'Do the filetitle
Openfile.lpstrFileTitle = lstrcpy(FileTitle, FileTitle)
Openfile.nMaxFileTitle = Len(FileTitle)
'temp
Filter ="Excel workbook"&Chr$(0)&"*.xls"&Chr$(0)&Chr$(0)
Openfile.lpstrFilter = lstrcpy(Filter, Filter)
'temp
lReturn = GetOpenFileName(OpenFile)

If lReturn = 0 Then
    longerror = CommDlgExtendedError
    'MsgBox longerror
    xls_FileName=""
Else
    'msgbox xls_FileName
    'msgbox Filetitle
End If
End Sub
```

An Example of the CSDDT Framework _____

The Web/FTP site that supports this book contains an example based on our testing tool of choice, Rational Suite TestStudio. The importance of this example is that, when implemented, it works in the same manner as the data-driven approach does in real automated testing projects. This example is based on the ClassicCD demo that Rational Software has provided for its customers. The reason we are using this example and not one from a client is that we wish to respect the privacy and confidentiality of our clients.

You must have Rational Robot in order to implement this data-driven example. The following information will help you install and run the ClassicCD example. Please read all readme files prior to your installation.

Script File List

DDMain Template.rec

DDWindow_Select.rec

DDTab_Select.rec

DDPerform_Action.rec

DDProcess_Error.rec

DBUtility.rec

get_db_connect_str.rec

DBFileQuery.rec

Convert.rec

Ini_Acess.rec

Manual Test Dialog.rec

Openfile_Txt.rec

Openfile_Xls.rec

Library File List

DataDriven.sbh

global.sbh

excel.sbh

ini_access.sbh

Openfile.sbh

DBase_Util.sbl

DDKeyword_Sub.sbl

excel.sbl

global.sbl

Directions for Installing the Example Files

Step 1. Copy the *.sbh and *.sbl files to your default sqabas32 folder. Under Rational 2001, this should be the default path. For example:

```
C:\your repository folder.....\TestDatastore\DefaultTestScriptDatastore\TMS_Scripts\SQABas32
```

Step 2. Copy the *.rec files to your default script folder. Under Rational 2001, this should be the default path unless the administrator has changed it. For example:

```
C:\your repository folder.....\TestDatastore\DefaultTestScriptDatastore\TMS_Scripts
```

Step 3. After the script files have been copied, Robot will not be aware of these files. You must open Robot, and then select New Script. Type in the name of the script file exactly the same as the name of the file(s) that was copied over. When you click OK, the file should be displayed, already populated with the script commands.

The *.sbh, *.sbl, and *.rec files can be opened and edited with a standard test editor like Notepad.

After all the files have been created and then closed, go to Robot's file menu and select Compile All. Provided all files have been copied to the proper location, the scripts should be able to be executed at this point.

Conclusion

The information in this chapter is designed to get you up and running with the Archer Group's CSDDT framework. The templates, which are also included on the Web/FTP site that supports this book, can be copied quickly and modified for your use. We have found this method to be an effective way of jump-starting an automation effort in organizations using Rational Suite TestStudio (1). If you are using a different suite of testing tools, it can easily be translated into the native test scripting language associated with your tool of choice. However, some of the functionality that Rational Robot provides through the built-in features of SQABasic may have to be programmed if they are not supported.

References

1. Mosley, Daniel J., and Bruce A. Posey. *Building and Executing Effective Real-World Test Scripts with Rational Suite TestStudio 2001*. Workbook from seminar offered by CSST Technologies, Inc., and the Archer Group.

2. Rational Software Incorporated, Rational Testing Products, *SQABasic Language Reference*, Ver. 2002.05.00, Part number 800.02125.00, 2001, *www.rational.com/docs/v2002/sqabasic.pdf*

Facilitating the Manual Testing Process with Automated Tools

9

Introduction

It has been shown statistically that randomly generated test cases find only one out of every three errors present in the software. This means that test cases not based in requirements are unproductive and are essentially worthless when it comes to producing a return on the organization's investment in their development. This fact is also compounded by further data that reveal two-thirds of all errors contained in software programs are of the more serious type—errors in logic (1,2). These are the errors related to mistakes made when defining the requirements or to errors made when designing the software to reflect the requirements. Only a third of all errors are due to oversights made during programming.

Of course, the goal of testing is discover all of the errors. In practice there is a differential rate at which different types of errors are discovered. Logic errors are the most difficult to uncover, and discovering them requires the most planning and resources. The current manual testing process does not allow for the up-front planning required to effectively identify logic errors.

In this sense manual testing is random and tests at a very superficial level. Software applications must be tested in depth, and deep testing requires intelligently designing, building, and executing test cases that will exercise the software's logic.

There is a minimum amount of basic information that is necessary to ensure the effective testing of a program/module: validate GUI objects, test GUI-level edits, and validate business rules. Testing the GUI provides the user interface validation, but the depth and breadth that are provided by testing business logic are the core of any testing effort. The test conditions must cover inputs and processes and must ensure test coverage from both Black Box and White Box perspectives.

A testing group's manual testing activities are usually executed in an ad hoc manner that defeats the repeatability of the tests—for regression purposes, the tests must be executed exactly the same way each time the software is tested/retested. Furthermore, the current manual testing approach does not produce the documentation required for verification and validation purposes. In addition, test case design is inadequate because it is more or less at random. Finally, the current process does not lend itself to automation. Let's look at this further.

The software testing process must be repeatable (*repeatable* means documented; it also means automated). This indicates that the same test cases are executed in exactly the same way and with the same test data under the same environmental conditions each time the tests are executed. It also indicates that tests must not be susceptible to individual differences among testers because a different person may execute a test each of the times it is run. The human condition, e.g., lapses in memory as to what test cases were run under what conditions, also affects repeatability. Individual differences with respect to personality traits and skill sets also introduce variation into test execution. This affects repeatability.

The lack of documentation with present manual test approaches aggravates this problem. All tests should be documented. Test requirements should be documented so that they can be traced directly to system requirements. Test conditions should be directly traceable back to the test requirements, and test data should be directly linked to specific test conditions.

The information required to define and document test conditions prior to test execution should be gathered from documents such as the Functional Requirements Specifications, Functional Product Needs, High-Level Design Specifications, Low-Level Design Specifications, and/or other documents that are produced as artifacts of the software development process. In addition, required information that is not documented should be obtained through informal meetings with product managers, developers, database administrators, etc., who can supply the needed facts.

Semiautomated Manual Testing Process Steps

The following semiautomated testing process is presented as an alternative approach to current ad hoc manual processes. It was implemented using Rational Suite TestStudio 2000 (note that the TestLog summary reports mentioned below are no longer available as of TestStudio 2001 and later versions), but similar processes can be implemented using other commercially available automated testing tool suites. The only requirements are that the test scripting language has the capability to present dialog boxes and retrieve tester input from them.

In this semiautomated testing process, Steps 1 through 4 involve planning and pretest setup. Step 5 describes the test execution process using Rational Robot and Rational TestLog Viewer.

Step 1. Identify and document the test objectives.

The test objectives should be based in the system requirements. Use the Excel workbook's Test Objectives spreadsheet template on the FTP site under the Test Planning folder. Be sure to identify the links back to specific system requirements. Use the requirements document to derive the objectives. If there is no requirement document available or if it is incomplete, meet with the development group and try to uncover as much information about the requirements as you can through your discussions.

Step 2. Translate the test objectives into specific test requirements.

Each test object will result in one or more test requirements. Identify the area(s) of the system associated with each objective. The test requirements should be developed using the Test Requirements Notes template that also resides under the Test Planning folder on the ftp site that supports this book. Test requirements should be documented in a manner similar to the approach described in Chapter 3. The test requirements can be documented at any of these levels: program, module, window, or tab.

The contents of this document must provide a vehicle for designing test cases that can be used for manual tests as well as automated tests. The entries should be conceptualized as test conditions that have a direct relationship to the test cases. One test condition will have one valid test case and one invalid test case. In many instances, the relationship is one to many—one condition can result in one valid test case and many invalid test cases. The filled-in contents cover the inputs, processes, and outputs that must be tested to ensure test coverage from both Black Box and White Box perspectives. In some occurrences, the information tends to be Gray Box.

Step 3. Translate the test requirements into test conditions.

Use the second spreadsheet template to document the test conditions. Convert each row in the Client (GUI) Edits table (see Chapter 3) document into two or more (one valid and at least one invalid) test conditions that will be executed. Use Equivalence Partitioning, Boundary Analysis, and Error Guessing to identify the set of test conditions for the row. Each test condition results in one input test case.

In the same spreadsheet, use the Server Edits table (again, see Chapter 3) to develop test conditions for validating business rule logic. Once again, use Equivalence Partitioning, Boundary Analysis, and Error Guessing to identify the set of test conditions for the row. As above, each test condition results in one input test case.

Step 4. Construct the test data.

Using the third spreadsheet template, create the test data—one data record for each test condition in the Test Conditions sheet—until all of the test conditions are covered by one or more test data record. Use the following guidelines.

For each program/GUI screen include data input records that cover the following conditions:

1. Include at least one GOOD record where all fields contain valid data that pass global, relational, and file edits (all GUI- and server-level edits).
2. Include at least one GOOD duplicate record.
3. Include one INVALID record for each GUI edit defined in the test requirements.
4. Include one INVALID record for each server edit (business rule) defined in the test requirements (see Note below).

5. Include one or more records for each type of special processing described in the test requirements.

6. Include one or more records for each type of Y2K date processing described in the test requirements.

Note: At the lowest level (the GUI) the system processes equivalence class values are independent of one another, but keep in mind that business rules represent interactions between and/or among combinations of values from dependent equivalence classes.

Export the test data rows in the spreadsheet to a simple text (*.txt) file. You can then open the file with Word or Notepad and add comments and white space for readability if you want.

Step 5. Execute the manual tests.

The following screen shots are taken from our implementation using Rational Robot, and the directions as written were used with Robot. Start Rational Robot. Start playback of the Manual Test test script, as illustrated in Figure 9.1. Select the Manual Test script and click OK.

Be sure that the GUI Playback option is checked (see Figure 9.2) or the tests will not be captured. In the Log Information screen (see Figure 9.3), enter a unique name for the test log that will be created.

Click OK and use the File Open dialog box. Select the Input Test File (refer to Figure 9.4), which contains the directions and data for the test you want to execute.

Click OK and you will be presented with the Manual Test Procedure dialog box. It acts as a *teleprompter* that you will use during test execution (see Figure 9.5a–d).

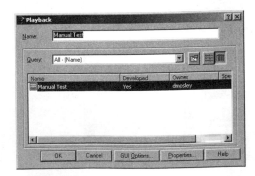

FIGURE 9.1
Test script selection dialog box

FIGURE 9.2
GUI Playback Options dialog box

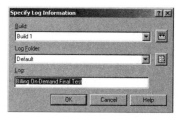

FIGURE 9.3
Test Log Information dialog box

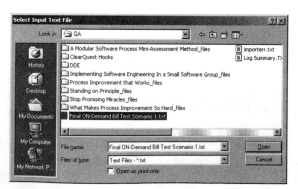

FIGURE 9.4
Select Input Text File dialog box

The main portion of this dialog box is a list box that displays the contents of the associated text file. It provides vertical scrolling but not horizontal scrolling. After you perform the steps listed in the display, you may select the buttons Pass, Fail, or Not Run. Doing so will create a log entry for the procedure indicating the Pass, Fail, or Not Run conditions.

At the bottom on the screen there is an edit box that allows the tester to add additional comments to the log file. If data are entered there prior to selecting the Pass, Fail, or Not Run buttons, it will be included in the log file.

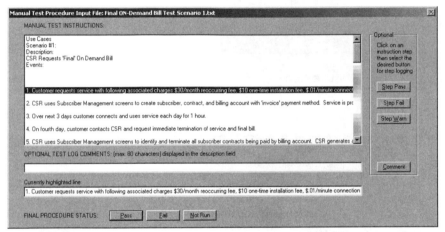

FIGURE 9.5A
Manual Test Procedures dialog box

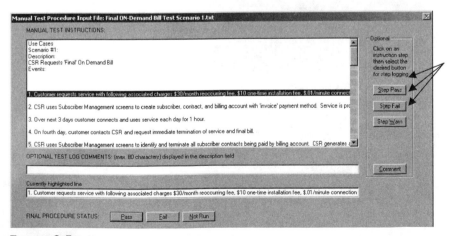

FIGURE 9.5B
Manual Test Procedures dialog box

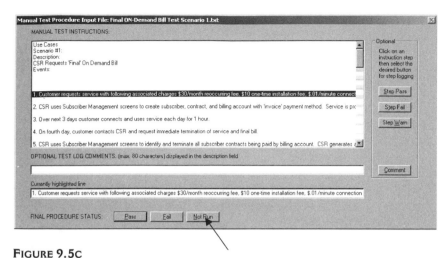

FIGURE 9.5C
Manual Test Procedures dialog box

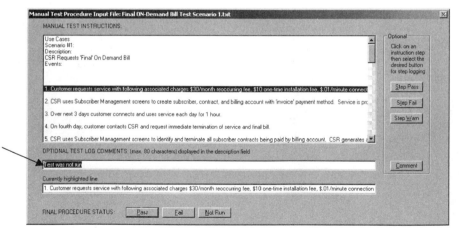

FIGURE 9.5D
Manual Test Procedures dialog box

During the performance of the manual test process, the tester may enter additional comments at any time by selecting the Comment button. This causes the comment to be logged and then clears the comment text box. It will *not* close the dialog box.

In addition to the comment box, the tester may, at any time, click on a line in the list box where the test instructions are displayed and then click on one of the four optional buttons:

Step Pass

Step Fail

Step Warn

Step None

The selected line in the display will be logged with a green Pass indicator, a red Fail indicator, a yellow Warning indicator, or, for Step None, no indicator. This functionality is provided for when it is desirable to indicate whether the step passed, failed, etc. The contents of comment line will be added to the log entry as well. Clicking on any of the four buttons will *not* close the dialog box.

Using the List Box

To use the manual testing process list box, highlight the test, or test step, you want to execute. Follow the instructions and use the test data presented for the test. Refer again to Figures 9.5a–d.

Bring up the AUT. Navigate to the appropriate screen or tab. Manually type the data into the corresponding input fields. After entering the data, note the result(s) of the test (behavior of the AUT related to the input values).

Alt+Tab back to the Manual Test Procedure dialog box and click on the command button that reflects the result of the test: Step Pass, Step Fail, Step Warn. Continue to alternate between the Manual Test Process dialog box and the AUT until testing is completed.

You may choose not to execute a test. When that is the case, click on the Not Run command button. Doing so terminates the tests and writes to the test log.

You can enter optional comments up to a maximum of 80 characters that will be written to the test log. It is important to comment the test results and especially so if the test failed or was not run.

When a step fails, the Pass command button is grayed out and the final result for the script is recorded as a failure.

The resulting test log highlights the failed steps in red. Refer to the example screen shot in Figure 9.6.

The test log should not be deleted or overwritten. If you are conducting a trial test run to fine-tune your test procedure, turn off the Robot playback option that writes the test log. Go to the Tools menu and select GUI Playback

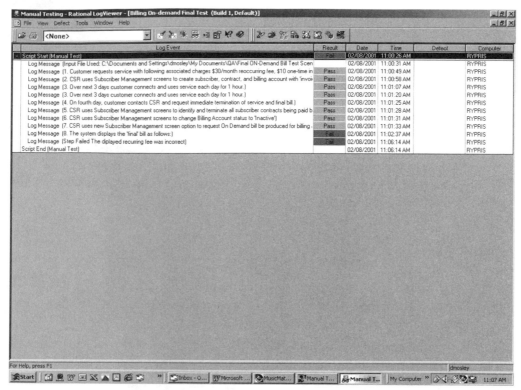

FIGURE 9.6
Test log

Options; choose the Log tab in the Options dialog box that appears. Be sure the box next to "Output playback results to log" is not checked.

The test log can printed to a file using the Quick Reports command if you are using TestStudio 2001 or an earlier version.

Manual Testing Artifacts

The following artifacts will be created during the manual testing process. They should be kept in a CM repository for future reference.

- An Excel workbook that contains the Test Objectives spreadsheet, the Test Conditions spreadsheet, and the Test Data spreadsheet will be developed during manual test planning and maintained throughout the manual testing process.

- An MS Word document that contains the Test Requirements Notes will be created and updated as needed.
- A text file containing test instructions and test data will be created.
- The Manual Test script will produce an automated test log as it executes.
- A TestLog Viewer Quick Report of the test results will be generated from the test log and printed to a file that will be saved in the CM repository (see Figures 9.7 and 9.8).

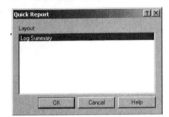

FIGURE 9.7
Quick Report dialog box

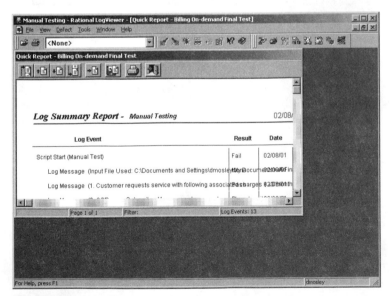

FIGURE 9.8
Example Quick Report

Conclusion

The advantages to a semiautomated approach to manual testing are numerous, but the two most important ones are repeatability of the tests and documentation of the test conditions, procedure, and results. The test results logs can be used to generate error reports, which in turn can be the source of test metrics. The reports can be used to monitor and guide further manual testing efforts. All of this is not possible when manual test is purely ad hoc (ad hoc being used in the true sense of its meaning, that each manual test execution is uniquely geared to the moment).

The test script that we used to implement the semiautomated manual testing approach in this chapter are also included on the FTP site that supports this book.

References

1. Mosley, Daniel J. *The Handbook of MIS Application Software Testing: Methods, Techniques, and Tools for Assuring Quality Through Testing.* Prentice-Hall Yourdon Press, Upper Saddle River, NJ, 1993.

2. Myers, Glenford. *The Art of Software Testing.* Wiley-Interscience, New York, 1979.

Managing Automated Tests

10

Writing Effective Test Scripts and Test Data

The following list of do's for writing effective automated test scripts is taken from the workbook of the advanced scriptwriting seminar offered by CSST Technologies, Inc., and Archer Group.

Test Scriptwriting Do's

Use framework-based script design.

Implement data-driven controls.

Develop and use scriptwriting guidelines.

Limit script sizes.

Break scripts down by functionality.

Document scripts well.

Organize test scripts into related groups.

Use shell scripts.

Include test parameters in data files such as *.ini files, settings files, and configuration files rather than as constants embedded into the test script.

Prompt users for input specifics with preset defaults.

Create error traps and provide the user with feedback.

Next are lists of do's and don'ts for creating effective test data.

Test Data Creation Do's

Use the test data design techniques listed in the section called "Functional Test Data Design" in Chapter 3.

Place the data in simple text files.

Document which tests are being executed.

Allow dynamic data input via placeholders.

Use input data to control test execution.

Test Data Creation Don'ts

Use capture/playback as the principal means of creating test scripts.

Use test scripts that individuals code on their own, without following common standards and without building shared libraries.

Use poorly designed frameworks.

Here are some additional scriptwriting tips and tricks.

Construct main test scripts for adding data records, deleting data records, updating data records, and verifying the edits.

Create separate test scripts for general menu properties, system menu properties, keyboard shortcuts, and toolbars.

Create additional scripts for object properties tests for all major GUI screens.

Develop and use test script templates for adding, editing, and deleting test data records.

Avoid hard coding items such as data paths, filenames, and constants. Instead, use global include files as header files (for example, *.sbh—SQA-Basic Header) for constants and definitions.

Use source files (for example, *.sbl—SQABasic Library) for executable code such as functions.

Avoid letting main script become too complex. Break complex testing activities/tasks into small pieces. Use subroutines, functions, and additional procedures when necessary. Convert subroutines that require input variables to functions. Back up scripts before making major modifications. Use a configuration management process/tool for test script version control.

Managing Manual and Automated Test Scripts _____

Because test scripts are fairly complicated and because many may be required during the test, it is best to organize them in *test case folios*. The test cases in the folio can be conveniently grouped according to the design objectives or requirements of the system they test. Based on Hetzel's earlier work, scripted test case folios should minimally contain (2)

1. Sections detailing the objects to be tested
2. Sections describing restrictions and limitations on script use
3. Sections with an overall description of the test scenario
4. Sections organizing groups of scripts according to purpose
5. Sections that describe the expected behaviors for each script

The test case folios can be constructed and maintained with many different desktop tools. All you need is a word processor and/or a spreadsheet. Of course, it is much better if the test case folio can be created with the testing management components of automated software testing tools. For example, Rational TestManager does not embed items such as the test plan or test case folio, but it does allow the user to set internal document locators to these items and displaying them in their native format.

In addition, GUI testing tools should include test management components that can organize test scripts and link them to test requirements. Two products that already have these capabilities are Rational Software's TestManager component and Mercury Interactive's TestDirector. Other vendors also have or are implementing new versions of their products to include testing management components.

Test Suite Maintenance _____

What most of us probably do not understand is that a suite of automated tests is really a software system itself with the same problems faced by the system it is designed to test. It is prone to errors and extremely sensitive to changes. So, any time a client-server system is tested with automated test scripts, you are really dealing with two systems that have to be maintained. This doubles the maintenance problem.

I worked with one Visual Basic programmer who had previously constructed and maintained an automated suite of test cases for a client-server system. The problem he encountered was that the features were never frozen, and he was constantly updating the test scripts to keep up with all of the changes. Of course, he never caught up. He swears he will never do testing again!

Steve Fuchs, the program manager for Microsoft Test (MS Test is currently a component in Rational Software's arsenal of software development and testing products), sees the macro recorder capabilities of the major test tools as causing several maintenance problems because testers can assume certain things (1):

1. That the software product will change during its life cycle
2. That, if it is successful, it will be reproduced in other languages
3. That the next version of the product will have a better user interface
4. That there will be less time to test subsequent versions of the product

He argues that the assumption on the part of testers that the product will change leads to scripts that will contain invalid events. He says the effort to isolate and rerecord those portions of the script will be substantial. He goes even further to say that the scripts will contain very little context information about the events, which makes maintenance harder, and that the scripts will contain hard-coded function calls that will require extensive updating for even minor user interface changes. He concludes that even simple changes can affect 50% to 90% of the test cases (2).

Fuchs arguments are valid because new system releases *do* impact automated test suites. Recorded test procedures will most likely require some updating when new versions of the system include changes to any of the system layers (interface layer, data layer, or function layer). Think of it this way: When we change a software module, we must ask what other modules are affected by this change. Now, when we change a software module, we must also ask what test scripts will be affected by the change. Automated test suites add a new constraint on the system itself. James Bach (in the USENET news group comp.software.testing) says, "Automation systems constructed from scripts are very complex and hard to maintain. The more complex a system is, the more likely it is to fail."(1) The implication here is that the test cases themselves can be prone to error. So what do we do— write test scripts to test the test scripts?

Another problem is the impact of software and/or hardware platform changes. Again Bach says, "Any change in such a platform will cause widespread failure of test automation, unless the change was specifically anticipated." Bach has experienced problems with test automation stemming from DOS updates and from changes to a Novell network. He was forced to add additional platform-related processes to the test automation in order to make it work. He found that only subtle configuration differences could cause automated test suites to fail.

To be fair to the automated test tool vendors, we must state that their products have come a long way since they were introduced. Many of the conditions that caused earlier test suites to fail are now trapped and logged, and the testing process continues. The test suites are much more robust than before.

An important piece of advice is to use plenty of comments. Insert a comment heading at beginning of the script for complex test procedures. Use a product such as Cyrano for documenting test suites.

Conclusion

Maintaining a suite of automated test procedures can become a full-time job in itself. This is true because even simple module/interface testing can require hundreds of test scripts. We recently tested an error routine using a driver module that presented a dialog box with a severity icon, an error message, and several different sets of command. Testing this small routine took just under a hundred test scripts.

Test suite maintenance begins far in advance of the actual testing. It is always advisable to start designing and constructing test scripts and test cases as soon as you have enough information to begin. The problem that you will encounter is that the test scripts and test cases must be revised each time the developers change the software. If there is little or no control over how developers insert changes during the analysis and design processes, it will drive you crazy trying to keep the automated test scripts up to date with the changes.

A compromise solution is to begin designing, but not constructing, test scripts and test cases as soon as possible. This eliminates 50% of the maintenance burden. You have to update only the design, and you do not have to rerecord or reprogram the test scripts. At some point as the actual test date nears, you have to begin construction, but the longer you can put it off, the less pretest maintenance you will have to do. In addition, constructing paper-and-pencil test scripts, which are easily modified when necessary, can enhance this approach.

This approach also addresses another problem that occurs frequently. Developers customarily do not deliver the functional software modules until right before the test date, and yet you are still expected to perform testing on time. But how are you supposed to construct automated test scripts without a working prototype of the software? Well, if you have the test cases designed and you have kept the design as up-to-date as possible, and if you have constructed paper-and-pencil test scripts, you will probably still be able to construct the test scripts in time to do the testing.

References

1. Fuchs, Steve. "Building Smart Testware." *Test Technical Notes* (Microsoft Technet CD) 4, no. 2, February 1996.
2. Hetzel, William. *The Compete Guide to Software Testing*. 2d ed, QED Information Sciences, Wellesley, MA, 1988.

Data-Driven Automation: User Group Discussion

The following online discussion on Data Driven Automation was held the week of May 17–21, 1999. It is about 7 pages in length in MS Word but contains excellent information on how (and how not) to implement Data Driven Automation using Rational Robot (or nearly any automation tool). [This discussion is being presented as is without any changes in format, spelling, or grammar.]

To get a visual of one possible architecture used in Data Driven Automation view the Architecture Notes. [This document is included in the DDE documentation that is available on the Just Enough Software Test Automation supporting ftp site.]

Named participants:

Carl Nagle   SAS Institute, Inc.

Dan Mosley   CSST Technologies

Elfriede Dustin   Computer Sciences Corp.

Gerry Kirk	TradeMark Technologies (?)
Mark Butler	Frank Russell Co.
Mike Tierney	Integrated Health Services, Inc.
Sarah Gleaton	Inmar Inc.

Carl:

Just got back from the STAR conference in Orlando and am curious to hear about successes or failures in developing the data driven engines described by Edward Kit and Linda Hayes and others at the conference. It sounds very promising, but wonder who has tried it or expanded on it and how well it has worked for you. Does it really get rid of writing all these scripts or does it just move them to a different part of the automation effort?

Mike:

I have a couple of test engines that accept GUI inputs only from .csv files. They're working pretty well. It's totally obvious to me what actions the input file is for without the use of action words, verbs, etc. I have not gotten into the action word thing yet. Myself and a couple of others are running the scripts and we are all script savvy. The advantage of the data driven engines for us is they eliminate all the calls to the re-useable procs we used to have in driving scripts. This makes maintenance easier and cuts down on the number of scripts we have.

I think testing with action words might be worth it if you had a large end user type tester population who did not deal well with scripting. In other cases like ours it might just increase script maintenance. If our whole suite had been designed as data driven with action words from the start it might be a different story.

Gerry:

We have implemented much of the framework to do "procedural-driven" or TM4 testing, whatever you want to call it, although its first real test will come later this week. Basically, the person writing the tests does not have to know (virtually) anything about SQA. The tester uses a concise verb dictionary to instruct the test engine what to do at each step: navigate to something, input something, click something, and verify something. The weaknesses right now are with

a. verifying object data lists, e.g., contents of a list—don't have a nice way to maintain such things

b. creating a GUI map of the application—right now, the tester must use a tool like SQA Inspector to get control ids of text boxes, etc. and then type them in a constants file.

c. syntax errors—the tester must type in the verb commands, constant names and ensure proper verb command structure. We've written a syntax checker tool that looks for mistakes, which should help (haven't used it yet).

All test scripts and constant files are maintained in Excel. A lot of time is saved converting a test plan to test scripts, because the test plan IS the test script. I'll let you know how the first real test goes.

Carl:
Using TestStudio, have you been very successful recognizing and automating the use of any custom objects with this type of engine? Or are all of your objects already known to TestStudio?

I am looking at implementing a Data-Driven/TM4/Next-Generation engine as well and I know that I will have custom objects not immediately recognizable to TestStudio. Since the goal of this engine is to make any object application/window independent I am interested to find out if others have dealt with this successfully and what methods were used.

Mark:
I have recently used data driven automation with great success and believe it has its place. There are many benefits to Data Driven Automation. BUT there are some negatives. It is those negatives I want you to think about.

Basic data driven automation consists of action steps along the line of "Click the Button" or "Enter Text". This basic level does little true testing but is where some people stop their development. The next level of data driven automation includes comparison values within the instruction set. The action steps to execute are followed by an instruction to compare a value in the input data file with that in one of the controls on the screen.

Maybe file comparisons would also be included. A more sophisticated level will allow for the retrieval and comparison of additional object properties and the inclusion of comment lines in the log file. I contend that this level is the minimum for good testing. An advanced implementation of data driven testing will allow the user to perform complex multi-object, multi-property comparisons. This would include list and data table comparisons.

In data driven automation the steps that are to be executed and any comparison values are kept external to the automated tool. When using a tool like Visual Test that's all fine and dandy. There is also no problem when you use it with Robot but use Robot like Visual Test.

But TestStudio is a suite of tools. There is the ability to create and describe an association between different parts of the test suite. A test requirement can be associated to a script. The development, execution, and the success or failure of that scripts execution can be tracked within the tool also. A comparison baseline, a.k.a. TC or VP, is kept within the tool and the tool controls its existence and configuration. The pass/fail results of a comparison can be directly tracked to the baseline of the comparison and to the instruction(s) that led up to that comparison from the resulting test log. You give up most, if not all, of this when you use data driven automation. Other items I believe are negatives to data driven automation:

- I do not believe conditional statements or looping instructions can be successfully implemented with data driven automation. If the test case designer wishes to instruct the application to repeat a series of steps then each of those repetitions must be indicated in the input data file.

- There is a lot of startup work required before useful results are to be realized. (There are contract test developers that have libraries that they have created that greatly reduce this startup time. I'm not one of them.)

- Data driven automation, like many types of test automation, is often not completely understood and, because of that, is not implemented to a sophisticated enough level.

- As mentioned above, you lose the ability to associate test assets to each other and to track their status through the cycle in a single place.

When I originally looked into data driven automation I felt it had no place in an environment where there was an intention to use TestStudio. Within a few months of stating that conviction I came across a situation where data driven automation was the best solution. I was very glad to have it at my disposal.

One good place I know of for data driven automation are applications like a Human Resources system where there can be a great number of combinations of scenarios. With data driven automation a subject matter expert can create these combinations during the original implementation, or later on, to see if the system will handle, and continue to handle, a particular scenario as expected. When used in combination with other test automation techniques a thorough test of the application can be accomplished.

Some proponents of data driven automation maintain that it is the best solution to all situations. It isn't. It is a good one with a variety of advantages. I recommend that you look into, and understand, what this approach to test automation means to your situation.

Carl:

Thanks for your perspective on this. Your points are well taken and were discussed at the conference.

Generally, if you do use the playback tool in the manner we have described, you *do* lose many of the nice hooks into the rest of the TestStudio product offerings (Planning, Organizing, Defect Tracking, etc.).

However, my situation does lend itself to implementing a data-driven engine in a variety of ways. And actually, I may need to implement a few.

I will be working with application testers to help automate as much as is possible while their traditional testing goes on. I will be doing this across several different unrelated applications and more than likely on more than one automation toolset. (We have internal tools capable of automation.)

One of my goals is to make the application/tool-independent test framework as universal as possible so that testers can move from one project to another with minimal impact on productivity. Thus if their data table structure, dictionary, and other core features are similar across toolsets and applications we hope to have a jump on these transitions.

Additionally, we use an in-house Defect Tracking system and Requirements are yet to be discovered in this corner of the company. So our implementation of automation is generally going to be effective use of the playback engine(s) and other sources (Flat File, Excel, SAS, and Napkins) for planning, data, and metrics.

We'll just have to see how well this works out and how workable this scenario really is.

Dan:
The concept of data-driven testing as Bruce Posey and I teach it (and I know you are not referring to our class so I am not being defensive here) is not as superficial as you have described. Data-Driven really refers to two things: control data (what button to click next, etc.) and test data (testing GUI, server, and database level validations).

The heart of this approach is in the test data not the control data. The type of testing you refer to below is not what we do. We only use Rational Robot's built-in test cases when necessary. The majority of our tests are built into the test data itself. In fact, we use one test script for basic GUI tests to be sure of the applications operability, and another that does object test on the GUI, but these are not data-driven. We run functional test scripts that are data-driven. They are data-driven in the sense that the test data causes the program to behave in a specific and expected way. The test results are how the application reacts to our test data.

The following objectives are but a sample of what you can use to set up data-driven test data.

For Each GUI Screen Include Data Input Records That Cover The Following Conditions:

1. At least one GOOD record where all fields contain valid data (Passes all GUI and Server-level edits)

2. Include at least one GOOD Duplicate record

3. Include one INVALID record for GUI edit defined in the test requirements

4. Include one INVALID record for each server edit (Business Rule) defined in the test requirements

5. Include one or more records for each type of special processing described in the test requirements

6. Include one or more records for each type of Y2K date processing described in the test requirements

The following format is used for input data records to SQA scripts:

- An input data record is considered to be one line in a text file.

- The first five fields of each data record are used for control purposes and the remaining fields are for data to be input to a given screen.

- Each field is enclosed in double quotes "x" and is delimited from the next by a comma (example: "field 1","field 2","field 3")

Field 1 Record Type

Field 2 Control 1

Field 3 Control 2

Field 4 Data Field Count, where data record field 6 is the first data field.

Field 5 Comment

Field 6 through Field x are data fields.

Example Data

```
"H","Ctl1","Ctl2","3","Comment","fld1-deal status","fld2-approverId","fld3-deal number"
"G","New","Ctl2","3","New Deal WIP","DEAL","tester1","00000001"
"H","Tab","Ctl2","11","Comment","start date","Expire
date","initiator","Category","Type","Duration","sell comp","sell
trader","buy comp","buy            trader","notes"
"G","Deals","Ctl2","11","fill in deals
tab","10/13/1998","10/30/1998","us","product","sell","longterm","clark","ed_
w","ayers","bob_a","NOTES"
"G","New","Ctl2","3","New Deal WIP","WIP","tester1","00000001"
"G","New","Ctl2","3","New Deal WIP","TEMPLATE","tester1","00000001"
```

You are right when you say there is a big up front investment if you are going to implement data-driven automated testing. As you can see from the short example above, the majority of the work is in capturing test requirements and developing test data based on those requirements. Writing the test scripts is simple and reasonably quick because there are many similarities across scripts for different applications and for screens within the same application. The control fields serve only to navigate the application under test and the majority of SQA test cases are used to verify the test script's location in the AUT, or that a particular test case elicits a response that we expect, etc.. We go into much more detail with examples in our seminar, but this should be enough to demonstrate how our scripts work. We do most of the verification by writing to the test log, by file comparisons, and by opening the database and downloading the updates tables to spreadsheets.

Elfriede:

I have to agree with Mark, in that there is a time for data driven testing and then there isn't. I will always use data driven testing using "test data" (see *www.autotestco.com* for one example of how we've used Robot for Y2K data testing), but very rarely will use data driven testing using "control data." The reason being is that it's tedious to implement and the effort only pays off if the test can be reused many times over in subsequent releases.

I inquired with Ed Kit after his presentation at the STAR and he agreed with me that the efforts of implementing this approach often don't pay off until after the 17th run. (Yes, that's the number he gave.)

A while back, one of my coworkers in a previous job had just received training on this data driven testing approach. It took that person 3 weeks to implement the data driven approach. There were lots of nice tables with commands/controls and data to read. But in the end it boiled down to that the test would have been much more efficient using simple record and playback and modification of the recorded script, since the test wasn't used repeatedly. The effort in this case was a waste of time. You will have to use your judgment and remember that it does not always pay off to implement a complex data driven framework for automated testing.

Carl:

I would have to agree on almost every aspect of this, but must also argue that no amount of automation is cost effective if it is not *INTENDED* to be repeated. In fact, to break even on a 17th iteration sounds great. On a build verification performed nightly that's 17 business days (or less) and all in the same release!

Dan:

I beg to disagree with you (Elfriede). Data-driven testing does require the up front investment that you indicated, but it does pay off big dividends during build-level regression testing. I have been there and I have seen it. We had to test 100+ transaction screens (each one was a window in itself) for a financial application. We developed over 7,000+ data-driven tests which each took approximately 3 to 5 days to create and debug, but which ran in 1–2 hours when played back between builds. We usually received one build a week and we were able to replay 100+ test scripts and 7,000+ test records each week and finish on time.

We did not attempt to build all of the test scripts and data records at once. As the application functionality was developed, we created data-driven tests for the features that were delivered. As we progressed over time we ended up with the large number of test scripts and test data records. My point is that it is important to start developing test scripts and test data early in the development process even though you have to put up with feature creep. Furthermore, we could not have handled the ensuing changes to the AUT and completed our testing if we had not chosen a data-driven approach.

I do not agree with Ed Kit's approach in that he develops a test script that preprocesses the test data in the Excel spreadsheet before it can be used in the test script proper. His approach adds to the overall test script maintenance burden. Control data is the only way to go! It reduces test script maintenance and as long as you have guidelines as to how to code the control data it is not a big deal. The most time consuming portion of data-driven testing is the creation of the test data itself. Adding control data negates the need to have a pre-processor test script and does not add that much to the test data development overhead. Believe me I know as I am the one who designs and creates our test data.

I don't mean to offend any one, but all of the critical comments about data-driven testing seem to be coming from people who have very little experience with it, or who have not been able to successfully implement it. I think that it is getting a bad rap when it is the best, most effective and most efficient way to do automated software testing. I would say to those of you who have not tried it, or have not been able to make it work, you really need to attend a formal training class or to work with someone who has perfected it. It is not as simple as everyone seems to think. If you do not use a structured scripting technique with the data-driven approach, you can create very convoluted and ineffective data-driven tests and test scripts.

Bruce Posey and I independently evolved into data-driven testing out of necessity three years ago and have been using it since. We were using it before it became the trend and we didn't even know there was such a concept as data-driven when we first began. We did it because it was the only way to do testing that was more than just GUI testing. If GUI testing is all a tester does, the application is not being tested very well at all. The GUI is secondary to the application functionality (if you don't believe me, ask all of the developers and project managers I have worked for). What is most important is to test the breadth and depth of the application functionality.

We test the GUI once after each build with a single test script. To test the GUI further is counter productive.

To test application functionality, you develop test data records that are "functional variations" of the baseline feature. Some must contain valid data, but the majority must be invalid variations of the data. If you attempt to do this using a record only approach you must record one test script for each functional variation. If you do it in a data driven manner, you must develop one test script that is a combination of recording writing and one data file that has one record for each functional variation you want to test. This is a lot less time consuming and there is a lot less script maintenance. I can develop my data-driven test data a hundred times faster than I can record and debug multiple variations of the same test script. The maintenance is really keeping the data up to date in between changes to the application. Occasionally a change in the AUT will require a change in the test script, but that change is usually minimal.

Mike:

Dan—By control data, do you just mean a field in your spreadsheet or csv file that has a code or explanation for the specific test being performed? Can you give an example of what you mean by control data?

Dan:

In the example I sent yesterday, the first six fields are used to identify the test data record's intent (Field 1: record type. good data v. functional variant bad data), to tell the test script where to go in the UAT (Field 2: CTL1), and to tell the script what to do when it is in the correct window/dialog box (Field 3: CTL2), to tell the script how many data fields to read (Field 4: Data field count), to comment on the data record's purpose (Field 5: Comments), Field 6 through Field x: (These fields will contain the data to be input). By using control field 4 we can enter variable length data records.

We use pre-coded functions and subroutines that are available to all test scripts via SBL files and define everything in SBH files. The test script calls these routines which decipher the codes and control the test script's navigational behavior and how much data it enters. The same test script can go to different windows and enter different data without being modified.

Mark:

I'm really glad I took the time to say what I did in that earlier message. If I had the forethought to attempt to elicit a response then I would have tried to get the one Dan sent first. Dan clearly described how he and Bruce implement Data Driven Testing. Those of us that are paying attention can use that information to understand when and where the method should be used in our situations. There is no question that Dan and Bruce are pushing the envelope.

The main point I was trying to make with my initial posting was that few people understand the process well enough to make good use of it. Truth is, many people don't understand how to make the most effective use of test automation. I have to admit that I think I'm one of those. I've learned the ropes but I'm not yet an expert. A good example of this is right in this thread. The example Elfriede gave of the test that was developed but hardly repeated. Why was it automated at all if it wasn't going to be repeated? Let alone in a method that was new to the test developer? (Don't get me wrong. I'm not pointing fingers. I know that if I'm pointing one finger at you then there are three more pointing right back at me.)

What it amounts to is: Don't expect miraculous results from data driven testing, or any other automated testing for that matter, unless you understand what you are doing. That doesn't mean you can't get good results while learning but you do have to LEARN. I'll put this out for the world to see. I will, someday, take the class offered by Dan and Bruce. Because it's a well thought out method that I know I will be using. It's obvious that Dan knows what he's talking about.

Dan left out a bunch of good things about the method. Most of the effort is in creating the data. If you change test tools you just have to recreate the logic in the language of the new tool. It also works cross platform.

Recreate the logic in a test tool that works on the different platform and you can use the same test data. As the test data gets modified you probably wouldn't have to make any platform specific changes. Also, subject matter experts and not test tool experts that have only a foggy idea of what the application is supposed to do can develop the data. Once created, the expert in the test tool can be working on scripts that don't lend themselves to the data driven approach. If a scenario needs change then the subject matter expert does it.

Sarah:

I was remiss when I posted my class comparisons regarding RTTS and CSST Technologies, and regret doing so, as this data driven testing approach was the main reason I wanted to attend training with Dan & Bruce. They are true masters of this approach, and as you can see, are quite passionate when they tell you how effective it is to use. Although you will find people on either side of the fence when it comes to implementing a data driven approach (and no one on the middle of the fence), it appears that those who are the most against it have never successfully implemented this and are going by what others in the field tell them.

Please don't get me wrong, I do appreciate everyone's opinions—but there are many people on this list who are unsure of how to proceed with training in this field, and they should not be discouraged from pursuing all options! It is my suggestion that training be pursued—versus reading about it in a book, as Dan & Bruce really gear this toward "real life," and many benefits can be gained by attaining more knowledge.

I know the data driven approach was just what we were looking for when I attended the training in Sept., and this approach really streamlined and perfected all our scripts. For those of you who don't agree, you are entitled to your opinions as well, but I don't think it's always a good idea to "poo poo" approaches that have and will help a lot of testing professionals perform their scripting/testing in a better overall way.

Dan:
What we do to link up our data with the rest of the info in Rational's test data store (repository) are several things. First of all, we link the test plan, test requirements, and test data docs through the SQA Assets>Test plan menu selection. Any type of document including spreadsheets can be opened via the Test Plan Selector window. It is also project specific so you will see the test data files, etc. only for the project you have open. Second, we write lots of messages to the test log that document when and what happened for each failed data record. From there you can automatically generate a defect. Third, we enter test requirements into SQA via the Assets>Test Requirements menu selection. From there we associate a specific requirement to the test log entries. We also document the software structure so that we can relate specific defects back to the software components in which they occurred.

Writing messages to the test log allows us to generate test log reports, various defect reports, Test requirements/defect reports that are linked to our entries into the test log which are in turn linked to specific data records in the CSV file the script ran. We can even run the one report that lists all of the docs we have associated through the test plan selector.

Unfortunately, some of Rational's built in limitations, such as not being able to associate a test procedure with multiple requirements, force us to document some relationships outside of the SQA repository. As I mentioned above, when we do so, we link those documents so that we can open and examine them while in SQA Manager.

I would also say that you are absolutely correct when you say that data-driven testing is not some cure-all for automated testing aliments. It does work when used correctly and when used appropriately.

For some testing, which may involve recording/writing a small number of test scripts and for which not a lot of test data is needed, the approach is over-kill. The real trick is to know when it can and should be used. In fact, in some situations test automation in any form is over-kill.

The incident that Elfriede referred to was one in which data-driven testing may have involved too much effort and resources for the task at hand and that is why it did not pay off. In that instance simple record and playback may have worked. I have learned a very important lesson from our discussions and that is Bruce and I must update our seminar material to include a discussion of when to use data-driven testing and when not to use it.

Mike:

(Dan, on your record format for record types, what are those "G"s and "H"s?)

Dan:

The purpose of the record type is to identify good records from error records, and to mark records we do not want to execute during a test run.

You can use any code you like as long as the script is coded to recognize it. We used "G" for good data records, "E" for error records, and "H" to skip data records or to insert comment records. The codes allow us to process some records while skipping others, and to invoke special processing for exceptions. The advantage is that if a particular record causes an error to occur, you change the code to "H" and you can run the data set again to continue testing. We also found that you can use these codes to stop processing when you hit a certain record. We used "X" as the code. The "E" code was used for records we expected to cause error conditions to inform the script to look for and handle those conditions (error message boxes etc.). CTL1 is used to identify the window>child window>dialog box>tab where the test will occur. The test scripts have built in intelligence in that they check the next data record for location codes before they begin processing it. They determine if the data relates to the window/dialog box/tab that is the current test context and process accordingly.

In this manner the script does not needlessly navigate around the GUI from object to object. Context of the test only changes when it needs to change.

As for looping, it depends on where the looping occurs. Of course we use a read loop to put the data into the app and save it, to update, to delete it.

Now if you are talking about testing looping logic in the application itself, it is possible, but questionable. First, data-driven testing is really black box testing that we do at the build/integration testing level. Second, unit testing (which is where loop testing occurs) is by its nature white box testing and the data-driven approach lends itself best to black box. This is not to say that it can't be used to develop and execute unit test data. In our testing, we have used it for build/integration testing after the system has been installed in the test environment.

Testing loops tends to be something that is quite time consuming and can generate 10s of 1000s of combinations and permutations of the test data.

Using McCabe's Basis testing approach to create the test data and then executing the data via a data-driven test script that reads the data from a CSV file would be one technique I would try. It would assure that the loop was exercised and it would introduce a basis set of functional variations (One in each data record) for each iteration of the loop. There are many articles in the Computer Science testing literature that specifically address testing loops. Try searching one of the databases on the net I think STORM has links to several database search engines on their web site.

Gerry:
Correct me if I'm wrong, but I think what was meant by the term "looping" is the ability to repeat a set of actions in a test. The approach we've taken is to enable testers with no coding background to build their test plans and get test scripts with minimal extra effort. We designed a business-like language to write scripts to aid in readability and understanding for anyone building or reviewing a test plan. Yes, it's quite low-level details—the tester has to guide Robot by saying select this menu item, click this button, input this text, etc. However, because the language is small and intuitive, so far we've found people with minimal programming background can pick it up quickly.

The way looping is handled in the language is by using a keyword "RunTest," which takes a test id as a parameter. We have found this very useful when trying to build complex tests out of smaller ones. This could be easily extended to 'repeat' a series of steps by taking in a parameter to re-run, say the previous 3 steps.

Automated Testing Terms and Definitions

Many of the terms and definitions included here are based on those found in Rational Unified Process 2001. Those taken from RUP are indicated by an asterisk.

*Architecture.The highest-level concept of a system in its environment [*IEEE*]. The architecture of a software system (at a given point in time) is its organization or structure of significant *components* interacting through *interfaces*, those components being composed of successively smaller components and interfaces.

Artifact. Any, product, deliverable, or document a process creates.

*Build. A build comprises one or more components (often executable), each constructed from other components, usually by a process of compilation and linking of source code.

*Component. A physical, replaceable part of a system that packages implementation and conforms to and provides the realization of a set of interfaces.

Data-Driven Testing. An automation approach in which the navigation and functionality of the test script is directed through external data; this approach separates test and control data from the test script proper.

Functional Decomposition Approach. An automation method in which the test cases are reduced to fundamental tasks, navigation, functional tests, data verification, and return navigation; also known as the Framework-Driven Approach.

Key Word–Driven Testing. The approach developed by Carl Nagle of the SAS Institute that is offered as freeware on the Web; Key Word–Driven Testing is an enhancement to the data-driven methodology.

Performance Testing. A class of tests implemented and executed to characterize and evaluate the performance-related characteristics of the application under test. These tests include timing profiles, execution flow, response times, and operational reliability and limits.

*Procedure. A documented description of the course of action that is followed when performing a task; a step-by-step method that, when followed, ensures that standards are met.

Process. A series of steps that result in a product or service; the work effort that produces a product or service.

Process Control. Self-adjusting operations that that keep a product or service in conformance with specifications.

Product. Any artifact, deliverable, or document a process creates.

*Rational ClearCase. Software that provides configuration management.

*Rational ClearQuest. A defect tracking and change request management system.

*Rational Robot. Robot is the Capture/Replay component of Rational Suite TestStudio 2001.

*Rational TestManager. TestManager is the central console for managing all testing activities—planning, design, implementation, execution, and analysis.

*Rational Unified Process. A software engineering process that provides a disciplined approach to assigning tasks and responsibilities within a development organization.

Specifications. What is expected when providing a product or service to a customer.

*Test Artifact Set. Captures and presents information related to the tests performed.

*Test Case. A set of test inputs, execution conditions, and expected results developed for a particular objective, such as to exercise a particular program path or to verify compliance with a specific requirement.

Test Condition. The set of circumstances that a test invokes.

*Test Data. The actual (sets of) values used in the test or that are necessary to execute the test. Test data instantiates the condition being tested (as input or as pre-existing data) and is used to verify that a specific requirement has been successfully implemented (comparing actual results to the expected results).

Test Inputs. Artifacts from work processes that are used to identify and define actions that occur during testing. These artifacts may come from development processes that are external to the test group. Examples include Functional Requirements Specifications and Design Specifications. They may also be derived from previous testing phases and passed to subsequent testing activities.

*Test Plan. Contains information about the purpose and goals of testing within the project. Additionally, the test plan identifies the strategies to be used to implement and execute testing and resources needed.

*Test Procedure. A set of detailed instructions for the set-up, execution, and results evaluation for a specific test case (or set of test cases).

Test Requirement. A statement of the objectives associated with a specific test and the criteria that must be met to ascertain the pass/fail status of the test.

Test Results. Data captured during the execution of test and used in calculating the different key measures of testing.

*Test Script. The computer readable instructions that automate the execution of a test procedure (or portion of a test procedure). Test scripts may be created (recorded) or automatically generated using test automation tools, programmed using a programming language, or created by a combination of recording, generating, and programming.

*Test Strategy. Describes the general approach and objectives of the test activities.

Test Suite. The set of tests that when executed instantiate a test scenario.

*Test Workspace. "Private" areas where testers can install and test code in accordance with the project's adopted standards in relative isolation from the developers.

Example Test Automation Project Plan Using Rational Suite TestStudio

Introduction

This document is designed to communicate the implementation strategy for an automated software testing framework and its supporting test tools. It is intended to help a general audience understand the strategy for deploying the framework.

It must be accepted that automated testing is a full-time activity that requires dedicated resources. Only with this point of view will the effort be a success.

Documentation References

Internal Sources

The Quality Assurance & Testing (QA&T) Group's automated testing approach should be outlined with the following documents located. These documents and their content are subject to change or replacement as the automation effort matures.

- Software Testing Automation Plan
- Automated Testing Methodology
- Automation Strategy
- Automation Testing Guidelines

External Sources

1. Nagle, Carl. "Test Automation Frameworks," available at *members.aol. com/sascanagl/FRAMESDataDrivenTestAutomationFrameworks.htm*.
2. Zambelich, Keith. "Totally Data-Driven Automated Testing," Whitepaper available at *www.auto-sqa.com/articles.html*, the Automated Testing Specialists (ATS) Web site.

Automation Implementation

Rational Suite TestStudio includes a number of products that can be used to support the different phases of the testing process. These products are to be implemented and used as described in the following sections.

Test Management

Rational TestManager will be used across testing phases to manage testing activities.

Test Design Phase

Rational TestManager and Rational RequisitePro will be used during this phase to define test requirements, test scenarios, test cases, test scripts, and test suites. In addition, Microsoft Word and Microsoft Excel will be used to develop test plans and test data, respectively, for each application feature.

RequisitePro will be the tool for defining test requirements. Functional Requirements, High-Level Design, and Detailed-Level Design documents will be imported into RequisitePro. Test requirements will be identified from system requirements and design specifications statements, which these documents contain.

TestManager will use the RequisitePro-derived test requirements as its primary class of test inputs. A test plan folder will be created in TestManager that will serve as the high-level directory for all test-related objects for each application feature being tested. External test plan and test case documents will be associated with the internal test plan folder and the test artifacts that are created there.

The test plan folder will maintain information relating test requirements to test scripts and test suites for specific application build and test configurations. Test data pools will also be associated with particular tests at this level.

The external test plan will be constructed in MS Word using the test requirements in RequisitePro as a guide to defining the testing activities. A modified version of the Rational Unified Process Test Plan Template will be used. Somewhat in parallel with the test plan, but beginning after the initial draft of the test plan, the test cases will be prepared in MS Excel. The test plan and the test cases will be dynamic documents that will require updating as the system requirements change.

Test Implementation Phase

Both Rational TestManager and Robot will be used during this stage. Smoke test scripts and environmental setup scripts will be constructed in Robot. The Data Driven Engine (DDE) will be implemented and customized via Robot. At this level, test-specific GUI and feature tests will be implemented as Robot scripts that feed the DDE. The DDE will drive the actual tests. TestManager will be used to connect test script with test requirements for traceability and to monitor test coverage.

Test Execution Phase

Rational Robot will be the primary test execution platform, but the tests will be run from the test manager console interface. Test results will be captured and displayed in the TestManager test log window. Test results will also be printed and archived.

Automation Environment

The test automation infrastructure described herein is illustrated in Figure 1.2 in Chapter 1.

Test Development Workstations

The test automation engineers will require a test development and execution workstation with TestStudio deployed on it. This workstation is in addition to their normal NT desktop machines. This is because automated test takes control of the desktop, and running tests on the engineers' primary workstations would interfere with other work activities. One of the benefits of test automation is that the test can be executed unattended, leaving the testers free to do other work.

The script development workstation should be an NT/Windows 2000 machine with a minimum 60-GB hard drive and 396 KB of RAM. It should have MS Office installed.

Test Data Store Server

All projects in Rational Suite TestStudio are implemented as test project data stores. Each project data store contains the project repository files and the requirements repository files. Additionally, ClearQuest repository files can be associated with each TestStudio project. In this manner, tests, requirements, and defects are all coupled and traceable.

A separate project data store server is required. It should be used to permanently house all linked project files and repositories. The server should be added to the nightly backup schedule.

Test Execution Workstations

One or more test execution workstations will be required to run the tests. Each test execution workstation either can run a test suite modally or can be one of several workstations for distributed test execution.

Test Application Servers

These should be dedicated servers that emulate all of the target production server environments in which the application will reside. They should be used exclusively for automated test runs; they should not be used for integration testing or manual system testing, which should be done on their own servers. Any activities on the automation servers other than the specified tests will invalidate those tests.

Test Environment Requirements   The following information should be used to configure the test application servers and the test execution workstations (clients).

Servers

Hardware

    Info for All Target Platforms

        [Network]: Network configuration

[Server Type]: Server model and manufacturer

[Server Configuration]: Server configuration parameters

[Quantity]: Number of servers in system

[Required Installation Date]: N/A

Software

Info for All Target Platforms

[OS]: Windows 2000, Windows NT 4.0, etc.

[Server Applications]: Any and all software that runs at the server layer of the system

Clients

Hardware

Info for All Target Client Platforms

[Network]: Network configuration

[Workstation Type]: Workstation model and manufacturer

[Workstation Configuration]: Workstation software configuration description including OS

[Quantity]: Number of workstations that will be implemented

[Required Installation Date]: Implementation date

Software

Info for All Target Client Platforms

[OS]: Windows 2000, Windows NT 4.0

[Client Applications]: Purchased or in-house-developed application programs that execute in the client layer of the system

Organizational Structure

The project will be under the direction of the Test Automation Lead. The ideal team would consist of two senior test automation engineers, three test automation engineers, and perhaps one junior test automation engineer.

External Interfaces

The test automation project will interface with several other groups in the normal course of its activities. The groups include:

- The QA&T group
- Development groups
  - ✗ Management
  - ✗ Core development
  - ✗ Support and maintenance
- Configuration management team

Roles and Responsibilities

Roles

Automated Tools Group Lead   This person is responsible for the day-to-day coordination of each group's projects (50% allocation). The lead is also responsible for participating in the daily work activities (50% allocation). His or her skill set should include all of the skills required at the senior engineer level.

Senior Test Automation Engineer   This individual has advanced expertise in all skill sets required. She or he may be a subject matter expert and/or a methods and tools expert. His or her skill set should include all of the skills required at the engineer level.

Test Automation Engineer An individual at this level has intermediate-level knowledge in his or her areas of expertise and should have good overall product knowledge. His or her skill set should include knowledge of the hardware and software platforms in use.

Junior Test Automation Engineer/Intern   An individual at this level possesses entry-level knowledge of information systems basics and/or fundamental knowledge of Quality Assurance and/ or Quality Control and Testing.

Responsibilities

Primary responsibilities of those planning and implementing a data-driven test framework for functional testing include developing:

- Modular automated test utility libraries with components for framework-based test script design and construction

- Database initialization functions
- Database access functions for test verification
- Miscellaneous application functions (e.g., select a menu choice, Dialog box tab navigation, window existence verification, and so forth)
- Miscellaneous common functions (e.g., file open, file close, and start applications)
- Participate in the design and implementation of automated test scripts for
  - ✘ GUI tests
  - ✘ Properties tests
  - ✘ Functional tests
  - ✘ Back-end server-based tests
  - ✘ Reliability tests
  - ✘ Performance tests
- Non-GUI-based test scripts for testing back-end capabilities

Project Estimates

MS Project will be used for all project-related estimates.

Test Automation Project Work Plan Template

Work Breakdown Structure

Project Start-Up Phase

Past Project Evaluation   Thoroughly evaluate the lessons learned from the previous automation project. From this, a draft for the new Automation Test strategy may be documented.

Scope   Outline the preliminary scope of the testing goals and objectives for the next automated test project.

Sizing   Outline a preliminary test effort sizing based on the planned scope of automation.

Team Composition   Develop an automation test team composition analysis and automation test engineer job description.

Recruiting   Conduct interviews for the planned team and develop the team.

Early Project Support Phase   Conduct meetings with other teams and stakeholders to determine their automation needs, as well as communicating a realistic expectation of the deliverables.

Goals and Objectives   Further define the goals and objectives and review with all stakeholders.

Constraint Examination   Review constraints (e.g., short time to delivery, limited resources).

Testability Review   Review the problems with the development of the application and tools used to automate the testing, which may impact the testability for automation.

Requirements Review   Ensure that the software development requirements for automation testing are documented and published.

Test Process Analysis   Analyze the current test process and determine how the automation testing life cycle will be included.

Organization Involvement   Discuss the automation plans with all test and development groups, and accept input for targeted test cases to automate.

Test Automation Planning Phase

Test Requirements   Document all of them in an automation test plan.

Automation Test Strategy   Define the automation test process, methodologies, and strategies to be used. Include considerations for the defect management process and script version control.

Deliverables   Define the project deliverables after the automation test life cycle is complete.

Test Program Parameters   Define the test program parameters such as the assumptions, prerequisite activities, system acceptance criteria, and test program risks. This can be included in the automation test plan.

Training Plans   Document what training will be needed and a proposed schedule for it.

Technical Environment   Document the technical environment in which the application under test will be tested by the automation.

Automation Tool Compatibility Checks   Document the incompatibilities of the automation tool with the AUT, as well as the work-around solutions needed.

Risk Assessments   Perform risk assessments in support of project management reviews.

Test Plan Document   Assemble and package the test planning documentation into a complete automation test plan.

Automation Test Data   Document the test data required for automation and plans for developing and maintaining its repository.

Automation Test Environment   Identify and document the requirements for an automation test lab for the AUT and the personnel needed for setting up and maintaining it.

Roles and Responsibilities   Define and document the team members' roles and responsibilities for the automation testing effort.

Automation Test System Administration   Define all tools needed for automation and outline the requirements for setting up and maintaining them.

Test Automation Design Phase

Prototype Automated Test Environment   Prepare and establish an automation test lab to support the design and development of the automation. Verify its functionality.

Automation Techniques and Tools   Identify the testing techniques and strategies of the automation system to be applied to the project.

Automation Design Standards   Prepare the standards and guidelines to be used for the automation project.

Automation Script Planning   Develop a hierarchy of scripts to be developed. Identify which test cases cannot be executed with automation.

Test Automation Library   Define which scripts can and should be included in a common library for reuse.

Automation Development Phase

Automation Script Assignments   Assign the planned scripts to the team. Use MS Project to track the development progress.

Script Peer Reviews   Review the design and development of the automation scripts, and ensure that they are developed consistent with the established standards and guidelines.

Test Tool Improvements   Create a database for bugs and enhancements for the automated test scripts.

Test Script Configuration Management   Ensure that configuration control is performed for test scripts and test data, as well as a repository backup plan.

Automation Integration Phase

Environment Setup   Define a process for setting up an environment for executing the automation test scripts for each new build of the AUT.

Test Phase Execution   Execute the automation scripts targeted for each phase of testing.

Automation Test Reporting   Prepare test reports based on results of script execution.

Issue Resolution   Debug tool and/or script issues found during the execution of the automated test scripts.

Automation Process Improvement Phase

Tool/Script Evaluation   Evaluate the efficiency, accuracy, and performance of the test automation processes.

Lessons Learned Reviews   Conduct a session after each test cycle and gather information to improve the automation process.

Maintain a Test Process Repository   Maintain a repository of test process assets, such as standards, procedures, test tool evaluation reports, historical test effort records, lessons learned, test effort metrics, and analysis reports.

Automation Intranet Site   Develop an intranet Web site for communicating automation efforts to the rest of the organization.

Continued Training   Participate in test tool user groups, test conferences, and seminars and promote information sharing in the automation group.

Timeline

This work breakdown structure will be dynamically maintained as in MS Project Gantt chart showing the allocation of time to the project phases or iterations.

Major Milestones   The major milestones should be illustrated in the MS Project document previously described.

Implementation Iteration Objectives

The automation framework will be implemented in incremental steps. Critical system components will be identified, prioritized, and scheduled for automation. These application features will be automated in the first stepwise increment. Other features will be implemented by priority in subsequent iterations.

Project Schedule

The project schedule is illustrated in the MS Project document previously described.

Project Resources

Staffing Plan   The automation group will require the following staff: two senior test automation engineers and three test automation engineers.

Resource Acquisition Plan   The automation project will require dedicated hardware resources. They include test engineer workstations and test automation servers. These resources should be acquired as soon as possible as some scheduled automation tasks are well under way.

Training Plan   All test automation engineers will be trained in the Rational Unified Process, in Rational Suite TestStudio and all of its components, in the functional decomposition test automation framework, and in the data-driven test automation approach.

The training vehicles will include in-house seminars, Rational public seminars and conferences such as the Rational Users Group conference, the International Software Testing Conference, and the STAR conference.

Budget

Test automation is not an inexpensive proposition. A substantial investment in tools, schedule, and expert tool users is required.

Project Monitoring and Control

Automation Effort Estimation

The estimation process for predicting the time to automate AUT's environmental setup, smoke, and regression testing is broken down on a feature-by-feature basis. The estimates will be developed and placed in an Excel workbook with each type of automation in separate sheets.

Schedule Control Plan

The progress of the project will be monitored with the MS Project tool. A weekly status meeting will be held and the schedule will be updated. If the project begins to slip behind schedule, the Team Lead will take steps to correct the schedule, which may include additional hours, additional personnel, or personnel changes.

Budget Control Plan

The budget estimates will be reviewed and revised at each project milestone.

Reporting Plan

Progress will be reported to the Test Manager at the weekly status meeting.

Measurement Plan

The metrics provided in the Suite TestStudio products will be implemented and monitored.

Supporting Processes

Configuration Management Plan

All test automation framework artifacts and test baseline information will be placed under change control using Rational ClearCase LT, which is a component of the TestStudio.

Defect Tracking and Problem Resolution

Once the automation framework is implemented, defects will be entered manually by the test engineers and /or generated automatically from the TestManager test logs that are created for each automated test run.

Framework Evaluation

An annual process improvement review will guide the evolution of the automation framework.

Framework Documentation Plan

The test automation engineers will document the test automation framework as each component is completed and implemented. They will identify each component by purpose, scope, special features it may contain, pretest conditions that must be met before test execution, and any necessary post-test cleanup.

Process Improvement

The test automation framework will be reviewed at least once a year and recommendations for improvement will be documented and implemented.

Index